AF573443

The Healthy Gourmet

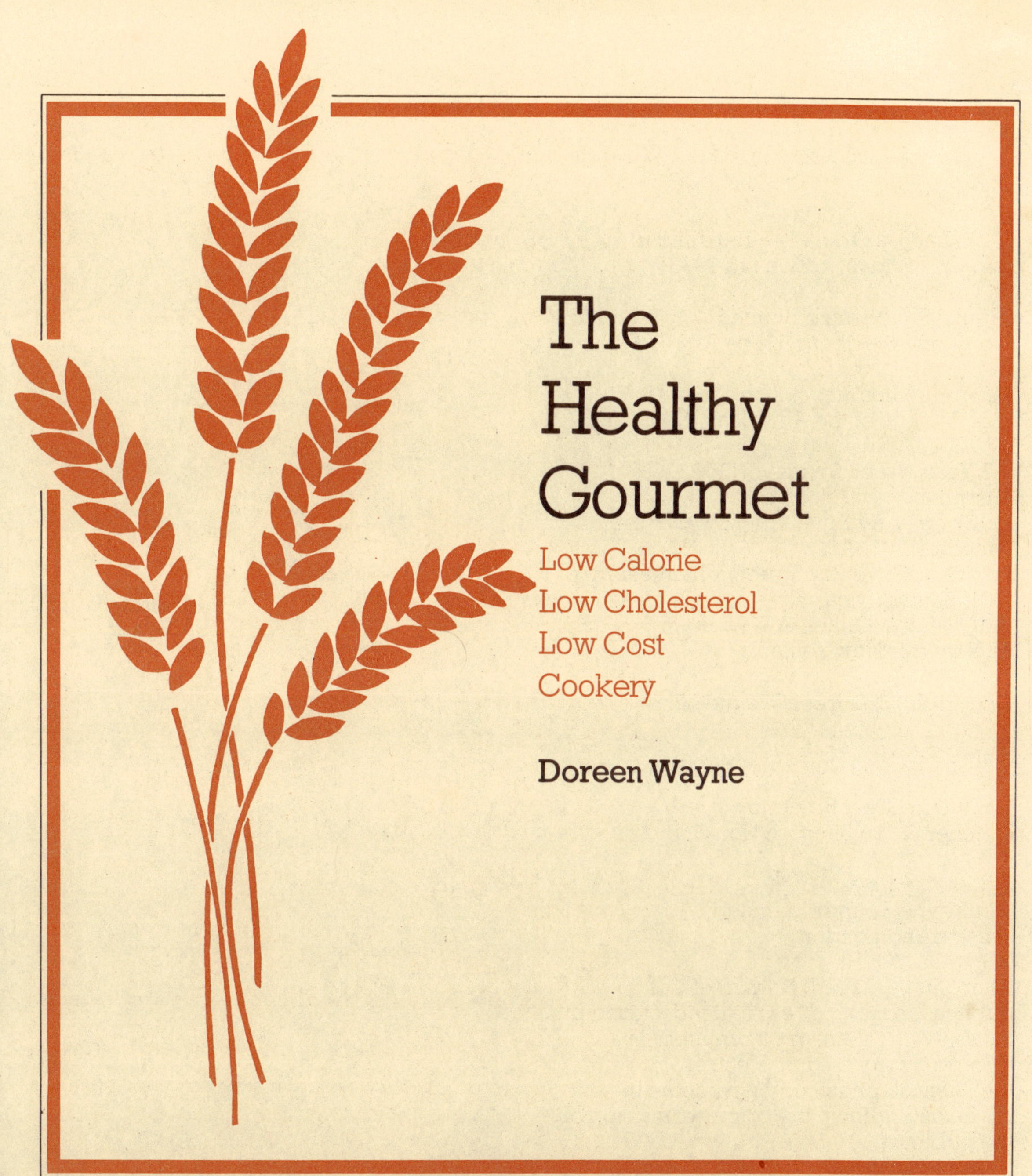

The Healthy Gourmet

Low Calorie
Low Cholesterol
Low Cost
Cookery

Doreen Wayne

HART-DAVIS, MACGIBBON
GRANADA PUBLISHING
London Toronto Sydney New York

Published by Granada Publishing in
Hart-Davis, MacGibbon Ltd 1978

Granada Publishing Limited
Frogmore, St Albans, Herts AL2 2NF
and
3 Upper James Street, London W1R 4BP
1221 Avenue of the Americas, New York,
NY 10020, USA
117 York Street, Sydney, NSW 2000,
Australia
100 Skyway Avenue, Toronto, Ontario,
Canada M9W 3A6
Trio City, Coventry Street, Johannesburg
2001, South Africa
CML Centre, Queen & Wyndham,
Auckland 1, New Zealand

ISBN 0 246 11032 5

Printed in Great Britain by
Fletcher & Son Limited, Norwich.

Typesetting by
Mouldtype Foundry Limited,
Preston and London

Contents

Acknowledgments

My sincere thanks to Mr Denis P. Burkitt for the help and advice he gave so generously. I am grateful to Dr Barry Lewis ; also, for their private help or published papers, to Dr D. A. T. Southgate, Dr K. W. Heaton, Mr N. S. Painter, Dr K. Ball and Dr J. Hill ; to their colleagues at The Royal College of Physicians and the British and American Heart Foundations, and to many others whose efforts have improved the quality of life for all of us.

To Jerry, who ate it all up

Introduction

Introduction

Do you remember when roast beef on Sunday and steak or chops a few times a week were standard fare, when 'inflation' was a game for politicians and there was more food available than we ever thought we'd eat?

Today, meat's a luxury, food prices rise constantly and there are shortages and warnings of famine not only in under-developed countries but right here at home.

Do you remember when Fat was Beautiful?

Now most of us are struggling to get slim.

Yesterday, eggs, cheese, butter, milk and cream were foods for health. Today we're told they contribute to heart disease.

It's a changing world and we're having to change with it. Already we're cutting out roasts and switching from steaks to stews and stews to mince. But what next? Textured soy protein? Even imitation meat is far from cheap, so do we start cutting down portions or eat two meals a day instead of three? How about living free off the land, as it says in the magazines? We can all go out and gather nettles (assuming there are enough to go round) and then, if we don't get stung to death picking them, there'll only be one small problem left. How do we persuade our families to eat them?

Perhaps we should just eat more of the safe old standbys like spaghetti and potatoes. But if the extra pound in our pockets is matched by one on our hips, haven't we compounded the problem?

A lot of questions, so how about some answers? Is there a single, simple solution to the complex problems of rising prices and shortages, obesity and other food-related health hazards?

Yes, there is. It's cooking *The Healthy Gourmet* way.

This book shows how you can eat satisfying quantities of delicious food, lose weight, feel well, *be* well and save money into the bargain.

The meals are appetising, satisfying, quick and easy to prepare, widely varied and made with good, basic, usually familiar foodstuffs. No nettles or other oddities here.

This is not a vegetarian, nor a 'health food' diet though it *is* supremely healthy and includes many vegetable recipes. It does *not* include the hefty dollops of philosophy, mysticism or other off-putting features found in 'fad' diets, because it's *not* a fad diet but a sensible, down-to-earth way of eating well while cutting food bills by a third or even more.

It is also a safe and reliable way of losing weight permanently without unhealthy crash diets or semi-starvation. You can enjoy satisfying thick soups, tasty casseroles, sweet desserts, stuffed fish, paprika chicken, savoury rice and apple pudding–and get slim.

The diet is based on the scientific discovery that many of our modern foods are too fat, too easily absorbed into the body or are just 'empty' calories, so that we're victims of over-nutrition (which means over-weight) and it's not really our fault. We now live on a diet which has been made possible by advances in technology, a highly refined diet which allows us to take in vast numbers of calories in a couple of gulps and a swallow. As an example, we'd have to munch through four good-sized apples to take in the same number of calories as we get from one tin of cola drink.

Introduction

Putting the FIBRE, or roughage, back into our diet in place of those empty calories is the most valuable aid to slimming yet discovered–or I should say *re*-discovered for high-fibre foods were our ancestor's natural ones. They didn't have the milling techniques to produce white flour or the refining methods for white sugar or the scientific farming, refrigeration and transport to make meat and high-fat dairy products widely available. So they ate 'natural' foods: wholewheat bread, whole-grain cereals, fruits and vegetables. And they were slim.

Modern methods gave us white bread, sweet cake, fizzy drinks, thick cream and 'frosted' breakfast flakes and research shows that 'modern' illnesses promptly followed. Constipation, haemorrhoids, appendicitis, diabetes, heart disease, bowel cancer and many other illnesses are now linked with our highly refined–and highly priced–foods.

This diet is not a magic cure-all, but eminent researchers are now convinced that cutting down certain fats and putting the fibre back into our diet–which means eating what is, after all, our traditional food –will minimise those health-hazards which were once unknown.

What exactly is dietary fibre? It's a complex group of substances which form the 'walls' around the cells of all plants. It gives fruits and vegetables their structure and texture, the strength to stand erect and the pliability to bend over, as our skeletons do for us, except that the plant skeleton is outside the cells, not inside. A grain of wheat is one example ; it has a 'wall' of rigid fibre (bran) around the white starchy centre. This crispy bran and the fairly obvious fibre in crunchy carrots, celery and lettuce, are probably the reason for the term 'roughage' being used for fibrous foods, but tomatoes, bananas and all the soft, juicy fruits and vegetables have fibre-skeletons, too, of one kind or another. Dried peas, beans and lentils, the softest and tenderest of foods when they're cooked, are among the richest sources of dietary fibre, while fluffy, tender-cooked whole grain cereals are the best source of all.

How does fibre actually work? It is not broken down by the digestive enzymes and so it is not absorbed into the body. Since about 10 per cent of whole-grain cereal is dietary fibre, this means we can eat 10 per cent more brown rice than white rice for the same number of usable (absorbable) calories. To be more practical, we can eat 10 per cent *less* brown rice and *cut* usable calories, without feeling hungry.

We generally feel empty when we're hungry, because our previous meal–instant cereal with milk and sugar, or a white bread sandwich and fizzy drink, or steak and kidney pie, a glass of wine and baked jam roll–have all been absorbed *into* us, down to the last crumb. In fact we *are* empty. But fibre is not absorbed. It collects and holds water, growing bulkier as it passes through the body, so that we keep the feeling of fullness until it's time to eat again, while the bulky matter is rapidly evacuated.

Wholewheat flour actually contains 5 per cent fewer calories (and 9 per cent more protein) than an equal weight of white flour and we can't devour wholewheat bread in two gulps and a swallow–it has to be chewed. This is very good for the teeth and jaw ; it also makes us eat more slowly and stimulates gastric juices and the secretion

Introduction

of saliva. These are important aspects of slimming, because the liquids make the food in your stomach swell, so that you feel fuller sooner.

Since all whole grains, legumes, fruits, vegetables, nuts and seeds are high in dietary fibre you can eat a generous portion of these bulky, filling foods, combined with fish or fowl (deliciously prepared according to the recipes here) and lose weight. Then, once you've achieved your correct weight you can maintain it.

The purpose of this book is to show you how to substitute high-fibre foods for over-refined ones, cheaper foods for high-priced ones, beneficial fats for unhealthy ones, valuable calories for 'empty' ones, without becoming a food faddist or crank in the process. You don't have to give up anything without a satisfactory substitute being recommended, and you certainly don't have to give up your pleasure in a mouth-watering meal. I am invariably told that this food is much too appetising and enjoyable to be healthy (working on the popular theory that what's good must be bad for you !) but healthy, satisfying and delicious it most certainly is.

So perhaps it is a little magical, after all . . .?

Counting the Cost

When I began looking for a different kind of diet my aim was to cut costs without cutting corners, which meant finding appetising substitutes for the more expensive items in my shopping basket. Clearly the first thing to be replaced was the item that cost most, and that was meat–beef, pork, lamb, veal, mutton, organ meats, smoked meat, salted meat–all meat.

Finding substitutes wasn't difficult at all. The problem lay in convincing myself that it was possible to make a meal without meat when to me food *meant* meat. Dinner meant hot meat, lunch meant cold meat and breakfast meant cured meat. I was convinced that if I didn't eat meat I would not only be hungry and undernourished but also socially inferior. What kind of people couldn't afford meat? What would I give my publisher when he came to dinner–*cauliflower*?

Yes, I had hang-ups about meat. We all have, and it's not surprising after centuries of mystique which have given meat a status out of all proportion to its food value.

From the moment when Man fashioned the first spear there was no holding him. It was meat, meat, all the way, though he ate it raw, because fire hadn't yet been invented, and it must have tasted vastly inferior to the fruits and vegetables he had been used to. Presumably this was when Man, rationalising his odd behaviour to Woman, started the Meat Myths–that blood gave you strength, entrails conferred supernatural powers (especially when worn around the neck), flesh made you virile, no one can make a meal without meat, and so on.

Throughout history meat has been a status symbol, even when lack of refrigeration meant it went off long before reaching the table. The Romans spent most of the money they got from sacking other people's countries on massive, meaty banquets to impress their friends, serving specialities like camels and dormice. The Ancient Britons spread a special paste on their meat, undoubtedly to hide its rank odour and taste. Even the paste–made of the blood and entrails of fish, salt, vinegar and herbs, all left to go putrid in the sun–didn't put them off their meat dinners.

Since then we've learned how to keep meat fresh and boost supplies by using wonder-drugs. So why aren't we swamped with cheap meat?

Because millions of people whose natural diet has always been rice and vegetables are suddenly investing the proceeds of booming economies in 'Western' food, particularly meat. They may believe, as many of us still do, that it makes them strong and virile. They certainly believe it gives them status. So the demand–and the price–continue to rise.

We pay another price for meat too. A farmer can produce enough cereal to provide a protein-rich diet for, say, fifty people. The same cereal fed to cattle will produce enough beef to feed only about ten people. So the switching of whole populations from rice to beef is a real threat to us all unless we learn right now that it *is* possible to make meals without meat, and marvellous meals at that.

I haven't mentioned 'cruelty', 'eating dead flesh', 'morality', or any of the other spectres normally evoked when 'cutting out meat' and 'improving health' are mentioned in the same breath. Though I wouldn't want to spend my holidays in a slaughter-house, the breeding and killing of animals for food doesn't spoil my dinner.

Counting the Cost

What does spoil it is a plate containing two vegetables and a gap which I simply cannot afford to fill with meat. I know that a lot of antibiotics, chemicals and other possibly harmful matter get into meat these days, but it was the cost that set me looking for appetising substitutes. Amazingly enough, after a few weeks I didn't miss meat at all, probably because there were ample alternatives available.

For a start, take chicken and turkey (and in this book you'll find out-of-the-ordinary chicken and turkey). Most of us know a couple of convenient ways to cook a bird and dish it up the same way every time which makes for instant boredom.(How many Christmasses have been ruined by interminable roast turkey?). There are thousands of different recipes for fowl and I've tried to give a variety–keeping preparation simple, since most cooks have other jobs as well–all of which I've developed or adapted to the high-fibre, low-fat concept, while stretching the birds to their absolute maximum to save money.

Another delicious food included here is fish. Apparently fish is only popular when it's oblong, covered with crumbs and hiding in a rocky batter, or swamped in a heavy butter-and-cream sauce. But the fish recipes in this book *prove* that fish is a real delicacy, that it smells good even when cooking and that the many varieties available can provide an astonishing range of mouth-watering meals.

Fish isn't cheap, of course, but I've learned how to stretch it in unusual dishes, combine it with unexpected ingredients and generally make it both economical and tasty.

My family now rate fish among their favourite foods, and I think yours will, too.

First Steps

There is a rumour, at home and abroad, that British people are not interested in their health. Yet a television programme only has to suggest that something is good for us and by nine-thirty next morning every scrap of it is sold out. Clearly millions of us *are* interested and, while not being cranky about it, would like a healthier diet.

I became aware of the health bonuses in low-fat, high-fibre foods only when a series of publications by eminent doctors indicated that the style of eating I'd been enjoying for some time could cure or prevent many chronic ailments.

Of course I knew the diet was keeping us slim, and that obesity was unhealthy as well as unattractive (a mere 10 per cent more weight than is recommended for one's height and frame can mean the risk of heart disease). But it was a surprise to learn that around 50 per cent of the people in Britain were overweight and worried about it–just as I had been.

In the 'bad old days' I was always either stuffing or starving–more often the latter, it seemed– and switching from one 'miracle' diet to another: bananas-and-milk, meat-and-water, grapefruit, cotton-wool bread, meal-in-a-biscuit–but nothing worked. After a few days I'd be sick of the permitted foods, my mouth tasted like fried dishwater and I was famished to the point of downing enough calories to fatten an army. I'd have given anything just to eat normally and maintain my correct weight. What I decided to 'give', as the first step, was sugar. After cutting it out and learning to live without it I discovered that sugar not only makes you fat but is also widely believed to contribute to ulcers, dyspepsia, fatty livers, heartburn, enlarged kidneys, tooth decay and–because its 'empty' calories encourage obesity–to heart disease.

Whether or not we actually want to eat sugar it's automatically added to many tinned and dried soups, baked beans, tinned meats, breakfast cereals, tinned vegetables–a long list of foods which we'd never associate with sugar...unless we read the labels.

It is also added to most baby foods, so that the taste for sugar is planted virtually at birth. Perhaps this is why a lot of us think we're actually *born* with a taste for sweet things.

It's hard to imagine giving a child a carrot or a strip of green pepper as a reward for being good, but one mother who did this says that now she can't keep a salad in the house for five minutes. Her daughter is as mischievous, lovable, active, noisy and repellant as any other child, but she has glossy hair, translucent skin, a slender, healthy body and magnificent teeth–not one of them a sweet tooth.

I'm not deluding myself that by giving up sugar I'm going to look like her–that would take plastic surgery and several miracles. But even if sugar is only half as harmful as doctors say, why risk it? Everyone knows it contains *absolutely no vitamins, minerals or food value of any kind*, and that applies to brown sugar, too, which looks more wholesome because of its pretty colour but is merely a little less refined than its white sister, or is dyed with caramel.

The least unhealthy sweetener I've found is honey. It costs more than sugar, but you use less–and then less and less as you follow the recipes in this book and discover that fruits and vegetables have a natural, delightful sweetness of their own that's been hidden under the sugar all this time.

It does take a little while to lose one's taste for over-sweet things, but honey can satisfy the most abject craving and I ought to know–I was a chocolate-cake junkie.

At the last count, every man, woman and child in Britain was gulping down, in one form or another, about 103 lbs of sugar a year, which is about six ounces a day. Since I don't take any, somebody is eating even more.

Can anything sweeten that statistic?

More about Fats

There is no cream in the recipes in this book, no butter, no whole milk, little cheese and few eggs, because, apart from their cost, all these foods are extremely high in saturated fat.

There's virtually no doubt among world medical opinion that a diet high in saturated fat raises our blood cholesterol level and can lead to Coronary Heart Disease.

To explain the medical terms a little more clearly:

Saturated Fats

Fats which are fully saturated with hydrogen. These include all dairy produce, meat, meat products (sausages, pork pies, tinned meats, etc.) organ meats, suet and lard, fish roe, duck, goose, and hardened (or hydrogenated) margarines, also coconut oil, palm oil, cashew nuts and chocolate.

Though the terms 'animal fats' and 'saturated fats' are apparently used interchangeably, this is for convenience since *most* saturated fats come from animals. However, as you'll see from the above list, some do not.

Polyunsaturated Fats

Fats which are not wholly saturated with hydrogen. They are usually liquid, usually of plant origin. The most valuable are Sunflower Oil, Safflower Oil and Corn Oil. These fats are recommended to replace saturated ones. Most fish oils and nuts are polyunsaturated.

Cholesterol and Triglycerides

Fat-like substances which are found in the blood. Both are measured in a blood-count and both are found in raised levels in people who suffer from heart disease. Often 'cholesterol' is used as a collective term to mean both substances. (Cholesterol is found in animal foods but not plant/vegetable foods.)

Hydrogenation

A method of treating liquid oil to harden it. If a polyunsaturated oil is treated this way it becomes a saturated oil–i.e. saturated with hydrogen.

Most foods contain a mixture of fats: saturated, mono-unsaturated (considered to be a neutral fat) and polyunsaturated. In beef the saturated fats greatly outweigh the polyunsaturated fats. In fish the reverse is true.

In spite of all this, since I'm not a food crank I'd go along with the people who say: 'A little of what you fancy does you good'. But we don't eat a *little* butter, cream, milk, etc. We've gone absolutely overboard on them. This may be due to deprivation during and after the war, or to persuasive advertising by the marketing boards, but it's hard to find a recipe nowadays which doesn't call for pints, dollops or chunks of these fatty foods.

The Finnish Government undertook a national campaign to persuade its citizens to cut down on saturated fats, while Americans have greatly reduced their intake and it's almost impossible to find real cream in a supermarket there. When I asked for it, they said 'You must be English.'

The College of Physicians 1976 report confirmed that high cholesterol, which is

More about Fats

positively linked with the percentage of saturated fat in the diet, is a major cause of Coronary Heart Disease.[1]

So isn't it time we started ignoring recipes that begin 'Take half a pint of cream...'?

Heart disease is now attacking men in their mid-thirties and is increasing every year. In 1973 (the final year covered by the College of Physicians report), 52 per cent of all the men who died in the 45-54 age group and 41 per cent of the 35-44 age group, died of heart disease. Next time you're at a large party or gathering, try to imagine what the room would look like if half the men suddenly vanished–and then imagine that one of those missing is your husband or son. Frightening, isn't it? Even if fatty foods are only partly responsible, isn't it worthwhile trying to cut them out, or at least down?

And the sooner we stop serving saturated fats to our children the better their chance of a long, active life, for the problems of high cholesterol start early and grow with us. Experts say that a low-fat diet can be given to children from the second year onwards.[2] This means no special cooking or fussing: the entire family eats the same meals.

Ideas about nutrition are changing; ideas about health are changing; ideas about farming, preserving, processing–all are changing. But we go on using the cow as a food-factory and struggling harder all the time to keep up with the bills. Yet fowl and fish provide just as good a protein and both these foods contain the desirable polyunsaturate fats. Soups don't need cream, milk doesn't need fat, sauces don't need butter and people don't need oodles of eggs and cheese. True gourmet dishes can be prepared without them, as you will see when you reach the recipe section.

And now a word about olive oil: it's expensive. Another word: it's unnecessary. Also, though it comes from a plant, it is not rich in polyunsaturates, as are sunflower oil, corn oil and safflower oil. So use whichever of these healthy oils is cheapest in your area. They make marvellous salad dressings and are perfect for frying, grilling, marinading and even baking. Though all oils are expensive, these are much cheaper than olive oil. So ignore the old saying, 'only olive oil will do', because in the light of medical discoveries–and rising prices–it won't do at all.

I use corn oil for cooking, sunflower oil for baking and salad dressings and polyunsaturate margarine wherever margarine, butter, lard or shortening might previously have been used. Polyunsaturate margarines are very versatile, as you'll have gathered, and since they have a mild flavour they can also be used as a spread.

Yes, I do mean in place of butter, but before a howl of woe goes up, let me say that the degree to which you switch to this new style of eating is entirely up to you. If you can't give up butter–okay. If you must eat some meat–all right. Or you can jump in at the deep end and then cheat if you get a yearning for something you haven't tasted in a while, like butter or meat.

I'll say a bit more about cheating later on

---

[1] Other factors: smoking, obesity, lack of exercise and stress (with stress being least established as a contributor to CHD)

[2] Royal College of Physicians Report Vol. 10 No. 3 April 1976 p. 49.

More about Fats

but, briefly, this is not a fad diet or a crash diet which makes the body behave in an abnormal way. It is our *natural* diet, so the occasional addition of a 'forbidden' food can't possibly 'undo all the good you've done'. You've been eating normally and added something not normal, that's all.

Whichever way you choose, all the way in or just a toe, you'll be cutting costs, cholesterol and calories. And you'll probably find, as I did, that once you start eating these delicious, satisfying meals and begin to feel the health bonuses you just won't want to stop being a healthy gourmet at all.

More about Fibre

As we've already discussed, 'miracle diets' –or just cutting down sugar and fats–won't permanently knock the pounds off. In fact, replacing sugar and fat with lean beef and other proteins sticks pounds *on*–to the household budget, making reducing a costly business. A friend told me: 'I've spent half my life and a small fortune knocking off the same 10 lbs !'

What makes it work? Experts now believe that what's needed to keep us healthy, slim and satisfied is a reduced intake of fat combined with a large increase in dietary fibre.

As we know, fibre is removed during the refining of flour and the polishing or processing of rice and other grains. Modern methods leave these foods whiter than white, quick to cook, soft and pulpy to eat and vitamin- mineral- and fibre-free.

Recently someone proved that popular breakfast cereals actually contained less nutrition than the boxes they came in–they were just empty calories to fatten up the children. (Children *are* fat, not cuddly or rounded, and a fat child becomes a fat adult, with all the misery that entails.) Since then some synthetic vitamins and minerals have been added to cereals to replace the natural ones lost in processing. In a similar manner white bread is 'enriched'.

There's no evidence to suggest that synthetic vitamins and minerals are less effective than natural ones, despite shouts of horror from the health food suppliers, but the third item removed from our foods–the fibre–is *not* replaced. Though our palates have adapted only too well to highly refined 'modern' foods–pure starch, sugar and fat–it's now evident that our bodies have not. Hence the obesity and other 'modern' ailments that we suffer from today.

Until roughly a hundred years ago, most foods were eaten in a pretty natural state. Only the rich could afford exotic white bread (then hand-milled), so it became highly desirable and, like meat, a status symbol. When milling techniques improved, more people could eat the now cheaper white bread–and they did. Today, about 95 per cent of the bread we eat is white (though status-wise, packaged-sliced-white must be considered something of a comedown !)

I think a lot of people would prefer bread with old-fashioned bite and flavour to it but are put off by the wild claims of Wholewheat Missionaries. To clear the matter up, dark, chewy wholewheat bread is not a cure-all, nor is it noticeably good for the soul. But it tastes marvellous, it's nutritious and it's a valuable source of fibre, as are oats, barley, maize and other whole grains.

Ninety-five per cent of us have switched from these fibrous foods to white bread and frosted snap-crackle-pops. As a direct result 95 per cent of us suffer from the first 'modern' complaint I'd like to talk about, a complaint linked in turn with many other painful, debilitating, possibly fatal ailments. That complaint is constipation.

Is there any other controversial subject so seldom mentioned in public? Oh, we joke about constipation but do you know anybody who admits to suffering from it? Next time you're on a bus with ten people, look around you. Nine of your fellow travellers are fellow-sufferers and they all live on a diet (*we* all live on a diet) of highly refined and high-fat foods devoid of fibre. Fibre-deficient diets cause constipation.

To emphasise this point, a fibre-free diet was deliberately fed to Astronauts, so as to *cause* constipation and reduce the 'bath-

More about Fibre

room' problem in space. And in a scientific experiment rabbits were fed a diet of white bread and butter, milk, sugar and vitamin supplements. Their general condition deteriorated and they quickly became constipated, then developed diverticular disease–'blow-outs' in the wall of the colon which can, and do, become infected. If diverticular disease is a serious problem for rabbits it's a worse one for people. About a third of the adults in Britain suffer from it.

There's considerable evidence that constipation–irregular, insufficient or just plain slow evacuation of the bowel–may be a cause of bowel cancer, which kills more people than any cancer other than bronchial. There's little doubt that retaining noxious waste in the colon for long periods, as constipated people do, can be dangerous.

Other complications come from straining at stool, which sets up pressure in the abdomen and can cause venous disorders like varicose veins ; or hiatus hernia ; or that scourge of the Western World–haemorrhoids.

Since constipation can lead to such complications, why don't doctors insist that we have a daily bowel movement? They always used to, but now they're more relaxed about it altogether...aren't they?

The idea, apparently, is that *we* should be more relaxed about it. Doctors were insisting we should have regular motions though the food we ate made them virtually impossible. Naturally we started to get anxious about it, anxiety made our problem more severe and it was essential to get us to relax, or we'd cease functioning altogether. Resorting to laxatives only compounds the problem, as 95 per cent of us have learned to our cost.

Another ailment which is linked with the bowel is appendicitis, most commonly found in countries where the diet is highly refined, like ours. It was almost unknown in Africa until Western foods were introduced. Then the rise in consumption of 'our' diet was matched by the rise in appendicitis. In America, in the 1930's, whites living in New Orleans had four times the appendicitis rate of blacks, the poorer members of the community. The blacks fought for a living wage, got it, and promptly switched to 'white man's food', rejecting the wholewheat flour, legumes, yams and the other high-fibre foods of their traditional diet. Appendicitis among blacks became more common and today blacks and whites in the U.S.A. have more or less identical incidence of this complaint.

In rural Africa today the traditional low-fat, high-fibre diet is still eaten–and gallstones are virtually unknown. And here cholesterol comes back into the picture, for that's what gallstones are mainly composed of. At the last count British gallstones were 60 per cent cholesterol and American ones 74 per cent, so they win–but we're both in the First Division !

From the evidence now available to us we must conclude that a diet deficient in fibre contributes to diseases related to the bowel, while a diet rich in sugar and saturated fats creates an excess of fat and contributes to fatal diseases like coronary heart disease.

More and more doctors are recommending that a diet which includes fibre but reduces saturated fats and sugar has to be eaten for the sake of our health. The recipes in this book are just what the doctor ordered.

Wasting and Saving

Statistics show that we waste about 20 or 25 per cent of the fresh food we buy–good, edible food–simply because it doesn't look quite as we'd like it to, or because it's more than we can eat at one meal. The wastage is partly due to certain kitchen myths, and the first one I managed to explode is the home-made soup myth.

I always had an image of permanent stock-pots, unpleasant odours, stirring and simmering, literally days of labour to produce what is available in tins to start with.

It's nonsense. Soup can be made in the time it takes to clean the basic ingredients and put them on the stove. You turn down the burner, go away and, in a few minutes, with no more help from you, a nutritious and tasty soup is ready.

What's in it? Well, what *can* be in it is the 20 per cent of fresh food that most of us throw away: outside leaves of lettuce, wrinkled tomatoes, hard bits of cabbage, limp carrots and leftover cooked vegetables. All these are chock-full of vitamins, minerals and flavour, foods that can be combined with other ingredients, spiced up and seasoned to taste good and do us good instead of going into the dustbin and costing us money. Which explodes another myth: vegetables don't have to be 'dewy morning fresh' to be tasty and healthy.

Home-made soups contain no sugar, no white flour, no starch, no saturated fats, no artificial flavourings, preservatives or chemicals–and are so delicious that you'll wonder how you ever ate the tinned kinds.

To cut fuel costs you can cook soup in large quantities and freeze part of it in one- or two-person portions, making healthy, home-made soup just as convenient as tinned. Simply take out the quantities you need, gently heat through and it's ready to be eaten. If you don't have a freezer you can still make a good quantity of the vegetable-based soups in this book and keep them in the refrigerator, because foods that don't contain meat or animal fats can be kept safely without fear of toxicity. You can then ring the changes: today's onion soup can easily become tomorrow's minestrone, at the cost of a few pence, and the following day–it's barley soup.

The myths about bread-making had me convinced that it was an operation only slightly less tricky than brain surgery.

Again, it's nonsense. The breads in this book are as quick and easy to make as 'instant' bread, many of them not even requiring kneading, but they are twice as good as any shop-bought bread and cost about half as much. Again, baking a large quantity and freezing a few loaves is a money-saver. No freezer? Well, before mine came I shared with a neighbour. We took turns to do the baking, shared the bread we made and lived happily ever after.

Fuel is so expensive these days that any bulk cooking is a big saving. Grains and beans, both important items in this diet, can be cooked in fairly large quantities and stored in your refrigerator, whereupon they become a great 'convenience food'. Cooked rice, for example, can be 'fried', Chinese style ; spiked with onions and herbs, Spanish style ; stuffed into marrows or peppers, English style–or simply used as a bed for a tasty sauce. 'Instant' meals at ridiculously low cost, and with virtually no preparation time–yet absolutely delicious.

Wasting and Saving

Another money-saver is a pressure cooker. It's invaluable for beans, chestnuts and other long-cooking foods, while vegetables can be cooked in minutes. But, if you don't have one, gentle simmering on the burners is not the most costly way of cooking.

What is? Pre-heating the oven and keeping it hot for hours. So in this book you'll find a wide variety of dishes which can be cooked on top of the stove. And when the oven absolutely has to be used the trick is to put your entire meal into it. For the same fuel cost, you can heat soup, roast chicken and bake apples all at once.

So you can save money by buying cheaper foods, by cutting out waste, by cooking in bulk, by saving fuel generally–and when you add up what you've saved in cold, hard cash by switching to this diet you'll find a number of unexpected bonuses.

For example: over one year the average family spends a considerable sum at the chemist's on laxatives, heartburn mixtures, indigestion tablets, etc. None of these will be needed when you eat this diet.

Thousands of working days are lost each year because of food poisoning, 'upset stomachs' and other non-specific aches and pains which are directly linked with food–usually contaminated processed meats, underdone pork or other meats and meat products which have been improperly prepared, re-heated or just gone off. Clearly no such ailments will trouble you on this diet. (An 'epidemic' of headaches in America was directly attributed to the chemicals used to preserve hot dogs.)

I should point out that it's not possible to compare the cost of this diet with your usual one by isolating specific items and not relating them to the diet as a whole. For example, certain nuts may cost 80p a pound, which could be more per pound than certain meats. But nuts contain no fat or bone and they don't shrink in cooking. Secondly, a light sprinkling of nuts–barely an ounce–makes a dish more satisfying and increases the protein content at a cost of just a few pence. Thirdly, even where nuts make up the bulk of the dish–like chestnut roast–a half pound of nuts (225g) will feed four people. How much beef would you need to do that?

When you casserole meat you add various other ingredients. When casseroling cauliflower you do the same. So although cauliflower may seem pricey on a given day you must remember that a single cauliflower (plus the other ingredients mentioned earlier) will be feeding four people. It's not a side-vegetable any longer ; it's replacing meat as the centre-piece of your casserole, and you have to weigh the price of a cauliflower against that of $\frac{3}{4}$ - 1 Kg ($1\frac{1}{2}$ - 2 lbs) of meat.

Of course it's impossible to calculate like this with every item you buy. The thing to do is ease your way gradually into the diet (see next section) and then, when you're on it completely, to stay on it for a month. At the end of that time the considerable savings–also the health bonuses noted earlier–will be abundantly clear. By that time, too, your craving for meat, fat and sugar will have virtually vanished, taking your weight problem with it.

This diet will make you slim and keep you slim if you approach it sensibly.

If you've been eating two slices of lean beef and a lettuce leaf for dinner, or cottage cheese and a cracker for lunch, being able to tuck into a thick, tasty soup, a chunky vegetable stew, a bowl of brown rice and fish fritters or a fruity dessert will be almost intoxicating. Just don't get too intoxicated and eat the whole lot at once !

A glamorous actress friend came to a buffet party one evening and enjoyed the food so much she ate five main courses over several hours. Yes, *five*. Next day she complained that she'd gained a pound. Imagine eating, at one meal, a full portion of lamb stew, roast beef, steak pie, macaroni-cheese and bacon and eggs, and also imagine how many pounds *that* lot would have put on my friend.

The doctor-author of a slimming book told readers they could have as much chewing gum as they wanted. One woman complained that the diet hadn't worked. It turned out she'd been chewing more than 200 sticks of gum a day.

We're all inclined to eat too much. Though a high-fibre diet makes this harder, don't feel you have to try! If you're overweight it's better to make a meal of soup, a main dish and salad or, alternatively, a main dish, salad and a sweet, than to eat all four courses. When you achieve your desired weight you can add extra dishes if you want them.

Bearing in mind that you eat bread on this diet, you can be sure you'll never suffer the pangs of 'slimmer's starvation'. Eat only the foods in this book and only until you are satisfied. By the time your weight is normal and your body is functioning as it should you'll have found the level of intake that suits you. At that point throw away those old crash diets. Your weight problem and related health problems will be solved.

Changing Over

It's best to change over gradually. I'd suggest serving only dinner from this book for the first week, breakfast and dinner the second week and all your meals after that. A quicker change-over might cause gassy stomachs which is a completely natural reaction but one that can be avoided by a slow transition to high-fibre foods.

While eating this 'mixed' diet, I'd recommend that weight-watchers select from those recipes that give a calorie count though as I said before, once you're a full-timer you won't need to think about calories at all.

If your major problem is constipation, as it is with most of us, then eat wholewheat bread from the very beginning and buy some natural wheat bran from a health food shop. (Once we all start demanding it, supermarkets will stock it, too.) Bran is so mild-tasting it can be sprinkled onto cereals or sandwiches, added to soups and stews or cooked into rice or fruits. It's a food, not a laxative, so you can keep increasing the quantity you eat until a large, soft, daily bowel movement is achieved. Start with one teaspoonful of bran three times a day and increase this to several tablespoonsful, if necessary. Take it until you are eating a variety of high-fibre foods at every meal. Then you'll be feeling the full benefit of this diet and surplus bran will no longer be needed–but I usually add some to my wholewheat bread as a booster and eat Bran Crunch for breakfast several times a week, simply because I like it.

Cheating

The trouble with most diets is their failure-rate.

At first we conscientiously eat nothing but protein or nothing but carbohydrate or nothing but grapefruit, but after a few days the very unnaturalness of such regimes makes us crave the one thing we mustn't eat in any circumstances if we're to 'burn off the fat'. We eat it, we 'put the fire out'– and we're back where we started.

When you're living on this diet and you feel an overpowering desire to cheat– *cheat*. Nothing will happen. You won't 'put out the fire' and you won't go back to where you started. Of course you won't save money either, or lose weight (depending upon what it is you've craved) but there's no other penalty. I believe that an ice-cream in time saves nine, so when I can't resist one I have one. I'm talking now about the period *after* your first full month on the diet. During that first month you'll probably feel much too full to cheat, and in any case you should really wait to see how well you *can* feel and how much you *can* save before you lick that ice-cream.

Eating out can be a problem to dieters. When I dine out I eat whatever I'm given– suddenly noticing how awfully *sweet* the sweets are–and the following day, usually with relief, I go back to my normal diet.

At *my* dinner parties I serve *my* food and I have learned to keep a stack of recipes, neatly typed, ready to hand to departing guests.

I particularly treasure the memory of an acquaintance telling everyone at the table that she couldn't possibly serve her husband nuts for dinner, then, as she left, insisting on the recipe for 'that marvellous whatsit'. Oh yes, the whatsit was made of nuts.

I spend about one-third less on food than my friends do, yet at my dinner parties it's the *meal* that everyone talks about. This style of cooking seems to be turning into a kind of status symbol, as meat and white bread were when they were ahead of their time, and an astonishing number of people are switching over.

Food *should* be satisfying and sustaining. Food *should* keep us fit as well as alive. Food *should* be filling without being fattening. Food *should* be reasonably priced. Food *should* be a joy and a delight to eat. And this is the only diet I've ever heard of that fills all of these essential requirements.

Kitchen Equipment

Kitchen Equipment

In lots of cook-books this section starts by saying you only need the minimum amount of equipment–then lists two hundred items you 'can't manage without'.

Gadgets are nice and the right one for the job can save time. A food processor, for example, that chops, shreds, minces, liquidizes, grinds and so on is the equivalent of two live-in maids, and you don't have to feed it–though you do have to pay for it, and the price can be steep. A pressure cooker is a wonderful aid and a great saver of time and money–eventually. But in the beginning it, too, must be paid for. So start this new diet by making do with the equipment you already have except for the following items, which are vital.

1. **A blender/grinder.** Mine is the cheapest brand available. It has only one speed and no fancy buttons for chopping, puréeing, liquidizing, etc., but it does all those things and does them efficiently. A coffee-grinder attachment, included in the price, is perfect for nuts and cheese as well as coffee beans, and it turns grain into meal or flour in seconds.

You can't make the full range of health-boosting, money-saving soups given in this book without a blender and it will earn its keep in a matter of weeks.

2. **Measuring cups and spoons.** These are essential. The metric system is easy to cope with if you have a proper measuring cup, clearly marked in steps of 50ml. All you need is a cheap lightweight plastic cup that you can more or less see through ; if it will take boiling water that's an advantage.

Measuring spoons cost very little and are a great aid. Not only can you measure the precise amounts called for, but by using the same set of spoons for each spoonful of the different ingredients you can keep the balance correct. Buy light-weight, spoon-shaped spoons on a 'key ring', not thick, chunky or oddly-shaped spoons which won't fit into your salt or herb containers.

3. **A scale.** Throwing in a handful seems to work for some people, but when I throw in a handful I usually throw out a panful, so a scale saves me time and money. If you're buying one for the first time, or buying a new one, buy metric. Converting is time-wasting, also confusing, since the equivalents given are only approximate.

4. **A stiff nail brush.** With this tiny investment you'll make a big saving. Instead of peeling your vegetables and wasting a good part of them, scrub away the dirt and outer skin. It's quicker and easier than peeling, too.

5. **A heat diffuser.** This can be an asbestos pad or–costing a bit more but far preferable in health terms–a metal diffuser. This sits on your burner and spreads the heat, so that foods which need minimum simmering heat, like grains, won't burn and stick to the bottom of the pan.

6. **A chopper.** You can chop vegetables quite well with a sharp knife, but a light-weight, easy-to-handle chopper is more efficient and quicker–and you can chop fish and other foods with it, too. Choose the kind that's best for you. I can't manage the curved-blade kind with a handle at each end, but I fare quite well with a hatchet-shaped chopper or the type that has a handle on top of a large, flat blade.

Don't buy until you've handled all the

types available. The most expensive item in a kitchen is one you don't use.

7. **A salad basket/drier.** You'll be eating a lot of salads on this diet and you won't get the full flavour of your dressing unless the basic ingredients–lettuce, cabbage, spinach or whatever–are thoroughly dried after being washed. There's a pretty good gadget available, a lattice-work basket with handles. You put in the lettuce, grasp the handles and shake or swing the basket, letting the drops fly–preferably out of doors for obvious reasons !

Another, slightly more expensive but very efficient drier is a plastic bucket with an inner basket and a lid with handle attached. This works by centrifugal force–though with no force at all from you–and it spins the vegetables almost bone dry without affecting their tenderness or crispness.

8. **A steamer.** I've never had a proper steamer or fish kettle, so I make do with improvised versions, the simplest being a colander on legs which I stand in a saucepan big enough to enclose it. The food–vegetables, fish and so on–goes in the colander. A half-inch of boiling water (about 1½cm) is poured into the pan (it mustn't reach the base of the colander or it might touch the food), the tight-fitting lid is put on, the pan is put on the stove and–it's a perfect steamer.

There's a fairly cheap steaming basket available which looks like a perforated stainless steel plate on legs when it's opened fully, but which curls up at the edges, rather like a flower, so that it can be used in a smaller pan than your rigid colander. Again, food goes into the basket, water below it, you put on the tight-fitting lid and start steaming.

9. **Pans with tight-fitting lids.** Saucepans and some frying pans have well-fitting lids when they're new, but after a few years of being bashed with spoons or dropped on floors they get out of shape. You waste money and goodness when steam escapes from your pans, and the stir-fry method of cooking vegetables, which is highly recommended in this book, won't work unless the lids fit.

Obviously you can't replace all your old pans, but as you buy new ones (preferably stainless steel, with good solid bases) try to avoid the spoon-bashing and dropping that dents the edges. Meanwhile wrap aluminium foil round the top edge of a pan, then press the lid on to it–a bit tricky to do but it helps to keep the heat, and goodness, in.

As a general rule read recipes from start to finish before doing anything, then collect together *all* the ingredients and *all* the equipment. Tragedies can occur because we're searching for the sieve while the vegetables are drowning !

Weights and Measures

Weights and Measures

Though the change-over from pounds and ounces to the metric system has been traumatic for a lot of us, it may prove to be a blessing in disguise, for we can now standardise the quantities we use in the kitchen and all know exactly what's meant by them. For example–what is a teaspoonful? I use bits and pieces of three sets of cutlery, which means three sets of teaspoons, all three of different sizes. Which do I use for '1 teaspoon'? And when the recipe says 'a rounded teaspoon' or 'a heaped teaspoon'–how round is round, how high is heaped?

Metric spoons are all *level* spoons. When the recipe calls for 1×5ml spoon (the closest measure to our various old teaspoons) you simply dip your 5ml measuring spoon into the salt, or whatever you're measuring, bring it out piled high, then run the back of a knife-blade across the top of the spoon. Result: 1 level spoonful–a perfect 5ml of salt. (Don't forget to hold the spoon over the container to catch the surplus!)

And now to pints. Were those old recipes based on a 16-oz pint or a 20-oz one? And what on earth's a gill? And did the ½-cup mark on my old measuring cup mean half an 8-fluid-oz cup or half a 10-fluid-oz one? Is it any wonder that my cakes often turned to soup and my bread dough to clay?

Measuring litres is foolproof. Take your metric measuring cup, find the amount called for in the recipe–say 100ml–fill the cup with liquid to the 100ml mark and proceed with the recipe. It's simple and accurate.

Volume: Though milli*litres* are really a liquid measure, when it's convenient they're also used to measure dry ingredients, as in spoonfuls. '5ml salt' and '5ml water' are both 1 teaspoonful. In the same way our metric measuring cup can be used to measure '1 cup' of liquid or of dry ingredients.

In this book '1 cup' means 250ml. You simply find the 250ml mark on your measuring cup, fill to that point with liquid *or dry* ingredients, and that is '1 cup'. (I've actually painted a line on my cup with red nail varnish so that I can see my 250ml '1 cup' at a glance.)

The cup, or volume, method is easier and quicker for certain foods–like grains, for example, which need one part grain to two parts water. Instead of having to take out a scale *and* a measuring cup in order to prepare this simple food I just take out the cup. I fill it to the 250ml mark with grain (1 part), then fill it to the 250ml mark *twice* with water (2 parts).

In the following recipes, this is written as:

1×250ml cup (1 cup) rice
2×250ml cups (2 cups) water

A comparison of the Volume and Weights methods for brown rice is as follows:

Volume
1×250ml cup (1 cup) rice
2×250ml cups (2 cups) water
½×5ml spoon (½ tsp) salt

Weight
100g (4 ozs) rice
500ml (16 fl.ozs) water
½×5ml spoon (½ tsp) salt

Length
1 in=2½cm

When following the recipes here don't switch from the metric column to the Imperial one or you'll run into trouble. The two weights *can't* be converted accurately, so use one column or the other. But do try to get used to the metric system; it really is easy–and it's here to stay.
The numerals under each recipe heading indicate the number of servings.

Soups and Starters

Soups and Starters

Almost everybody likes good soup, but a lot of people won't eat it because they think it's fattening. Usually they're right. Soups thickened with potato, 'enriched' with butter and 'swirled' with cream are very fattening, and it's hard to find recipes that don't call for some or all of these calorie-boosters.

In the recipes that follow thin soups are transformed into thick ones simply by putting the ingredients through a blender; a push of a button that cuts out hundreds of calories while giving you cream soup that never came within a mile of cream.

Many of the soups here are based on water. Those calling for stock do not mean you have to suffer the smells, bother and expense of a permanently boiling and reboiling stock-pot. If you have a freezer you can cook your chicken or vegetables according to the recipes given, then freeze the liquid in one-serving portions and have instant, home-made stock. Or you can use cubes. There are several brands of chicken cube on the market and you should try them all. I was sure they were all alike until I tried them and found out otherwise: some taste of chemicals and salt while others really do have a flavour to match the picture on the pack. Vegetable stock cubes can be found in health food shops and they're okay for an emergency but rather expensive considering that you can make your own stock for the price of a few withered carrots, a couple of ribs of discoloured celery, a medium onion, a bayleaf and a few cups of water. I'm not suggesting you *have* to use vegetables that are a bit off, but you can make excellent stock with these foods instead of producing costly, vitamin-enriched garbage.

I never throw left-over cooked vegetables away, either. Three mushrooms, eight peas and a bit of cauliflower can improve the taste and texture of practically any soup. I never throw one spoonful of cooked rice or other grain away. It can add a little high-fibre thickening. I never throw the outside leaves of lettuce or cabbage away. They make distinctive and distinguished soups, with a little help from their friends (carrots, onions, etc.), and at the same time put a smile on the face of your Bank Manager, whether he's dining with you or not.

Some of these thick, tasty, satisfying soups are astonishingly low-calorie and can be eaten confidently during your change-over to this diet. Once you're a full-time participant, enjoy all these unusual, delicious soups whenever you want them.

Soups and Starters

1
Minted Carrot Soup
(4-5)

1 × 5ml spoon (1 tsp) oil
1 small onion, chopped
2 ribs celery, chopped
225g (8 ozs) carrots, cut in matchsticks
1 litre (36 fl.ozs) water
2 × 15ml spoons (2 tbs) tomato paste
$1\frac{1}{2}$ × 5ml spoons ($1\frac{1}{2}$ tsp) salt
ground black pepper
3-4 × 15ml spoons (3-4 tbs) fresh mint, chopped

In soup pan heat oil, stir-fry onion and celery. Add carrots, stir fry for 2 mins. Pour in water, tomato paste and seasoning. Bring to boil, cover, simmer gently for 30 mins or till carrots very tender. Stir in mint and serve immediately. *or* sprinkle mint on top of each serving bowl as a pretty green garnish.
Cals: 36

2
Lettuce Soup
(4)

1 × 5ml spoon (1 tsp) polyunsaturate margarine
1 small onion, finely chopped
1 carrot, finely chopped
225g (8 ozs) lettuce leaves, finely chopped
1 × 15ml spoon (1 tbs) wholewheat flour
450ml (16fl.ozs) skimmed milk
250ml (8 fl.ozs) water
1 × 5ml spoon (1 tsp) salt
$\frac{1}{2}$ × 5ml spoon ($\frac{1}{2}$ tsp) paprika
$\frac{1}{8}$ × 5ml spoon ($\frac{1}{8}$ tsp) ground nutmeg

Melt margarine in soup pan, sauté onion, carrot and lettuce gently for 5 mins. Sprinkle in flour and stir, then add milk, water and seasonings, stirring as soup comes to boil. Reduce heat and simmer gently, stirring occasionally, for 10 mins. Adjust seasonings and serve.

A green-speckled, slightly crisp soup that makes delicious use of throw-away outside lettuce leaves.
Cals: 80

3
Mushroom Soup
(4-5)

1 × 5ml spoon (1 tsp) oil
1 med onion, chopped
1 clove garlic, chopped
225g (8 ozs) mushrooms, sliced
700ml (24 fl.ozs) chicken stock
1 × 15ml spoon (1 tbs) cottage cheese
Sprinkle paprika

Heat oil and gently sauté onion till silver, then garlic and mushrooms till golden. Pour in stock, reduce heat to minimum, simmer for 15-20 mins. Cool slightly, put through blender with cottage cheese until creamy. Return to pan, warm through *without boiling* and adjust seasoning. Pour into serving bowls and sprinkle top of each with paprika for colour.
Cals: 35

4
Watercress Soup
(4-6)

1 × 5ml spoon (1 tsp) polyunsaturate margarine

2 med onions, chopped
225g (8 ozs or 2 bunches) watercress
450ml (16 fl.ozs) chicken stock
250ml (8 fl.ozs) skimmed milk
Salt and pepper

Melt margarine, gently sauté onions for 5 mins. Meanwhile trim coarse stems off watercress, wash and drain, then add to onions, cover pan and simmer for 4 mins. Add stock, bring to the boil, then remove from heat and add cold milk. Put through blender until creamy, then return to pan and gently heat through without boiling, adjusting seasoning, if needed.

This has the texture and flavour of a creamed, thickened soup–but with none of the disadvantages !
Cals: 40

5
Cabbage Soup
(6)

2×5ml spoons (2 tsp) oil
500g (1 lb) light green cabbage, shredded
2 med onions, chopped
1 litre (36 fl.ozs) water
600ml (20 fl.ozs) tomato juice
1×5ml spoon (1 tsp) honey
1×15ml spoon (1 tbs) salt
$\frac{1}{4}$×5ml spoon ($\frac{1}{4}$ tsp) ground black pepper
1×5ml spoon (1 tsp) caraway seeds

Heat oil, sauté cabbage and onion together gently for 15 mins, stirring occasionally, then add all other ingredients *except* caraway seeds and simmer very gently for 1 hour. Add seeds for last five minutes of cooking time.

This Russian speciality is interesting with a dollop of yogurt in it if you like the sharp flavour.

If you're making this soup to freeze, don't add the seeds. They can be added when you're warming the soup, 5 mins before serving.
Cals: 62

6
Green Pea Soup
(6)

1×5ml spoon (1 tsp) oil
1 lge onion, chopped
2 ribs celery, chopped
2 carrots, sliced
300g (11 ozs) green split peas, washed and drained
1.4 litres (48 fl.ozs) water
1×5ml spoon (1 tsp) salt
2×15ml spoons (2 tbs) Tamari soy sauce

Heat oil, sauté onion till silver, then celery and carrots till pale gold. Add split peas and water, bring to boil, then simmer very gently, covered, for 1$\frac{1}{2}$ hours. Add salt and Tamari for last 15 mins.

I like this with the split peas melted and mushy. If they don't do it put the soup through the blender until it's creamy–but first take out the carrot slices. They look lovely floating in the soup when you serve it.

7
Thick Lentil Soup
(6)

1×5ml spoon (1 tsp) oil
1 lge onion, chopped

2 ribs celery, chopped
1 lge carrot, chopped
250g (9 ozs) green or brown lentils
1.1 litre (40 fl.ozs) water
1 × 5ml spoon (1 tsp) salt
2 × 15ml (2 tbs) Tamari soy sauce

Heat oil, stir-fry onion for 2 mins, then celery and carrots for 2 mins more. Add lentils and water, bring to boil, then reduce to simmer, cover and cook for 1½ hours, adding salt and Tamari for last 15 mins.

Lentils should be tender but firm and this soup *almost* qualifies as a main course soup. If you were to add a cup of cooked grain and 100g (4 ozs) fresh string beans 10 minutes before serving, it would certainly make it.

8
Curried Lentil Soup
(5)

1 × 5ml spoon (1 tsp) oil
1 med onion, chopped
1 green pepper, chopped
1 med carrot, grated
1 litre (36 fl.ozs) water
175g (6 ozs) red lentils, picked over, washed and drained
¼ × 5ml spoon (¼ tsp) celery seed
1¼ × 5ml spoons (1¼ tsp) salt
1-1½ × 5ml spoons (1-1½ tsp) curry powder
75g (3 ozs) fresh peas

Heat oil, stir-fry onion for 2 mins, green pepper and carrot for 3 mins more. Add water, lentils, celery seed, salt and curry powder. Bring to boil, reduce to barest simmer and cook for 20 mins, covered. Stir in peas, cover, cook for 10 mins more or until peas firm/tender. Adjust seasoning and serve. (Frozen peas will need only about 2 minutes cooking time)

This is a savoury, warming soup. The small quantity of curry powder gives a subtle, not really curried, flavour and the almost chewy peas should contrast with the soft lentils.
Cals: 140

9
Tomato Soup
(4)

2 × 250ml cups (2 cups) Tomato Sauce (No. 309)
2 × 250ml cups (2 cups) vegetable stock (No. 147)

Combine, heat through, adjust seasoning and serve with crispy croutons (No. 211).
Cals: 80

10
Fresh Pea Soup
(5)

175g (6 ozs) outside lettuce leaves (or ½ crisp lettuce)
1 small onion
450ml (16 fl.ozs) chicken stock
225g (8 ozs) peas, fresh or frozen
sprig fresh mint
1 × 15ml spoon (1 tbs) polyunsaturate margarine
2 × 15ml spoons (2 tbs) wholewheat flour
450ml (16 fl.ozs) skimmed milk
1 × 5ml spoon (1 tsp) salt
pinch nutmeg
ground black pepper

Roughly chop lettuce and onion. Add to stock with half the peas and sprig of mint and bring to boil, then reduce heat and simmer till peas tender. Remove mint. Cool soup slightly, put through blender until creamy. Clean pan then melt marge in it, stir in the flour, cook for 1 min then gradually add milk, stirring continuously. Bring to gentle boil and add remaining peas, salt, pepper and nutmeg. Simmer until peas just tender, then stir in purée from blender and gently heat through. Adjust seasoning and serve.

A spring-time soup that's thick and satisfying enough for the heartiest appetite. And it's spring in winter if you use frozen peas.

Cals: 110

11
Creamed Carrot Soup
(4)

350g (12 ozs) carrots, chopped
½ small onion, chopped
1 clove garlic, chopped
1 × 15ml spoon (1 tbs) tomato paste
½ × 5ml spoon (½ tsp) salt
ground black pepper
pinch dried thyme
700ml (24 fl.ozs) chicken stock
250ml (8 fl.ozs) water

Garnish
2 ribs celery, finely chopped
1 × 15ml spoon (1 tbs) parsley, chopped

Combine all ingredients (except garnish) and bring to the boil, then reduce heat and simmer for 30 mins. Put through blender. Adjust seasoning if required, pour into individual bowls and sprinkle garnish on top of each.

Thick and sweet, with lovely crispy bits in it.

Cals: 35

12
Onion Soup
(4)

3 med onions
1 × 5ml spoon (1 tsp) oil
900ml (32 fl.ozs) vegetable stock
1 × 15ml spoon (1 tbs) fresh parsley, chopped
2 × 5ml spoons (2 tsp) yeast extract
Or
2 × 15ml spoons (2 tbs) Tamari soy sauce
Salt and pepper
1 × 5ml spoon (1 tsp) lemon juice

Thinly slice onions, sauté gently in oil for 15 mins, covering to prevent them burning. Then add stock, parsley and seasonings and simmer for 10 mins more. Stir in lemon juice and serve.

This is particularly good served with a slice of wholewheat bread that you've sprinkled with Parmesan cheese and toasted crisply. Float it in the soup. Or, if you like thick onion soup, take out half the onions when the soup is ready, put them through blender, then return to pan and heat through.

Cals: 45

Soups and Starters

13
Chicken Soup
(6)

1 small chicken, cut into eighths
Water to cover by 1 in
1 large onion, cut into eighths
2 large carrots, sliced
1 large rib celery, sliced
1 chicken stock cube
1-2 sprigs parsley
Salt and pepper

Into large pan with lid put chicken pieces, cover with water and bring to boil, skimming off all froth that rises to the top. When clear add all ingredients except salt and pepper, reduce to gentle simmer and cook, partly covered, for about 1 hour. When chicken is falling off the bone add salt and pepper, remove fat and serve. (See P. 60 for removing fat).

I make this often so as to have great soup *plus* cooked chicken for the various recipes calling for it. Always serve the sliced carrots with your soup, the onion too if you like it. For more substantial soup add a few spoons of cooked grain or noodles to each bowl.
Cals: clear, about 75

14
Celery Soup
(4)

8 lge ribs celery with leaves, chopped
1 med onion, chopped
3 sprigs parsley
1 bayleaf
800ml (28 fl.ozs) chicken stock (or vegetable)
2 × 15ml spoons (2 tbs) cottage cheese
Salt and pepper

Gently simmer celery, onion, parsley and bayleaf in stock for 30 mins. Remove bayleaf. Pour soup into blender with cottage cheese and purée till creamy. Return to pan and gently re-heat without boiling, adding a sprinkling of salt and pepper if necessary. OR take out parsley before blending and return it to pan when re-heating. It will break up and add pretty green flecks to your soup.
Cals: 56

15
Chestnut Soup
(6-7)

1 × 15ml spoon (1 tbs) polyunsaturate margarine
1 med onion, chopped
3 ribs celery, chopped
1 sharp eating apple, chopped
500g (1 lb) cooked chestnuts (No. 109)
700ml (24 fl.ozs) water
450ml (16 fl.ozs) skimmed milk
3 × 15ml spoons (3 tbs) wheat bran
$\frac{1}{4}$ × 5ml spoon ($\frac{1}{4}$ tsp) nutmeg
ground black pepper
1 × 5ml spoon (1 tsp) salt

Melt margarine, sauté onion, celery and apple for 5 mins. Put this mixture into blender with chestnuts and about 450ml (16 fl.ozs) water and blend till creamy. Return soup to pan. Stir in nutmeg, pepper and salt, remainder of water and the milk. Simmer gently, uncovered, for 10 mins. Stir in the bran, simmer for 5 mins more and serve.

This is such a sweet, creamy soup, so rich and filling, that only a small bowl is needed. I sometimes reserve one-third of the chestnuts and blend the remainder as above till creamy, then add the remaining third and just give a brief buzz in the blender so that the finished soup has little chestnut bumps in it.

16
Gazpacho
(3)

3 lge ripe tomatoes, sliced
½ green pepper, seeded, sliced
½ mild, small onion (or 1 slice of med onion)
8cm cucumber (about 3 in), sliced
1 clove garlic
1 × 5ml spoon (1 tsp) salt
¼ × 5ml spoon (¼ tsp) ground black pepper
100ml (4 fl.ozs) cold water
3 × 15ml spoons (3 tbs) wine vinegar
1 × 15ml spoon (1 tbs) oil

Combine all ingredients in blender and blend till smooth. Chill, and serve with diced cucumber and onion or crispy wholewheat croutons (No. 211) sprinkled on top.

This spicy, cold Spanish soup is unbeatable on a hot day.
Cals: 64

17
Chilled Beetroot Soup
(3)

225g (8 ozs) boiled beetroot, peeled
2 × 15ml spoons (2 tbs) onion, chopped
1 med eating apple, sliced
250ml (8 fl.ozs) buttermilk
1 × 15ml spoon (1 tbs) lemon juice
½ × 5ml spoon (½ tsp) honey
½ × 5ml spoon (½ tsp) salt
ground black pepper
3 × 15ml spoons (3 tbs) cold water

Combine all ingredients in blender and blend till creamy.

If you forget to buy the buttermilk use two-thirds natural yogurt mixed with one-third skimmed milk.
Cals: 85

18
Hearty Bean Soup
Main Course Soup
(8)

1 × 5ml spoon (1 tsp) oil
1 lge onion, chopped
2 carrots, chopped
2 ribs celery, chopped
1.4 litres (48 fl.ozs) vegetable or chicken stock
500g (1 lb) pulped tomatoes (or tinned)
1 lge bayleaf
75g (3 ozs) green lentils
500g (1 lb) cooked, mixed dried beans
2 × 15ml spoons (2 tbs) Tamari soy sauce
Salt and pepper

Heat oil, stir-fry onion for 2 mins then carrot and celery for 3 mins. Pour in stock, tomatoes, bayleaf and lentils and simmer uncovered for 15 mins. Add cooked beans and Tamari. Return to boil, reduce heat and simmer gently, uncovered, for 45–60 mins, stirring occasionally, adjusting seasoning 5 mins before cooking is completed.

Soups and Starters

If your pre-cooked dried beans are a bit mushy just give them 20-30 mins in the soup. Ideally they should be firm-tender for a 45-min cooking time. I always make this quantity and freeze half. It seems to taste even better after re-heating.

Special Garnish (optional)

Combine:

2 × 5ml spoons (2 tsp) grated lemon peel
1 × 5ml spoon (1 tsp) finely chopped garlic
2 × 15ml spoons (2 tbs) fresh parsley, chopped.

19
Chicken Gumbo

Main Course Soup
(6)

1 lge onion
500g (1 lb) tomatoes
2 med green peppers, seeded
225g (8 ozs) okra
50g (2 ozs) wholewheat flour
$1\frac{1}{2}$Kg (3 lb) chicken, cut in 2 in pieces, skinned
2 × 15ml spoons (2 tbs) oil
1.4 litres (48 fl.ozs) chicken stock
1 × 5ml spoon (1 tsp) salt
$\frac{1}{4}$ × 5ml spoon ($\frac{1}{4}$ tsp) pepper
175g (6 ozs) sweet corn kernels
75g (3 ozs) cooked brown rice or other grain

Chop onion, tomatoes and one green pepper. Cut second green pepper into matchsticks, set aside. If okra are large, slice into 1 in pieces. Put flour into a bag, drop in chicken pieces a few at a time and shake till coated lightly with flour. Heat oil in large soup pan with lid. After shaking excess flour off chicken put each piece into oil and sauté, removing when golden. In same oil stir-fry chopped pepper and onions for 5 mins, scraping up any bits of crispy chicken sticking to pan and stirring in. Add tomatoes, stock and seasoning, part cover and simmer for 1 hour or till chicken very tender. Stir in corn,[1] green pepper matchsticks and okra. Return to boil, cover and simmer gently, part-covered, for 25 mins. Add rice, cook for 5 mins more, serve.

This is a glorious, traditional dish from America's Deep South. A salad before it and a fruity dessert to follow is all you'll need.

Cals: 340

20
Turkey Soup

Main Course Soup
(6)

Reserve 75-100g (3-4 ozs) cooked turkey pieces cut off carcase
Make stock from carcase (No. 73) and strain
1 × 5ml spoon (1 tsp) oil
1 lge onion, chopped
2 carrots, chopped
2 ribs celery, chopped
2 sprigs parsley
75g (3 ozs) raw barley, washed, drained
Salt and pepper

In soup pan heat oil and stir-fry onion for 2 mins, carrots and celery for 3 mins more. Pour strained turkey stock over vegetables, add parsley, barley and a little salt. Bring to boil, reduce heat, part-cover and simmer

---

[1] If using tinned corn, add with rice.

for about 1 hour. Add turkey pieces and heat them through, adjust salt, add pepper to taste and serve.

For variation a few fresh green peas or string beans are good.
Cals: 103

21
Mulligatawny
Main Course Soup
(6)

1 × 5ml spoon (1 tsp) oil
1 lge onion, chopped
2 ribs celery, chopped
2 med carrots, chopped
1 × 15ml spoon (1 tbs) curry powder (or to taste)
1.1 litre (40 fl.ozs) chicken stock
225g (8 ozs) tomatoes, chopped
1 med cooking apple, chopped
$\frac{1}{8}$ × 5ml spoon ($\frac{1}{8}$ tsp) ground nutmeg
$\frac{1}{8}$ × 5ml spoon ($\frac{1}{8}$ tsp) dried thyme
2 whole cloves
$\frac{3}{4}$ × 5ml spoon ($\frac{3}{4}$ tsp) salt
1$\frac{1}{2}$ × 250ml cups (1$\frac{1}{2}$ cups) cooked, diced chicken
75g (3 ozs) cooked brown rice

In large soup pan heat oil and stir-fry onion, celery and carrots for 5 mins. Stir in curry powder, cook for 2 mins. Add stock and tomatoes, simmer uncovered for 20 mins. Add all remaining ingredients and simmer uncovered for 25 mins more over minimum heat. Adjust curry powder and salt, remove cloves and serve.

This knife-and-fork soup is so subtly flavoured that guests play 'what's in it' down to the last drop of their seconds (and sometimes thirds).

To serve as a soup course, add 250-450ml (8-16 fl.ozs) more chicken stock and you'll feed two more on the thinner, but still wonderfully tasty soup.
Cals: (6) 132

22
Barley Soup
Main Course Soup
(4)

1 × 5ml spoon (1 tsp) oil
1 med onion, chopped
1 rib celery, sliced
1 carrot, sliced
1 clove garlic, chopped
100g (4 ozs) mushrooms, sliced
75g (3 ozs) whole raw barley, washed and drained
900ml (32 fl.ozs) chicken or vegetable stock
1 sprig parsley
1 × 5ml spoon (1 tsp) salt
ground black pepper
1 × 15ml spoon (1 tbs) Tamari soy sauce
100g (4 ozs) fresh green beans, 1$\frac{1}{2}$ in pieces
1 × 5ml spoon (1 tsp) lemon juice

Heat oil, stir-fry onion, celery and carrot till turning golden. Add garlic and mushrooms, stir-fry for 2 mins more. Add barley, stock, parsley, salt, pepper and soy sauce. Reduce heat, cover and simmer for about 1 hour, till barley chewy-tender. Add grean beans and cook for 5-10 mins till they are firm-tender. Stir in lemon juice and serve.

This needs no garnish, but for special occasions try Special Garnish from No. 18 instead of using lemon juice in the soup.
Cals: 128

Soups and Starters

23
Nut Pâté
(350g, 12 ozs)

2 med tomatoes, skinned
75g (3 ozs) soft wholewheat breadcrumbs (No. 206)
½ small onion
1 × 15ml spoon (1 tbs) fresh parsley
1 × 5ml spoon (1 tsp) polyunsaturate margarine
½ × 5ml spoon (½ tsp) salt
generous ground black pepper
50g (2 ozs) roasted peanuts, finely ground
50g (2 ozs) walnuts, finely ground

In blender, purée all ingredients except nuts.[1] Transfer purée to bowl, stir in nuts, chill.

Serve as a starter on a bed of crisp lettuce or as a dip (thin slightly with tomato juice) or spread on crackers. It's very good on Corn Crispies, No. 210.

24
Chickpea 'Nuts'

2 × 5ml spoons (2 tsp) corn oil
175g (6 ozs) cooked chickpeas (No. 103)
½ × 5ml spoon (½ tsp) salt
½ × 5ml spoon (½ tsp) garlic powder or dried, ground garlic

Heat oil, sprinkle in salt and garlic and cook for a moment or two. Pour in beans, stir and shake to coat them, then cook over med heat until they turn golden–about 10 minutes. Stir to prevent sticking, but don't mash the beans.

Serve as a cocktail snack, hot or cold, instead of cholesterol-rich nibbles.

---

[1] If your blender will take a very thick, firm mixture, process all ingredients at once, including the finely ground nuts.

25
Pear Starter
(4)

2 large ripe pears
½ fresh lemon
225g (8 ozs) low fat cottage cheese
2 × 15ml spoons (2 tbs) raisins
50g (2 ozs) chopped walnuts

Cut pears in half, rub cut edges with lemon to prevent darkening, then slice lemon to use as garnish. Combine cottage cheese and raisins. Scoop core and seeds out of pears and put big spoonful of cottage cheese mixture in centre of each, sprinkling nuts on top. Decorate with lemon 'wheels'.

26
Mushroom Pâté
(Starter: 4 Dip: 8)

225g (8 ozs) mushrooms
1½ × 15ml spoons (1½ tbs) polyunsaturate margarine
3 × 15ml spoons (3 tbs) wholewheat flour
250ml (8 fl.ozs) skimmed milk
1 × 15ml spoon (1 tbs) skimmed milk powder
½ × 5ml spoon (½ tsp) salt
¼ × 5ml spoon (¼ tsp) grated nutmeg
ground black pepper
pinch paprika
3 × 15ml spoons (3 tbs) natural yogurt
Garnish: chopped chives or toasted nuts

Chop mushrooms, sauté gently in ½ × 15ml spoon (½ tbs) margarine. Make roux: melt remaining spoonful margarine, stir in flour, then add milk gradually. Add milk powder and stir till creamy. Season, simmer for 2 mins more, then stir in mushrooms and all juices from pan. Cool, chill, stir in yogurt, adjust seasoning. Put a mound on a lettuce leaf for each person and sprinkle garnish over. To serve as a dip, thin slightly with skimmed milk, pour into pretty bowl, garnish, then set dish in centre of table with Corn Crispies (No. 210) to dip in.

27
Cheese Dip and Crudités
(6)

225g (8 ozs) low-fat cottage cheese
75ml (3 fl.ozs) skimmed milk
¼ × 5ml spoon (¼ tsp) salt
generous ground black pepper
1 × 15ml spoon (1 tbs) Parmesan cheese
1 spring onion, chopped
2 × 15ml spoons (2 tbs) chopped fresh parsley
Put all ingredients except onion and parsley into blender and blend till creamy. Add onion and parsley and blend till green speckled–but don't over-blend or you'll lose the colour and crispy bits. Chill for 30 mins, then spoon into a bowl, place in centre of table.

Crudités:

bite-sized pieces of fresh, crispy, raw vegetables.
Select your favourite vegetable, dip one end into the cheese dip and enjoy a delightful, low-calorie munch.

Select from: Cucumber chunks, carrot strips, celery strips, cauliflower florets, radishes, baby mushrooms, green or red pepper strips, etcetera.
Variation: Make Cheese Dip as above. Finely dice about 3 in chunk of cucumber and stir it in. Then set out a plateful of Corn Crispies (No. 210) and Rye Crackers (No. 209) and dip those instead of vegetables.

28
Stuffed Celery

Scrub large ribs of celery and chill them.
Fillings: 1. Cottage cheese topped with sliced olives or chopped dates and walnuts.
2. Nut Paté (No. 23)

29
Avocado Vinaigrette
(2)

1 ripe avocado pear
4-6 × 15ml spoons (4-6 tbs) Vinaigrette (No. 304)

Simply cut the pear in half, carefully remove the stone and put the halves on two small plates. Spoon the dressing into the centre cavity–and enjoy a gourmet start to a meal.

About once a year there's a glut of avocado pears and the price comes down. Then I make the following Mexican-style dip:

Soups and Starters

30
Guacamole
(4-6)

2 very ripe avocado pears, peeled, mashed
$\frac{1}{2}$ × 5ml spoon ($\frac{1}{2}$ tsp) chili powder
1 × 15ml spoon (1 tbs) lemon juice
1 spring onion, finely chopped
1 ripe tomato, skinned, finely chopped
pinch garlic powder and paprika
Salt and pepper to taste

If using immediately mash the pears, combine with all other ingredients and either pile on to crackers or spoon into a bowl to serve as a dip with Corn Crispies (No. 210). If preparing in advance combine all except the lemon juice and put into a bowl. Brush the lemon juice all over the surface and cover tightly before refrigerating. This stops the top from turning dark. Stir well before serving to distribute the lemon juice.

Fish

Fish

The real secret of success with fish is to have a good fishmonger. We can seldom prod a fish nowadays to be sure it's firm, open its gills to see if they're pink or sniff it to be sure it smells only of the ocean. We have to trust the person behind the counter. If you are sold inferior fish at your local shop go back and complain very strongly. If it happens again–buy elsewhere! Spend your money only where you get good quality and service, which means the fish being gutted, beheaded, scaled, filleted–whatever you want done–so that you just have to rinse it and cook it when you get home. All good fishmongers give this service if asked–and don't forget to request that the skin, head and bones be wrapped up with your fish; you've paid for them and they'll make a wonderful stock. Fish stock can't be bought in a cube, so these trimmings–and any others your fishmonger has available–are worth having Just simmer them with a few vegetables and you have a rich, flavourful liquid that can make all the difference to fish entrées and soups.

There are occasions when you have to cope with cleaning, skinning or filleting at home, either because a fisherman friend lands you with his catch or, as is often the case with me, you change the menu when it's too late for your fishmonger to help. You'll find a little advice on this, as well as some basic ways of cooking fish, at the beginning of the recipe section.

If you can't get fresh fish then frozen is fine. It's often frozen right there on the trawler, or certainly very soon after being caught, so it's very fresh indeed. The full flavour can be preserved by thawing it out in its freezer wrappings in the refrigerator rather than at room temperature, then cooking it as soon as the ice crystals have melted. I usually transfer it from the freezer to fridge early in the morning for that evening's meal or, with large, whole fish, the night before. Should you de-frost fish and find you can't use it that day, don't leave it uncooked for another twenty-four hours. Poach it lightly or grill it, then refrigerate it. You can use it next day in a 'cold' recipe and it will have a fresh, lovely flavour.

The texture of fish is at its most delicate when it comes out of the ocean, so you don't have to cook it to tenderise it. On the contrary, over-cooking can toughen and spoil it. A short cooking time and gentle heat are all that fish needs for perfect taste and texture. Could there be a better food for keeping down the fuel bills?

Of course, the price of fish has risen along with everything else, but there are so many different kinds–many of them ignored by us because we're reluctant to try the unfamiliar–that some variety is always 'running', which means plentiful and cheap. My family eat a lot of herring, mackerel and mullet, rich, oily fish that can be cooked in dozens of appetising ways. We also enjoy coley, bass, hake and whiting–fish that needs dressing up a little but is marvellous dressed; while cod, haddock, plaice and all the other more familiar fish are eaten regularly, price permitting. I don't recall the last time we ate salmon, turbot, halibut or any other 'fashionable' fish, because they're just too expensive–and honestly, you don't need them. When the recipes here call for 'any white fish', that means *any* white fish. They are all mild in flavour and respond similarly to gentle cooking with simple flavourings. When a recipe says 'any fish', you can make

Fish

the same dish twice in a week, using herring the first time and skate the next, and nobody will guess what you've done because the taste will be so different. I hasten to say that you don't *have* to do this– there are enough recipes here for you to ring all the changes you like–but don't be afraid to experiment. Try fish with funny names and odd appearances. You'll be agreeably surprised at their good flavour.

There is no fish at all that needs to be smothered in butter and cream. Fish-as-it-comes is low-calorie and high-protein, a perfect food to keep you slim and healthy. Once the smothering starts, you're simply adding calories plus saturated fat (not to mention cost), whereas wonderfully tasty and nutritious fish soups, stews, bakes and pies–a wide variety of dishes–can be prepared without any unhealthy fat at all. Remember that fish oil is polyunsaturated, which doubles its value to our diet.

Fish itself doesn't contain any dietary fibre, so unless the recipe you choose actually includes grain (like Fish with Wheat, No. 44 or Stuffed Fish, Nos. 55, 57, 59), you must always serve a grain with it. Millet is particularly good with white fish and buckwheat is marvellous with the oily species, but all whole grains add fibre as well as a taste and texture that wonderfully complement fish.

There is no seafood (shellfish) in this book. Seafood is high in cholesterol and even higher in price, so I've cut it out completely. Remembering the pallid prawns, tasteless crab and rubbery odds-and-ends in shells that used to disappoint me, this has been no loss at all.

Smoked fish, on the other hand, is a very valuable addition to this diet. Since it is already cooked it doesn't feature in the recipe section, but do eat kippers, smoked trout and buckling, scrumptious smoked mackerel– really, any fish at all (other than seafood) that has been cured. They make great breakfasts, good appetisers and tasty main courses once they are combined with a grain, a steamed vegetable and a raw salad.

Finally: leftovers.

I never freeze cooked fish, or re-heat it. If there's some left over, I keep it in the refrigerator overnight and use it next day in one of the cold fish dishes. Fish-in-Aspic Flan (No. 68) is perfect for this ; a dish with such eye-appeal that you can confidently serve it to guests without anyone suspecting the fish of giving a repeat performance.

Fish

31
To Clean Fish
Spread newspaper in your sink and put the fish on it. With a medium-sized knife scrape the skin until the scales begin to fly off – and fly they will, so run a little cold water on the fish as you work to keep them down. Next cut off the fins and sharp bits, then slit open the belly and remove the innards until the backbone is cleanly exposed. Pile these into the newspaper with the scales, gather it together, throw it away and you've a nice clean sink in which to run cold water and wash the fish, inside and out. Behead it, if you wish, pat it dry and it's ready to be cooked.

32
To Bone Thick Fish
(already cleaned) like mackerel, herring, trout, etc.
Cut off the head. Place slit side down on a board and firmly, with your thumbs, press down along the backbone from head to tail. You'll feel it give under your pressure. Turn the fish over–and the backbone, plus a lot of attached little bones, will easily pull out.

33
To Bone Flat Fish
You will end up with four fillets cut away from the flat bone. First take a small, sharp knife and make an incision down the centre, lengthways. Then slip the knife under the flesh at the head end and, pressing down onto the bone, slide the knife towards the tail end, raising the flesh as you go. Repeat this motion as you work from the centre to side of the fish, and when you arrive at the row of tiny edgeing bones cut off your first fillet. Repeat with the second side, then turn the fish over and do it all again.

34
To Skin Fillets
Place the fillet skin-side down on a board, the tail towards you. With a sharp knife raise a little of the flesh at the tail end, so that you can see the inside of the skin underneath it. Now place the knife under the raised flesh at an angle against the skin and, pressing firmly, work your way towards the head. The flesh will come neatly away from the skin as you go.

35
To Skin Whole Fish
With a sharp knife make a slit in the skin along the backbone from head to tail, then raise a little of the skin at the tail end, scraping it from the flesh. Grasp this raised skin firmly in your hand and pull, and with a bit of luck the skin will pull cleanly off this side of the fish. Repeat with the second side.

36
To Poach Fish (I)
Pour your poaching liquid into a fish kettle or pan (I use a large, deep frying pan) and heat it to just warm. Put in the fish and let the heat increase till the water is just shivering, which means the bubbles rise but don't pop through the surface. Once this simmering point is reached, time your fish as follows:

small fillets or fish with total weight of under 900g (2 lbs) .... about 8 mins

Fish

1-2 kg (2-4 lbs) .... about 15 mins
2-3 kg (4-6 lbs) .... about 20 mins

...and so on, adding about 5 mins for each kilo (2 lbs) of fish. I'd cook the fish in two lots if I had more than 3 or 4 kg (6 or 8 lbs) so that it would fit into the pan in one layer.

Whatever you do, don't *boil* the fish. Water that's 150°F will cook fish and boiling point is 212°F![1] All we want to do is change the texture of the fish from transparent and 'wet'-looking to opaque and just-firm.

To Poach Fish (II)

Wash and pat the fish dry, place it on aluminium foil large enough to cover well, sprinkle it with salt, pepper and lemon juice, plus thyme, fennel or whatever herb you like, then wrap the foil around the fish, sealing it well so that the water won't get in and the juices won't get out. Now put the package into a pan of cold water, bring it to the simmering point and keep it there for the times given above.

Really small fillets, or cutlets up to one inch thick ($2\frac{1}{2}$cm), don't need to simmer at all. Wrap them as above, put them in cold water, bring the water to the boil, then put on a tight-fitting lid and immediately remove the pan from the heat. Let the fish stand for about 10 minutes if you want to eat it hot; cool it in the liquid and then refrigerate it if you want it cold.

37
To Grill Fish

Contrary to popular belief you don't need to smother fish in butter to grill it properly. A transparent coating of oil or margarine painted on before seasoning will help the skin to crisp, but even that isn't strictly necessary if, for example, you're changing over and watching calories. However:

Lightly brush the fish with melted polyunsaturate margarine or oil, generously sprinkle lemon juice (which will keep the cooking smell down), add salt and pepper to taste, stand on grill tray or rack and pop under a heated grill.

Whole small fish, like mackerel, codling, trout, etc...
about 7 minutes each side

Flat fish like plaice, sole, dab, flounder, etc. (If especially thick, allow 1 minute more each side)...
about 5 minutes each side

Cutlets or steaks about 1 in thick...
about 6 minutes each side

Fillets of flat fish ..
about 7 minutes altogether without turning over

Fillets of thicker fish...
about 7 minutes on flesh side. Turn, give about 3 minutes on skin to crisp slightly.

Remember, we're not trying to 'tenderise' fish, merely to change its texture. So try these timings, then stick a skewer into the fish near the bone and lift. If flesh comes away easily and is firm and opaque it's done. Fillets will certainly be done.

38
To Bake Fish

While fillets or chunks of fish will generally bake in about 20 minutes at 180°-190°C (350°-375°F, Gas 4-5), a medium-sized fish needs about 30 minutes and a large one about 40. You can bake with or without a

[1] 60°C . . . 105°C

lid, depending on whether the dish is supposed to be crisp and brown or tender and white, or bake *'en papillote'*, when fish and seasonings are wrapped securely in foil or paper. All these methods are used in the following recipes and all give delicious results. If you want to do some experimenting the timings given above should help. I always bake fish in oven-to-tableware to avoid extra handling of this fragile food.

Baking costs more than poaching or grilling because of pre-heating and then maintaining a hot oven, but if your dessert is cooking at the same time (which means, of course, something calling for the same temperature) you'll be getting better value for money.

39
To Fry Fish

Though fried foods are somewhat hard to digest, at least when fried with polyunsaturate oil they're not bad for you– but do follow these rules:

1. Take fish out of the refrigerator 15 minutes before cooking so that it reaches room temperature.
2. If you're not using a batter make sure that the fish is dry, blot it on kitchen paper and dip it in wholewheat flour (seasoned with salt and pepper) before putting it into the frying pan.
3. The oil must be hot enough (about 190°C ;370°F) before the fish goes in. I've tried using a thermometer but it can only be used for deep frying and it's messy. I've tried dropping in bits of bread and timing their colour change, but that never works for me, either. So I just turn the heat to medium-high, wait until a thin wisp of smoke rises from the oil, then put the fish in. If it's thick fish I usually reduce the heat slightly, but without letting the strong bubbling diminish. When the fish is golden on both sides, I stand it on a rack to let as much oil as possible drip off, then put it on kitchen paper to blot it dry. If you use really hot oil, as described here, the fish will not absorb any grease at all, but will be tender and flaky inside and dry and crisp outside.
4. Always keep the lid of the frying pan close by. Don't *ever* use it while you're frying fish, but if the oil should accidentally catch alight *immediately* put the lid on the pan and the flames will die down.
5. So long as you don't let your polyunsaturate oil burn and turn black it can be used several times, for it doesn't retain the flavour of the fish. I let it cool in the frying pan then put it through a strainer lined with muslin, strain it twice, then pour it into a glass jar and store it in the refrigerator. (Never pour used oil back into the plastic containers it sometimes comes in.) Don't throw the muslin away or you'll always be buying it. Just wash it well in washing-up liquid, rinse, dry and re-use.

40
Fish Stock

500g (1 lb) head, skin and bones of white fish
1 litre (36 fl.ozs) water
6 whole black peppercorns
2×15ml spoons (2 tbs) lemon juice
1 med onion, sliced
1 carrot, sliced
1 bouquet garni (optional)
$\frac{1}{2}$×5ml spoon ($\frac{1}{2}$ tsp) salt

Fish

Combine all ingredients in saucepan, bring to boil then reduce and simmer very gently (water just 'shivering') for 30 mins. Strain well through fine sieve, or sieve lined with muslin.

If you have some white wine left over replace 1 cup of water with 1 cup of wine (about 250ml), and reduce lemon juice to 1 × 15ml spoon (1 tbs)

If you have no fish trimmings, make the following liquid to use for poaching fish:

41
Poaching Liquid
Court Bouillon

1 litre (36 fl.ozs) water
6 whole black peppercorns
2 × 15ml spoons (2 tbs) lemon juice
1 med onion, sliced
1 carrot, sliced
1 sprig parsley
1 bay leaf
A few mushroom trimmings (optional)
$\frac{1}{2}$ × 5ml spoon ($\frac{1}{2}$ tsp) salt

Combine and simmer gently for 30 mins, strain and use. As with stock, you can replace 1 cup of water with 1 cup white wine, reducing the lemon juice to 1 × 15ml spoon (1 tbs).

Once you have poached fish in this liquid you will have a magnificent stock to use for soup !

42
Basic Poaching Liquid
Basic Court Bouillon

Simplest of all, least tasty, but quite satisfactory if you want to poach fish in a hurry:

1 litre (36 fl.ozs) water
6 whole black peppercorns
1-2 × 15ml spoons (1-2 tbs) lemon juice
1 × 5ml spoon (1 tsp) salt

43
Plaice Suzette
(4)

Marinade:
6 × 15ml spoons (6 tbs) orange juice
3 × 15ml spoons (3 tbs) lemon juice
1 × 15ml spoon (1 tbs) finely chopped onion
1 whole clove
Pinch dried basil

4 lge or 8 small plaice fillets
Salt and pepper
1 × 15ml spoon (1 tbs) polyunsaturate margarine

Combine marinade and let it stand 1 or more hours. Lightly grease heatproof plate, arrange fillets on it, sprinkle with salt and pepper. Add a few dots of margarine, then strain marinade and spoon half of it over the fish. Grill for 4 mins. Spoon over remaining marinade and grill for 4 mins more. Serve.
Cals: 185

This simple dish has a really exotic flavour ; it can be garnished with a 'wheel' of orange and sprig of watercress for party eye-appeal.

Fish

44
Fish with Wheat and Mushrooms
(4)

500g (1 lb) fish fillets
Salt and pepper
Lemon juice

1 × 15ml spoon (1 tbs) polyunsaturate margarine
2 × 15ml spoons (2 tbs) wholewheat flour
300ml (10 fl.ozs) skimmed milk
½ × 5ml spoon (½ tsp) salt
¼ × 5ml spoon (¼ tsp) grated nutmeg
100g (4 ozs) mushrooms, sliced

100g (4 ozs) bulgur wheat
¾ × 5ml spoon (¾ tsp) salt
350ml (12 fl.ozs) water

6 spring onions, chopped
1 × 15ml spoon (1 tbs) fresh parsley, chopped

Sprinkle fish with salt, pepper and lemon juice and set aside. Melt margarine, stir in flour and cook over gentle heat for 1-2 mins. Gradually stir in milk and simmer for 5 mins. Stir in salt, nutmeg and mushrooms and simmer for 5 mins more. Remove from heat, set aside.

In saucepan combine wheat, salt and water, bring to boil, cover, turn to minimum heat–use diffuser– and cook for 10 mins.

Grease ovenproof dish (with lid), spread cooked bulgur wheat at the bottom and sprinkle over it the chopped onions and parsley. Place fish on top and pour mushroom sauce over. Bake for 30 mins, covered, in pre-heated oven–180°C (350°F, Gas 4).
Cals: (with whiting) 280

45
Pan-Fried Fish

1 small fish or 1 thick fillet per person (175g, 6 ozs) each
Paprika
Salt and pepper
Lemon juice
1-2 × 5ml spoons (1-2 tsp) polyunsaturate margarine
1-2 × 15ml spoons (1-2 tbs) chopped fresh herbs (optional)

Rinse fish and pat dry. Sprinkle one side with paprika, just to colour, then salt and pepper to taste and a little lemon juice. Melt margarine to bubbling, put in fish *seasoned side down* and cook about 1 min, meanwhile seasoning other side and sprinkling on the herbs. Turn fish over, immediately cover with tightly fitting lid and reduce heat to minimum. Cook 8-10 mins and serve with juices poured over.

Use a non-stick pan, or well seasoned frying pan, with tight-fitting lid.

The fish is delicately coloured by the paprika, pleasantly flavoured by seasoning and herbs and wonderfully moist and appetising. Frozen fillets become special cooked this way.
Cals: haddock, 188 mackerel, 344

I serve garlicky spinach and a grain; and calories are so low I usually follow with a lovely pudding, like Almond Rice Cream (No. 269).

Fish

46
Fishkebabs
(4)

100g (4 ozs) mushrooms, med caps
1 med green pepper
1 bunch fresh sage or fennel leaves
4 large, firm tomatoes
500g (1 lb) any firm fish, cut into 1 in cubes (about 16).

Prepare vegetables: Wipe mushrooms with damp cloth, leaving caps whole. De-seed pepper, cut into chunks, then drop into boiling salted water to blanch for 2 mins. Drain, rinse under cold tap to freshen. Wash herbs and shake dry. Cut tomatoes into quarters.

Sauce: Combine
2×15ml spoons (2 tbs) Tamari soy sauce
2×5ml spoons (2 tsp) oil
2×5ml spoons (2 tsp) lemon juice
ground black pepper

Dip fish into the sauce, turning it several times. Sprinkle prepared vegetables with salt and pepper. Lightly oil skewers and thread fish, herbs and vegetables alternately, making sure a leaf of the herb is beside each cube of fish. Heat grill. Place completed skewers on grill pan or over a roasting tin–anything with edges on which you can rest skewers and which will fit under the grill. Grill first side for 7 mins and second side for 5 mins, sprinkling the remaining sauce, or drippings from the grill pan, over the food as it cooks.

Place one skewer on a bed of brown rice for each diner.

Cals: white fish, 168 oily fish, 240

47
Fish Peperonata
(4)

1×5ml spoon (1 tsp) oil
2 med onions, sliced
2 green peppers, seeded and sliced
2 red peppers, seeded and sliced
500g (1 lb) tomatoes, chopped (or tin)
Salt and pepper
350g (12 ozs) fish fillets (any kind) in chunks
Paprika

Heat oil, sauté onion till turning brown, add peppers and cook gently for 5 mins, turning frequently. Add tomatoes, salt and pepper, cover and simmer for 10 mins. Place fish chunks on top, sprinkle with paprika and salt, cover again and cook gently for 10 mins more.

Serve on a bed of brown rice with a fresh green salad.

Or stir in a cup or two of cooked dried beans just before you add the fish.

48
Sweet and Sour Fish
(4)

This is a fantastic dinner-party dish. It looks like hours of work instead of about 10 minutes and the sauce is so delicious and rich that you can use really cheap fish (I use whiting or codling) and still have a feast.
A whole fish looks more imposing; get one which will give about 750g ($1\frac{1}{2}$ lbs) of edible flesh. So:

1 whole fish or 4 individual fish – rinse and pat dry.

Sauce:
$1\frac{1}{2}$ × 5ml spoons ($1\frac{1}{2}$ tsp) arrowroot
4 × 15ml spoons (4 tbs) cold water
2 × 15ml spoons (2 tbs) tomato paste
1 × 15ml spoon (1 tbs) Tamari soy sauce
2 × 15ml spoons (2 tbs) honey
2 × 15ml spoons (2 tbs) wine vinegar
1 red pepper, seeded, cut into matchsticks
Peel from $\frac{1}{2}$ orange, cut into matchsticks

Stir arrowroot into water, then combine with all other sauce ingredients in saucepan. Paint a thin coating of sauce on the fish, then put under hot grill for 10 mins. Turn fish, paint a coat of sauce on second side and grill for 7 mins. *Meanwhile* heat sauce gently, stirring until it thickens, 5-7 minutes, so fish and sauce will be done at the same time. Carefully transfer fish to a serving platter and spoon the sauce over it, complete with peel and peppers.

For additional colour, garnish with watercress or spring onions.

Rice-with-pumpkin-seeds and a bowl of steamed beansprouts are marvellous with this dish.

Cals: (white fish) 208

49
Smoked Haddock and Wheat Berries
(4)

75g (3 ozs) red lentils
350g (12 ozs) smoked haddock fillet
1 × 5ml spoon (1 tsp) oil
2 ribs celery, chopped
1 lge onion, chopped
1 green pepper, seeded, chopped
350ml (12fl.ozs) boiling water
$\frac{1}{2}$ × 5ml spoon ($\frac{1}{2}$ tsp) salt
350g (12 ozs) cooked whole wheat (No. 228)
3 × 15ml spoons (3 tbs) skimmed milk
3 × 15ml spoons (3 tbs) fresh parsley, chopped

Pick over lentils, wash and drain. Poach haddock: cover with cold water, bring to gentle simmer and cook for 10 mins. Drain, flake fish. Heat oil in large pan (with lid) and stir-fry celery, onion and green pepper for 5 mins. Add lentils, salt and boiling water, cover tightly, reduce heat to minimum–use diffuser–and cook for 25 mins. Remove from heat, stir in wheat and milk (adding more milk if very thick), then fold in fish and gently heat through. Spoon into serving dish and sprinkle parsley over.

A salad with, and a fruity dessert after, is all you'll be able to manage.

50
Bouillabaise
(6)

There are as many fish stews as there are varieties of fish. This one is not only delicious, it's also economical, which makes it hard to beat.

1 × 5ml spoon (1 tsp) oil
2 leeks, carefully washed and finely sliced
2 onions, chopped
2 ribs celery, chopped
2 large cloves garlic, chopped
2 carrots, cut into rough matchsticks
$\frac{1}{2}$ × 5ml spoon ($\frac{1}{2}$ tsp) each: dried thyme, celery seeds, fennel seeds, pinch saffron threads (optional)
3 × 15ml spoons (3 tbs) fresh parsley, chopped

1 × 5ml spoon (1 tsp) shredded orange peel (optional)
1 bay leaf
225g (8 ozs) tomatoes (or tin)
350ml (12 fl.ozs) cider or white wine
700ml (24 fl.ozs) fish stock (No. 40)
dash Tabasco
Salt and pepper
1-1½Kg (2-3 lbs) white fish, if possible 3 different varieties

Heat oil, gently sauté leeks, onion and celery until tender, but not brown. Add garlic, sauté for 1 minute, then add all other ingredients *except fish*, bring to bubbling boil and hold it there for 5 mins. Now add fish, bring back to a gentle boil and cook for 10 minutes. Serve.

This is marvellous with hunks of crusty rye bread, or garlic bread, to complete the 'peasant' quality of the meal.

51 Cod Normandy

(4)

4 cod steaks
2 × 15ml spoons (2 tbs) wheat bran sprinkled with salt and pepper
2 × 5ml spoons (2 tsp) polyunsaturate margarine
1 onion, chopped
½ clove garlic, chopped
2 med tomatoes, chopped
1 × 15ml spoon (1 tbs) fresh parsley, chopped
½ × 5ml spoon (½ tsp) dried tarragon
100ml (4 fl.ozs) cider

Coat cod with seasoned bran. Melt margarine and gently sauté cod for 1-2 mins each side, remove from pan. Now sauté onion and garlic till silver, then add tomatoes and herbs. Return fish to pan, pour in cider, cover and simmer very gently for 10 mins. Remove lid. If too much liquid, simmer uncovered for a minute or two. Serve.
Cals: 145

52 Tuna Bake

(4-5)

2 × 200g (2 × 7 ozs) tins tuna fish
75g (3 ozs) soft wholewheat breadcrumbs
3 ribs celery, chopped
2 cloves garlic, chopped
2 med onions, chopped
1 green pepper, seeded, chopped
6 × 15ml spoons (6 tbs) fresh parsley, chopped
1¼ × 5ml spoons (1¼ tsp) salt
¼ × 5ml spoon (¼ tsp) pepper
2 × 15ml spoons (2 tbs) peanuts (or more)

Carefully drain oil from tuna and flake fish. Combine all ingred., mixing well. Press into greased casserole or deep pie dish and sprinkle peanuts on top. Bake for 30 mins, 190°C (375°F, Gas 5).

53 Tuna Fish and Noodles

(3)

175g (6 ozs) noodles (No. 236)
or wholewheat macaroni pieces
Boiling, lightly salted water to cover well

Fish

Sauce:
1 × 5ml spoon (1 tsp) oil
1 lge onion, chopped
1-2 cloves garlic, chopped
1 lge green pepper, chopped
225g (8 ozs) tomatoes, diced
100ml (4 fl.ozs) water
8 × 15ml spoons (8 tbs) fresh parsley, chopped
1 × 5ml spoon (1 tsp) salt
generous ground black pepper
$\frac{1}{4}$ × 5ml spoon ($\frac{1}{4}$ tsp) dried oregano
$\frac{1}{2}$ × 5ml spoon ($\frac{1}{2}$ tsp) anchovy essence (optional)
1 × 200g (1 × 7 ozs) tin tuna fish

Heat oil, stir-fry onion, garlic and green pepper for 2 mins. Add tomatoes, water and parsley, salt, pepper, oregano and anchovy essence. Simmer gently, uncovered, for 15 mins. Well-drain tuna fish and flake it, then stir into sauce until heated through. Drop noodles or macaroni pieces into boiling salted water and cook, stirring occasionally, until 'al dente'–which means 'firm with a bit of bite'–about 6-10 mins. Drain in colander. Spoon the thick sauce on to a bed of noodles.

54
Fish En Papillote

Any fish at all responds well to being cooked in the oven in a tightly sealed packet containing its own juices and some good seasoning. Aluminium foil is perfect for making the packets, and this is the method:

1. Clean the fish and pat it dry. Sprinkle with salt, pepper, lemon juice and herbs.
2. Cut a piece of foil twice the size of the fish and paint it lightly with oil.
3. Put fish on to foil, bring edges together and seal them tightly. I make a squarish half-moon, or apple-turnover shape, so that I can seal the foil to itself while it's lying flat. This also ensures that a baggy parcel is made so that the fish has room to swell and there's space for the juices.
4. Pre-heat oven to 190°C (375°F, Gas 5).
5. Bake as follows:
   Fillets or flat fish–25 mins
   thick or whole fish–35 mins
6. **To serve:** Just put a foil package on each plate. Each person opens his or her own 'parcel' and gets that first wonderful aroma and all the natural juices.

55
Stuffed Fish En Papillote

Stuffing is a marvellous way of bringing fibre to fish, and en papillote is a moist, appetizing way of cooking it.

1. Whole flat fish. Make an incision along the centre backbone and raise the flesh alongside the bone. Stuff beneath it.
2. Fillets of flat fish. Put a dollop of stuffing in the centre and roll up the fillet around it.
3. Whole, small fish. Remove backbone and as many small bones as possible. Place stuffing down middle, lengthways, fold fish over–back to normal, whole shape–and fasten edges with skewers.
4. Thick fillets. Put a generous layer of stuffing on top of one fillet, 'sandwich' it with a second fillet, seal with skewers or toothpicks.

To cook: follow the method given for Fish En Papillote.

Fish

And here's a stuffing we particularly like.

56
Chestnut Stuffing for Fish

1 × 5ml spoon (1 tsp) polyunsaturate margarine
½ small onion, chopped
100g (4 ozs) mushrooms, chopped
150g (5 ozs) cooked chestnuts (No. 109)
2 × 15ml spoons (2 tbs) wheat bran
½ × 5ml spoon (½ tsp) grated lemon peel
⅛ × 5ml spoon (⅛ tsp) ground mace
¼ × 5ml spoon (¼ tsp) dried thyme
½ × 5ml spoon (½ tsp) salt
ground black pepper
3 × 15ml spoons (3 tbs) cold water

Melt margarine, gently sauté onion till silver. Add mushrooms, sauté for 2 mins more, then stir in chestnuts, bran and seasoning. Remove from heat, stir in water. Stuff into fish.

Or use Raisin Stuffing (No. 58) or Apple Stuffing (No. 60).

57
Stuffed Mackerel

(4)

2 med mackerel or 4 small ones.

Remove backbone, rinse and pat dry. (If fishmonger fillets for you, make sure he leaves fish whole.) Sprinkle with salt, set aside. See Recipe 58 for stuffing.

58
Raisin Stuffing

1 × 5ml spoon (1 tsp) polyunsaturate margarine
½ med onion, chopped
175g (6 ozs) cooked brown rice
2 × 15ml spoons (2 tbs) raisins, halved
2 × 15ml spoons (2 tbs) broken roasted peanuts
2 × 15ml spoons (2 tbs) wheat bran
¼ × 5ml spoon (¼ tsp) salt
ground black pepper

Melt margarine, gently sauté onion till turning gold. Remove from heat and combine with all other ingredients.

To stuff fish: Lay fish flat, flesh side up. Pile stuffing down centre, fold fish in half (back to normal shape) and hold edges together with skewers. Make 3 cuts in skin on top. Grease baking dish, place fish in it and bake for 30-40 mins depending on whether med or small fish, in oven pre-heated to 180°C (350°F, Gas 4).

This succulent stuffing adds fibre and extra protein to one of the tastiest fish of all–and it looks lovely with its crispy, crinkled skin.

59
Stuffed Herring

(4)

4 herrings, cleaned and boned

Pat dry, sprinkle with salt, set aside. Approx. 100ml (4 fl.ozs) cider–set aside. See recipe 60 for stuffing.

Fish

60
Apple Stuffing

50g (2 ozs) soft wholewheat breadcrumbs
1 eating apple, chopped
¼ small onion, finely chopped
1 rib celery, chopped
1×5ml spoon (1 tsp) salt
¼×5ml spoon (¼ tsp) grated nutmeg
1×5ml spoon (1 tsp) lemon juice
Generous ground black pepper

Combine all ingredients.
To stuff fish: Lay one fish flat, put a quarter of stuffing in centre and roll up from tail to head, enclosing stuffing. Hold with toothpick. Repeat with other fish. Place in greased dish. Pour in enough cider to rise ¼ in from bottom of dish. Bake for 25 mins in pre-heated oven 180°C (350°F, Gas 4).

Try this Eastern style, with Russian Beetroot Salad (No. 294).

61
Fish Chunks and Chickpeas
(4)

350g (12 ozs) fish fillets in bite-sized chunks
Lemon juice
Paprika
1×5ml spoon (1 tsp) oil
175g (6 ozs) cooked chickpeas (No. 103)
350g (12 ozs) cooked brown rice (No. 227)
100ml (4 fl.ozs) skimmed milk
Salt and pepper
2×15ml spoons (2 tbs) fresh parsley, chopped

Sprinkle fish with lemon juice and paprika, set aside. Heat oil, toss chickpeas in it till beginning to turn gold, then add rice and stir in skimmed milk. Place fish on top, sprinkle fish and grain with salt and pepper, then parsley. Cover tightly, reduce heat to simmer and cook for 10 mins.

Serve with crisp-tender steamed broccoli, or honeyed carrots–or both–for eye-catching colour (Nos. 121 and 125).

62
Fish and Grain Bouillabaise
(4)

1×5ml spoon (1 tsp) oil
2 med onions, chopped
2 cloves garlic, chopped
225g (8 ozs) tomatoes, chopped
4×15ml spoons (4 tbs) fresh parsley, chopped
1 bayleaf
¼×5ml spoon (¼ tsp) crushed fennel seeds
1×5ml spoon (1 tsp) dried thyme
Pinch saffron threads (optional)
2½×5ml spoons (2½ tsp) salt
Generous ground black pepper
3 matchsticks orange peel
1.6 litres (56 fl.ozs) water
75g (3 ozs) bulgur wheat, washed and drained (or 250g [9 ozs] any *cooked* grain)
500g (1 lb) any fish

Heat oil, stir-fry onion and garlic for 1 min. Add tomatoes, herbs and seasoning, pour in water and stir in bulgur wheat. Bring to boil and let bubble gently, uncovered, for 15 mins. Add fish (and *cooked* grain, if you're using it instead of bulgur) and let mixture bubble gently for 10 mins more.

I've used cod, coley, herring and whole fresh sardines for this–all very different but adding up to a hearty, peasant-style fish stew. If skin-and-bones give you problems,

Fish

use easier-to-manage filleted fish (any kind).
Cals: white fish: 205, oily fish: 309

63
Fish in Pastry
(6)

This is another dish that looks so magnificent you're reluctant to cut into it. It tastes as good as it looks and is a way of entertaining guests royally without breaking the bank.

1 × 5ml spoon (1 tsp) oil
2 lge onions, chopped
175g (6 ozs) mushrooms, chopped
350g (12 ozs) cooked brown rice
3 × 15ml spoons (3 tbs) fresh parsley, chopped
2-3 × 15ml spoons (2-3 tbs) toasted almonds or other nuts
½ × 5ml spoon (½ tsp) dill seeds
¼ × 5ml spoon (¼ tsp) ground nutmeg
1 × 5ml spoon (1 tsp) lemon juice
¾ × 5ml spoon (¾ tsp) salt
⅛ × 5ml spoon (⅛ tsp) pepper
100ml (4 fl.ozs) fish stock (No. 40) or water
1 × 15ml spoon (1 tbs) melted polyunsaturate margarine
500g (1 lb) cooked white fish, cut in bite-sized pieces

Pastry: 350g (12 ozs) recipe No. 272

Heat oil, sauté onions until silver, then mushrooms for 1-2 mins. Remove from heat and combine all ingredients *except fish*, mixing well. Now gently fold in the fish, trying not to break it up too much. On floured board roll approx. one-third of pastry to an oblong about 10 in × 6 in. Place this on greased baking tray and paint top of it with melted margarine. Pile filling on, leaving about ½ in clear all around edges. Press filling lightly with fingers to make a firm, flat-topped mound. Roll remaining pastry to about 15 in × 11 in. Dust top with flour, fold oblong in half lengthways and make four evenly-spaced 2 in-long diagonal cuts in the folded edge. Unfold– and you'll find a herringbone pattern. Place this pastry over mound of filling (it should reach bottom crust) and press edges to the bottom crust to seal well. Cut away any surplus from ends and corners– a neat, perfect 'brick' is the objective. Now paint generously with skimmed milk and bake for 25-30 mins 220°C, 425°F, Gas 7.

We like this just as it comes, but a sauce boat filled with Creamy Onion Sauce (No. 314) can be provided for those who want it.

64
Gefilte Fish
(5)

This is best known as a Jewish delicacy, but since it's low-calorie, high-fibre (cooked this way) and absolutely delicious–why shouldn't everyone enjoy it?

250g (8 ozs) coley fillets } or any other
250g (8 ozs) haddock fillets } two white fish
1 lge onion
50g (2 ozs) soft wholewheat breadcrumbs
1¼ × 5ml spoons (1¼ tsp) salt
⅛ × 5ml spoon (⅛ tsp) pepper
1 egg, lightly beaten

Finely chop or mince the fish and onion. Stir in salt, pepper, breadcrumbs and egg to make a soft but not wet mixture. (If wet, add more crumbs). Form into 10 patties, patting between damp palms for best results. In large pan, combine the following:

900ml (32 fl.ozs) water
2 carrots, sliced
1 onion, cut into eighths
1 rib celery, sliced
1 × 5ml spoon (1 tsp) salt
ground black pepper

Bring to boil, reduce heat and simmer for 30 mins. Now drop in patties, one at a time so that water doesn't cease its gentle bubbling. When all patties are in, simmer uncovered for 30 mins.

Allow the fish to cool in the liquid then transfer it to a serving dish, spoon over some of the liquid, which is a delicious sauce, add the sweet and tender carrots and some onion if you like it. Chill for an hour or more, and serve.

This is good with millet-and-chickpeas, plus a steamed green vegetable, or simply placed on lettuce leaves and accompanied by a crunchy Red Cabbage Salad (No. 280).
Cals: 2 patties, 144

65
Fish Fritters
(5)

These fish cakes are a great favourite with us, and are equally good hot or cold. (For parties I make baby ones and spear them on cocktail sticks).

1 recipe Gefilte Fish (No. 64)
Wholewheat flour, seasoned with salt and pepper
Corn oil to shallow fry

Make gefilte fish up to, and including, the making of patties. Heat oil to smoking point. Dip each patty in flour to coat thoroughly on all sides, then gently slip them into the hot oil. Watch carefully because they brown quickly, and try to turn just once. When both sides are golden, drain off as much oil as possible, then stand on kitchen paper to blot really dry.

66
Fish in Spinach
(5)

225g (8 ozs) fresh spinach
500g (1 lb) white fish
1 lge onion
1 lge carrot
2 × 15 ml spoons (2 tbs) fresh parsley
50g (2 ozs) soft wholewheat breadcrumbs
$1\frac{1}{4}$ × 5ml spoons ($1\frac{1}{4}$ tsp) salt
$\frac{1}{8}$ × 5ml spoon ($\frac{1}{8}$ tsp) pepper
1 egg, lightly beaten

Sauce:
500g (1 lb) tomatoes, pulped (or tin)
$\frac{1}{2}$ × 5ml spoon ($\frac{1}{2}$ tsp) salt
$\frac{1}{4}$ × 5ml spoon ($\frac{1}{4}$ tsp) dried thyme
ground black pepper

You need 10 large leaves of spinach or enough small leaves to patch together so that you wind up with 10 large 'envelopes'. Wash this spinach, drop into boiling, lightly salted water and blanch, covered, for 2 mins. Drain immediately and freshen in cold water, gently pat dry and set aside.

Finely chop or mince the fish, onion, carrot and parsley. Stir in the breadcrumbs, seasoning and egg and mix to a firm, sponge-like consistency. If it feels wet, add another few spoons of crumbs. Divide this mixture into 10. Put one portion into the centre of each spinach 'envelope', wrap up, and place join-side down in lightly greased ovenproof dish. When all 10 are in, combine the sauce ingredients and pour over. Pre-heat oven to 190°C (375°F, Gas 5) and bake, uncovered, for 45 mins.
Cals: 2 rolls=173

This has enough eye-appeal for a dinner party, and it certainly won't break the bank. Low-calorie, great taste, a very popular dish with us. I serve cooked dried beans, a grain and a salad with it; or just serve the grain, and follow with an Applesauce Cake (No. 266) for a real treat.

67
Sardined Beans
(4-6)

1Kg (2 lbs) cooked butter beans (No. 103)
6 spring onions, or bunch chives, chopped
2 ribs celery, finely sliced
2 firm tomatoes, diced
7 × 15ml spoons (7 tbs) Vinaigrette or Italian Dressing (No. 304 *or* No. 306)
1 × 15ml spoon (1 tbs) lemon juice
garlic salt
ground black pepper
2 tins sardines, well drained[1]
2 × 15ml spoons (2 tbs) fresh parsley, chopped

Cool beans (if freshly cooked) and combine with onions, celery and tomatoes. Spoon dressing and lemon juice over, season with garlic, salt and pepper, then gently stir without breaking beans. Chill for 1 hour or more, stirring occasionally to distribute dressing. When ready to serve, coarsely chop sardines and arrange on top of beans and garnish with parsley.

Variation: Try using different dried beans–kidney, perhaps, or chickpeas–and tuna fish instead of sardines.

68
Fish-in-Aspic Flan
(4-5)

Although there are three parts to this dish it's quite easy to make and is so beautiful that you won't want to cut it. Guests are always impressed and the cost is negligible. This recipe is for leftover fish. If you have none try this with well-drained, whole sardines.

1 × 9 in pastry shell, fully baked (No. 272)
250-350g ($\frac{1}{2}$-$\frac{3}{4}$ lb) cooked fish, any variety

Aspic:
$3\frac{1}{2}$ × 5ml spoons ($3\frac{1}{2}$ tsp) plain gelatin (1 × $\frac{1}{2}$ oz packet)
250ml (8 fl.ozs) water
250ml (8 fl.ozs) tomato juice
1 × 15ml spoon (1 tbs) lemon juice
$\frac{1}{4}$ × 5ml spoon ($\frac{1}{4}$ tsp) salt
Generous ground black pepper

---

[1] I spill away as much oil as possible while sardines are still in the tin, then trickle cold water into the tin and swish it around the fish. Spill away the water (and lots more oil), then stand the sardines on kitchen paper to blot dry, turning them once. They're firm, oil-free and delicious.

4 in chunk cucumber, 1 in sliced paper-thin, remainder diced
1-2 × 15ml spoons (1-2 tbs) chopped fresh herbs (basil, dill or any)
½ small onion, diced
Few sprigs watercress to decorate

Aspic: In a pudding basin sprinkle gelatin on to half the cold water and leave undisturbed for 5 mins. Now stand basin in pan of boiling water and stir over med heat until gelatin is dissolved. Remove basin from pan and stir into gelatin the remaining water, tomato juice, lemon juice, salt and pepper. (Amount of seasoning will depend on your tomato juice.) Let aspic cool until starting to set–it should have texture of raw egg-white–then spread the chopped vegetables and herbs into the cold pastry case and spoon three-quarters of the aspic over. Arrange fish on top, pressing gently into aspic without burying it, then spread remaining aspic in a very thin, transparent coating on top of the fish.[1] Arrange thin cucumber slices and watercress attractively on top, where they'll be gripped by the aspic without sinking. Chill in refrigerator about 3 hours, taking out just before serving so it won't melt in your warm room.
Cals: 320

---

[1] If tragedy strikes and your aspic gets too 'jelled'–put pudding basin into pan of hot water and very, very gently warm gelatin until if softens again . . . but don't overdo it, or you may have setting problems.

[2] You can use leftover cooked fish–350-500g (12-16 ozs) –in which case the liquid should be vegetable stock or skimmed milk, since you'll have no poaching liquid. Remember to adjust seasoning.

69
Fish Bake
(4)

350ml (12 fl.ozs) water
½ × 5ml spoon (½ tsp) salt
2 whole black peppercorns
½ bayleaf
1 × 5ml spoon (1 tsp) lemon juice
500g (1 lb) any white fish

Heat water to warm, add all ingreds. and raise heat to simmer–the liquid should just 'shiver'–cover and cook for 10 mins. Remove lid and let fish cool in liquid, which should then be strained and retained for use later.

Combine together:
The cooked fish, flaked[2]
6 × 15ml spoons (6 tbs) fresh parsley, chopped
1 med onion, chopped
50g (2 ozs) soft wholewheat breadcrumbs
50g (2 ozs) roasted peanuts, coarsely chopped
½ × 5ml spoon (½ tsp) salt
¼ × 5ml spoon (¼ tsp) pepper
250ml (8 fl.ozs) poaching liquid reserved earlier

Separate:
1 egg. Beat yolk and add to mixture, stirring well. Beat the egg white until stiff and gently fold into the mixture. Transfer to oiled baking dish, and bake for 35 mins in pre-heated oven 190°C (375°F, Gas 5).
Cals: 240

Fish

70
Herring Pie
(4)

1×5ml spoon (1 tsp) oil
3 lge eating apples
2 med onions
3 boned herrings
$\frac{1}{2}$×5ml spoon ($\frac{1}{2}$ tsp) ground black pepper
$\frac{1}{2}$×5ml spoon ($\frac{1}{2}$ tsp) ground mace
$1\frac{1}{2}$×5ml spoons ($1\frac{1}{2}$tsp) salt
water

Pastry: 100g (4 ozs) recipe No. 272.

Oil a deep pie dish. Slice apples and onions paper-thin, spread half of each in layers in dish, season lightly. Sprinkle herring flesh generously with salt, pepper and mace, fold in half (to look like whole fish), place in dish in one layer. Spread remaining apple, onion and seasoning on top and add enough water to rise $\frac{1}{2}$ in from bottom of dish.

Cover dish with pastry, make three cuts to allow steam to escape then brush with skimmed milk and bake in pre-heated oven for 50 mins, 200°C (400°F, Gas 6).

71
Soused Herring (or Mackerel)
(4)

4 herrings, cleaned and filleted
1 × 5ml spoon (1 tsp) salt
$\frac{1}{4}$×5ml spoon ($\frac{1}{4}$ tsp) pepper
100ml (4 fl.ozs) vinegar
100ml (4 fl.ozs) water
1 bayleaf
$1\frac{1}{2}$×15ml spoons ($1\frac{1}{2}$ tbs) honey
3 whole cloves
6 whole black peppercorns
$\frac{1}{2}$ lge onion, sliced in thin rings

Cut each fillet in half up centre lengthways and sprinkle with salt and pepper. Roll up, starting from tail end, and place neat, tight roll into ovenproof dish (with lid). Repeat with remainder. Into saucepan put all other ingreds., bring to boil, then simmer for 5 mins. Pour over rolled-up fish, cover dish with lid and bake for 45 mins, 180°C (350°F, Gas 4). When cooked remove from oven but leave closed until cool, then refrigerate and serve chilled.

This is a traditional dish in almost every country. Serve it on lettuce leaves for a hearty lunch, as a starter, or with a grain and a salad for a tasty, nutritious dinner.
Cals: 302

72
Herring in Oatmeal
(4)

4 herrings, cleaned and filleted
Salt and pepper
50g (2 ozs) coarse oatmeal
Oil to shallow-fry

Rinse herring and pat dry, sprinkle generously with salt and pepper. Spread oatmeal on to a plate and press fish on to it to get a good, thick coating on both sides. Heat oil to smoking point and fry herrings until golden brown and crisp, turning once. Drain well, then stand on kitchen paper to blot really dry.

Serve with lemon wedges, or a tart, fruity sauce. We particularly like Rhubarb Honey with this (No. 256)
Cals: 268

Chicken and Turkey

Chicken and Turkey

Once upon a time chicken was expensive and eaten only on special occasions. It was sometimes tough, because chickens fended for themselves in the farmyard and developed muscles doing it, but even the muscles were full of flavour and a plain, roast bird on a festive occasion was a treat indeed.

Today everybody can afford chicken and we eat it often. It's never tough, since battery chickens don't build muscle, and it cooks quickly–but there's been a sad falling off in flavour. A plain roast bird is all right once in a while with a delicious, moist and flavourful stuffing (Nos. 76-80) but as a regular diet it gets boring, so here is a wide selection of chicken recipes to liven up your taste buds again: chicken with fruit, with beans, with seeds and nuts, with grains ; leftover chicken in mouth-watering knife-and-fork main-course soups ; chicken stews, pies and pancakes ; ideas from all over the world for making chicken, even frozen chicken, a special-occasion dish again–this time for people on a tight budget.

Chicken itself doesn't contain dietary fibre so most of these recipes include ingredients that do. However, if there's no grain in the dish serve a grain *with* it–like chicken curry on a bed of rice, paprika chicken with a mound of bulgur wheat, and so on. Chicken and grain really go well together, and with the addition of a few vegetables plus a fruity dessert you have a meal fit for a king–a slim and healthy king, at that !

Like most animal foods chicken contains a variety of fats. The saturated fat lies in and just under the skin, a soft yellow fat which shouldn't be eaten. Simply skin the chicken (many people find the skin distasteful anyway), scrape away as much visible fat as you can, then cook the chicken according to the recipe.

When making chicken stock or soup skim any globules of yellow fat off the liquid. The best way is to cool and then chill it, so that the fat forms easily removed solid lumps on top. Thoroughly boil the stock or soup again before using or serving. If you haven't time to chill it take a wodge of kitchen paper and trail it across the surface of the soup to blot up the fat. You can get a special gadget for removing fat from soups and stews, a white mop that looks like raffia and which attracts all fat globules, even out of the air. Just stir your soup with it and voila !–it's fat-free. The mop is rinsed and used again, of course.

Do the best you can to skim, but don't worry too much about it if you have skinned the chicken and carefully removed the yellow fat–*unless* your cholesterol count is high and your doctor has put you on a very rigid cholesterol-lowering diet, in which case you must follow medical instructions.

The fat remaining in the chicken, the invisible fat, is rich in polyunsaturates, which means that chicken, like fish, is a valuable element in your diet. This is true of turkey, also, and all the recipes which follow are just as good if you use turkey instead of chicken.

You should not eat duck or goose ; both are very high in saturated fat which can't be removed satisfactorily. But with this selection of mouth-watering chicken and turkey dishes you'll never miss them. And think of all the money you waste when you take out of the oven only half the duck or goose that you put in, the remainder having become several inches of inedible fat in your roasting tin.

Chicken and Turkey

To clean chicken pieces I usually hold them under running water without letting them soak in it. I pull away any clinging bits of 'inside', then remove the skin and yellow fat. Pat dry, and the pieces are ready to cook. To clean a whole bird wash it as above, de-feather the legs and wings with a sharp knife and let running water pour into the cavity to clean it out, then pat dry. It's difficult to skin a whole bird without ruining it, or giving it sad-looking patches, so instead I stuff and roast the bird in its skin, but **prick it all over with a fork three or four times during cooking so that the fat can run away.** With a turkey, or a large chicken, spread a little polyunsaturate margarine onto the skin before you put it into the oven, so that the bird won't dry out during the longer cooking period.

By the way, don't make gravy out of the greasy pan drippings. See Nos. 74 and 75 for a delicious fat-free gravy with fibre and a clear gravy that's low-calorie.

Paprika is a valuable aid in cooking chicken or turkey that's been skinned, because it turns a delightful golden colour when it's fried or baked without adding noticeable flavour (unless you want it to, in which case you use much more). I don't like to add calories by using pints of oil when **browning chicken**, even if it's polyunsaturate oil, and a light sprinkling of paprika on the flesh means you don't have to. Place the red-sprinkled pieces in a few tablespoons of smoking corn oil and within minutes you'll have perfectly browned chicken to put into your casserole.

Do try the unusual dishes, like Moroccan Chicken, which combines the bird with prunes, and Peking Chicken, my version of exotic Peking Duck. I've served both of these at dinner parties and been paid extravagant compliments for a meal I'd prepared with minimum fuss and at amazingly low cost.

I think you'll find this true of all the chicken dishes here.

73
Chicken Stock/Turkey Stock

1 carcase, broken into pieces
1 lge onion, in quarters
2 carrots, sliced
2 ribs celery, sliced
1 bouquet garni
3 sprigs parsley
Mushroom trimmings (optional)
Water to well cover
1 × 5ml spoon (1 tsp) salt

Put all ingredients into large soup pan and bring to boil, skimming off any froth that rises. When surface is clear, reduce heat and simmer very gently (with water just 'shivering') for 2-3 hours. Strain, remove all fat (see Page 60) and stock is ready to use.

Giblets (not hearts or livers) can be added to make the stock richer, and for a really special stock you can use chicken portions and then use the boiled chicken in one of the dishes calling for it.

74
Thick Chicken Gravy

1 × 15ml spoon (1 tbs) polyunsaturate margarine
1 med onion, chopped
2 × 15ml spoons (2 tbs) wholewheat flour
250ml (8 fl.ozs) chicken stock
1 × 15ml spoon (1 tbs) chopped fresh parsley
Salt and pepper

Melt margarine and cook onion gently till turning golden. Sprinkle in flour and stir for a minute or two, then gradually add stock, stirring continuously. When gravy has thickened add parsley, reduce heat–use heat diffuser–and simmer for 10-15 mins, stirring occasionally. Adjust seasoning adding a little more stock if too thick, and serve.

75
Clear Chicken Gravy
(low-cal)

1 × 5ml spoon (1 tsp) oil
1 med onion, chopped
1 small carrot, chopped
1 small rib celery, chopped
350ml (12 fl.ozs) chicken stock
Salt and pepper

Heat oil, stir-fry onion until brown, then add all other vegetables are tender. Adjust more. Pour in stock, bring to boil, then reduce to simmer and cook gently for 20-30 mins or till vegetables tender. Adjust seasoning and serve. (I always serve the vegetables too, but you can strain if preferred).

For a richer, darker gravy add 1 × 5ml spoon (1 tsp) yeast extract–but remember to adjust the salt accordingly.

Stuffing, or dressing, is the most delicious way of adding fibre, as well as interest, to a bird. Don't wait until you roast one whole to enjoy a stuffing–just make up the one you want, put it in a greased dish, cover with foil and bake in the oven for an hour along with your chicken or turkey portions, or casserole. Or try skewering two chicken breasts together and stuffing the cavity.

Chicken and Turkey

76
Chestnut Stuffing
(about 8)

350g (12 ozs) cooked chestnuts (No. 109)[1]
75g (3 ozs) wholewheat breadcrumbs (No. 206)
1-2 ribs celery, chopped
2 × 15ml spoons (2 tbs) onion, finely chopped
3 × 15ml spoons (3 tbs) fresh parsley, chopped
¾ × 5ml spoon (¾ tsp) salt
½ × 5ml spoon (½ tsp) paprika
2 × 15ml spoons (2 tbs) melted polyunsaturate margarine
3 × 15ml spoons (3 tbs) chicken stock

Combine all ingredients and stuff into bird loosely so stuffing has room to swell, or bake in a greased dish, covered, for about 1 hour.
Cals: 125

77
Simple Bread Stuffing
(about 5)

1 × 15ml spoon (1 tbs) oil
1 lge onion, chopped
1 clove garlic, chopped
2 ribs celery, chopped
100g (4 ozs) soft wholewheat breadcrumbs (No. 206)
½ × 5ml spoon (½ tsp) salt
⅛ × 5ml spoon (⅛ tsp) pepper
¼ × 5ml spoon (¼ tsp) dried rosemary, crushed
2 × 15ml spoons (2 tbs) melted polyunsaturate margarine
3 × 15ml spoons (3 tbs) chicken stock

Heat oil, stir-fry onion for 2 mins then garlic and celery for 3 mins more. Remove from heat, combine with all other ingredients and stuff into bird loosely so it has room to swell–or bake in a greased dish, covered, for about 1 hour.
Cals: 124

78
Wheat Berry Stuffing
(about 6)

175g (6 ozs) cooked whole wheat (No. 228)
1 med onion, finely chopped
1 green pepper, finely chopped
2 × 15ml spoons (2 tbs) fresh parsley, chopped
50g (2 ozs) roasted peanuts, coarsely chopped
3 × 15ml spoons (3 tbs) raisins
1 eating apple, chopped (optional)
½ × 5ml spoon (½ tsp) salt
⅛ × 5ml spoon (⅛ tsp) pepper
2 × 15ml spoons (2 tbs) melted polyunsaturate margarine

Combine all ingredients and stuff into bird loosely so stuffing has room to swell–or bake in a greased dish, covered, for about 1 hour.

79
Buckwheat Stuffing
(about 6)

1 × 15ml spoon (1 tbs) oil
1 med onion, chopped
1 clove garlic, chopped

[1] Dried = 175–225g (6–8 ozs)

1 green pepper, chopped
100g (4 ozs) mushrooms, coarsely chopped
175g (6 ozs) cooked buckwheat (No. 230)
$\frac{1}{2}$×5ml spoon ($\frac{1}{2}$ tsp) celery seed
$\frac{1}{4}$×5ml spoon ($\frac{1}{4}$ tsp) dried basil
$\frac{1}{2}$×5ml spoon ($\frac{1}{2}$ tsp) salt
$\frac{1}{8}$×5ml spoon ($\frac{1}{8}$ tsp) pepper
2×15ml spoons (2 tbs) melted polyunsaturate margarine
3×15ml spoons (3 tbs) chicken stock

Heat oil, stir-fry onion for 2 mins, then garlic, green pepper and mushrooms for 3 mins more. Remove from heat, combine with all other ingredients and stuff into bird loosely so it has room to swell–or bake in a greased dish, covered, for about 1 hour.

Cals: 97

Any other cooked grain (rice, millet, bulgur, etc.) is just as good, and changing the grain changes the flavour, so this is a very versatile stuffing.

80
Barley Stuffing
(4-6)

1×5ml spoon (1 tsp) corn oil
$\frac{1}{2}$ med onion, chopped
1 lge carrot, chopped
1 green pepper, seeded, chopped
1 rib celery, chopped
2 sprigs parsley, chopped
75g (3 ozs) raw barley
550ml (18 fl.ozs) chicken stock
1×15ml spoon (1 tbs) lemon juice
ground black pepper
$\frac{1}{4}$×5ml spoon ($\frac{1}{4}$ tsp) dried thyme
$\frac{1}{4}$×5ml spoon ($\frac{1}{4}$ tsp) salt
Pinch ground coriander (optional)

Heat oil, stir-fry onion, carrot, green pepper and celery, in that order, for 1 minute each. Add all other ingredients, bring to boil, then reduce to minimum heat –use heat diffuser–cover tightly and simmer until barley is tender (about 1 hour).

I stuff this into the bird in the usual way, but don't bake it separately–it's so much better combined with cooking juices.

81
Roast Chicken or Turkey

Pre-heat oven to 230°C (450°F, Gas 8). Wash bird and pat dry. Stuff loosely so stuffing has room to swell a little. (Stuffings: Nos. 76-80) or try putting a whole apple or peeled onion into the cavity ; they help to keep the bird moist and add interesting flavours. Stand a rack in your roasting tin, stand the bird on the rack and spread a thin layer of polyunsaturate margarine on the skin. Put into oven and *immediately* reduce heat to 180°C (350°F, Gas 4). Allow 20 mins to the lb ($\frac{1}{2}$Kg). If the bird is over 6 lbs, cover breast loosely with foil after about 1$\frac{1}{2}$ hours to prevent drying out. 3 or 4 times during cooking prick skin thoroughly all over with fork so fat can run out. *Do not baste:* if bird looks dry spread a little more polyunsaturate margarine on it.

Don't make gravy with pan-drippings ; they contain all the fat that's melted off. For delicious, healthy gravies, Nos. 74 and 75.

A (3 lb) 1$\frac{1}{2}$Kg bird doesn't cook long enough to get really brown, so 15 minutes before cooking is complete sprinkle lightly with paprika for a glorious colour. (I sprinkle salt and garlic at the same time.)

Serve generous amounts of stuffing. It

Chicken and Turkey

tastes marvellous, and that's where the fibre is.

82
Chicken and Beans
(4)

1 × 15ml spoon (1 tbs) oil
2 med onions, chopped
2 cloves garlic, chopped
1 lge carrot, sliced
500g (1 lb) tomatoes, chopped (or tin)
1 × 15ml spoon (1 tbs) tomato paste
250ml (8 fl.ozs) chicken stock
1 green pepper, sliced thinly in rings
4 small portions chicken, skinned
1 × 5ml spoon (1 tsp) chili powder
$1\frac{1}{2}$ × 5ml spoon ($1\frac{1}{2}$ tsp) salt
600g ($1\frac{1}{4}$ lbs) cooked dried beans[1]

In oven-proof casserole heat oil and brown onion, garlic and carrot. Add tomatoes, tomato paste and stock, simmer for 5 mins. Add salt to taste. Place sliced green pepper on tomatoes and arrange chicken pieces on top of them. Sprinkle with chili powder and remaining salt. Cover. Bake for 1 hour, 180°C (350°F, Gas 4).
Remove from oven, gently lift chicken pieces and spoon beans into the sauce, trying not to break them. Replace chicken, cover and cook for 30 mins more. (This is almost as good cooked on the burners.)

[1]Dried = 275g (10 ozs). Use a mixture of butter beans, kidney and black-eyed peas, or any others you like. I keep a variety in jars and just take a handful of each to make up the quantity I need. To cook, see No. 103.

83
Chicken, Lentils and Barley
(6)

175g (6 ozs) green lentils
1.4 litres (48 fl.ozs) cold water
2 × 15ml spoons (2 tbs) oil
6 small portions chicken, skinned
1 × 15ml spoon (1 tbs) paprika
2 lge onions, chopped
1-2 cloves garlic, chopped
3 lge carrots, cut in chunks
50g (2 ozs) raw barley, washed and drained
$\frac{1}{2}$ × 5ml spoon ($\frac{1}{2}$ tsp) dried rosemary, crushed
700ml (24 fl.ozs) chicken stock, cooled
2 × 15ml spoons (2 tbs) Tamari soy sauce
ground black pepper
Garnish: 1 med orange, sliced cross-ways in 'wheels'.

Pick over lentils and cook with barley in the water about 1 hour till firm-tender, or pressure cook (See No. 104). Heat oil in casserole, sprinkle chicken with paprika and brown for 5 mins each side. Remove chicken. In same oil, sauté onion and garlic till silver, then carrot for 5 mins more. Stir in cooked lentils, barley, rosemary. Add stock, bring to boil, then simmer for 5 mins. Put chicken pieces on top, dribble soy sauce over, sprinkle pepper. Cover tightly, reduce heat to minimum and cook for 1 hour or till chicken and barley are tender. Garnish with orange, which looks beautiful with the lentils and tastes even better!

Chicken and Turkey

84
Oven Fried Chicken

Coating
50g (2 ozs) fine-ground wholewheat breadcrumbs (No. 206)
4×15ml spoons (4 tbs) cornmeal
1×5ml spoon (1 tsp) salt
½×5ml spoon (½ tsp) paprika
¼×5ml spoon (¼ tsp) garlic powder
¼×5ml spoon (¼ tsp) onion powder
¼×5ml spoon (¼ tsp) dried rosemary, crushed

4-6 portions chicken, halved, skinned
3×15ml spoons (3 tbs) oil

Pre-heat oven to 180°C (350°F, Gas 4). Combine coating ingredients and spread them on a plate. Wash chicken and pat dry, then use pastry brush to paint all over with oil. Press oiled chicken firmly into crumbs until you have a generous coating. Put on rack in roasting tin and bake (top of the oven) for 50-60 mins, turning the pieces over after 35 mins for a really crunchy, golden crust.

Children adore this and it's a perfect picnic dish since it's crisp and appetising hot or cold.
Cals: 460

85
Chicken Teriyaki
(4)

4 portions chicken, skinned
Marinade. Mix together
3×15ml spoons (3 tbs) honey
3×15ml spoons (3 tbs) hot water
2×15ml spoons (2 tbs) tomato paste
3×15ml spoons (3 tbs) Tamari soy sauce
2×15ml spoons (2 tbs) corn oil
1-2 cloves garlic, crushed
1×5ml spoon (1 tsp) grated ginger root (or 2½×5ml spoons (2½ tsp) ground ginger)
2×5ml spoons (2 tsp) lemon juice

Cut chicken into 1½ in pieces and marinate for 1 or more hours in the liquid, turning them occasionally. Grill for about 15 mins each side, brushing with marinade as they cook to keep them moist and well-covered.

A delicious, spicy chicken that's very quick and easy to cook. Serve with brown rice in which you've sliced spring onions, and a dish of mixed bean sprouts and mange tout peas.
Cals: 472

86
Chicken in the Pot with Dumplings
(6)

1½-2Kg (3-4 lb) chicken, in portions
Cold water to cover
1 lge onion, peeled, quartered
2 lge carrots, sliced
1 rib celery, sliced
1 chicken stock cube
½×5ml spoon (½ tsp) salt
⅛×5ml spoon (⅛ tsp) pepper

Put skinned chicken in soup pan with water to cover, bring to boil and skim off the froth as it rises. This is important for a clear golden soup. When froth stops rising (after about 10 mins) add all other ingredients, return to boil, part-cover and simmer very gently till chicken falling-tender, 1-1½ hours. (To remove fat see P. 60)

Chicken and Turkey

87
Dumplings
(16-18)

150g (5 ozs) wholewheat flour
1×5ml spoon (1 tsp) baking powder
$\frac{1}{2}$×5ml spoon ($\frac{1}{2}$ tsp) salt
Pinch pepper
100ml (4 fl.ozs) skimmed milk or water
1×15ml spoon (1 tbs) melted polyunsaturate margarine
Salted water

Combine flour, baking powder, salt and pepper. Stir margarine into milk and pour into flour, mixing to a heavy paste. In large pan bring salted water to boil. Roll paste in 5ml spoonfuls between palms and drop into water without letting boil stop. When all in cover tightly, reduce heat, cook for 20 mins. Lift dumplings out with slotted spoon. (I use a deep 10 in frying pan to give them room to swell.)

Serve everyone a bowl of soup with chicken, vegetables and dumplings in it, as a main course soup, or soup first, with a few spoons of rice in it, and chicken, dumplings and vegetables to follow. Marvellous meal–minimal washing up!

88
Chicken and Pineapple
(4)

4 portions chicken, halved, skinned
Paprika
1×15ml spoon (1 tbs) oil
1 med onion, chopped
1 rib celery, chopped
4 slices pineapple, cut in chunks (200g, 6-8 ozs.) If tinned, use fruit packed in water, not syrup. Use $\frac{1}{3}$ cup of this liquid in place of $\frac{1}{3}$ cup chicken stock.
1×5ml spoon (1 tsp) salt
$\frac{1}{8}$×5ml spoon ($\frac{1}{8}$ tsp) ground cloves
$\frac{1}{8}$×5ml spoon ($\frac{1}{8}$ tsp) ground allspice
$\frac{1}{8}$×5ml spoon ($\frac{1}{8}$ tsp) ground nutmeg
1×15ml spoon (1 tbs) lemon juice
1×15ml spoon (1 tbs) Tamari soy sauce
1×15ml spoon (1 tbs) honey
350ml (12 fl.ozs) chicken stock
4 sprigs watercress to garnish

Sprinkle chicken pieces with paprika. In casserole with lid heat oil and brown chicken on all sides. Remove. Brown onion and celery, then add pineapple and sauté gently for 2 mins. Now add all seasoning and stir well. Return chicken to casserole, pour in stock, cover and simmer till tender (about 1 hour).

Cals: 430

89
Chicken Curry Española
(4)

1×15ml spoon (1 tbs) oil
4 chicken portions, skinned
3 ribs celery, chopped
1 lge onion, chopped
2×15ml spoons (2 tbs) orange peel in matchsticks
1×5ml spoon (1 tsp) salt
$\frac{1}{4}$×5ml spoon ($\frac{1}{4}$ tsp) pepper
1×15ml spoon (1 tbs) wholewheat flour
1×15ml spoon (1 tbs) curry powder
250ml (8 fl.ozs) chicken stock

In frying pan heat oil and gently brown

chicken pieces, then transfer to a casserole. In same pan stir-fry onion and celery for 2 mins, then orange peel half a minute longer. Transfer to casserole. In same pan combine flour, curry powder and stock to a smooth cream. Pour over contents of casserole, sprinkle salt and pepper, then cover with a tight-fitting lid and simmer until chicken tender (about 1 hour). Alternatively, this can be oven-baked for $1\frac{1}{2}$ hours at 180°C (350°F, Gas 4).
Cals: 406

The perfect accompaniment to this is Millet with Nuts and Raisins, No. 237.

90
Chicken and Vegetable Curry
(4)

Make Mixed Vegetable Curry (No. 172). Fifteen minutes before cooking complete, stir in 225g (8 ozs) cooked chicken chunks.

91
Chicken Paprika
(4-6)

1-2 × 15ml spoons (1-2 tbs) oil
$1\frac{1}{2}$-2Kg (3-4 lb) chicken, in portions
Paprika
1 lge onion, chopped
1-2 cloves garlic, chopped
2 ribs celery (incl. tops) sliced
1 green pepper, sliced
100g (4 ozs) mushrooms, sliced
350g (12 ozs) ripe tomatoes, sliced
250ml (8 fl.ozs) chicken stock
1 × 15ml spoon (1 tbs) Tamari soy sauce
1 × 15ml spoon (1 tsp) salt
ground black pepper

Heat oil in frying pan. Sprinkle paprika very generously on one side of chicken and place that side down in pan to brown. Meanwhile liberally sprinkle second side, turn, brown second side and transfer chicken to a casserole. In frying pan gently sauté onion and garlic till soft, then celery, green pepper and mushrooms. Cook for a few minutes, stirring, then add tomatoes, stock, soy sauce, salt and pepper. Simmer gently for 10 mins, then pour over chicken in casserole. Cover with tight-fitting lid and simmer gently for $1\frac{1}{2}$ hours or until chicken tender.

The 'hot' paprika, which isn't really hot at all, but has a flavour, is essential for this dish, which is a great favourite of ours. I spoon the chicken and sauce on to a bed of buckwheat and sometimes make Indian Garlic Bread too (No. 205).
Cals: 4=340, 6=288

92
Peanut Butter Chicken
(4)

$1\frac{1}{2}$Kg (3 lb) chicken
2 × 15ml spoons (2 tbs) peanut butter
100g (4 ozs) chopped roasted peanuts

Pre-heat oven to 230°C (450°F, Gas 8). Clean and prepare bird as for roasting but don't put anything in the cavity. Stand chicken on tray in roasting tin, put into oven and immediately reduce heat to 180°C (350°F, Gas 4). Roast for 45 minutes, removing from oven three times to prick with a fork so that fat can run away.[1] After 45 mins take a knife and carefully spread a

[1]See page 61

layer of peanut butter over the entire surface of the chicken, then sprinkle liberally with peanuts (which will stick to the peanut butter) and replace the bird in the oven. Bake for 30 mins more.

When you carve make sure each person gets a fair share of the buttery nuts or there may be an outbreak of hostilities.

93
Chicken Sesame
(4)

1-2 × 15ml spoons (1-2 tbs) oil
1½Kg (3 lbs) chicken in portions, skinned
4 × 15ml spoons (4 tbs) roasted sesame seeds (No. 105)
1 × 5ml spoon (1 tsp) salt
1 × 5ml spoon (1 tsp) garlic powder or ground garlic
ground black pepper

Pre-heat oven to 200°C (400°F, Gas 6). Using a pastry brush, lightly oil the chicken all over. Spread sesame seeds on to a plate and press the chicken pieces firmly on to them to pick up a generous coating. Oil an oven-proof dish and put the coated chicken pieces in it. Put into the oven, reducing heat immediately to 180°C (350°F, Gas 4). After 40 mins sprinkle with salt, pepper and garlic (I use ground garlic for a heavier garlic taste) and return to oven for 10 mins more.

Sesame seeds have a delightful, highly distinctive flavour as well as an astonishing amount of protein, and they're rich in polyunsaturate oil.
Cals: 350

94
Chicken Siam
(3)

1 × 15ml spoon (1 tbs) oil
225g (8 ozs) skinned, boned chicken, cut into bite-sized pieces
½ med onion, chopped
75g (3 ozs) mushrooms, sliced
1 clove garlic, chopped
1-2 × 5ml spoons (1-2 tsp) grated ginger root
Pinch crushed coriander seed
½ × 5ml spoon (½ tsp) salt
350g (12 ozs) beansprouts, washed and drained

Sauce:
2 × 15ml spoons (2 tbs) Tamari soy sauce
2 × 15ml spoons (2 tbs) lime or lemon juice
1 × 15ml spoon (1 tbs) honey
In a large, deep pan or casserole heat oil and stir-fry chicken over medium heat for 2 mins. Gradually stir in onion, mushroom, garlic and seasoning. When all are added stir-fry for 2 mins more, then reduce heat to minimum, cover, and simmer for 5 mins. Meanwhile combine sauce ingredients in saucepan and heat through, then pour over the chicken-vegetables. Immediately add the beansprouts (as dry as you can make them, or they'll water down the flavour) and stir-fry for 2 mins. Serve at once.

In true Oriental style the chicken and vegetables should be prepared in advance and just thrown into the pot for cooking for the shortest possible time. Each retains its own flavour and texture, yet adds to the overall taste.
Cals: 260

Rice and Pumpkin-seeds, No. 240, plus crisp-tender green beans No. 116 will give you a perfect three-bowl dinner–maximum flavour and minimum calories.

95
Chicken in Red Wine

(4)

1 × 15ml spoon (1 tbs) oil
4 portions chicken, skinned, halved
Paprika
Salt
2 lge onions, chopped
150g (5 ozs) mushrooms, sliced
6 carrots, sliced
2 ribs celery, sliced
2 lge cloves garlic, chopped
1 leek, thinly sliced (optional)
large bayleaf
250ml (8 fl.ozs) red wine
450ml (16 fl.ozs) water, with
1½ chicken stock cubes melted in it
225g (8 ozs) fresh green beans in 1 in slices
Salt and pepper

Heat oil in pan. Sprinkle chicken pieces lightly with paprika and salt, brown them in oil and place in a casserole. In same oil brown onions and spoon them over chicken in casserole. Repeat with mushrooms, carrots, celery, garlic and leek. Add bayleaf, wine and stock, sprinkle lightly with salt and pepper, cover and cook for 1-1½ hours or until chicken is tender. Meanwhile, steam green beans in lightly salted water until crisp-tender–a little 'bite' is delightful in this dish– and stir them into the sauce just before serving. Or cook this in the oven at 180°C (350°F, Gas 4).

We have this treat when there's wine left at the bottom of a bottle or when I want to serve something special to guests without being the 'missing link' in the kitchen all evening.

Cals: 490

96
Chicken Tamale Pie

(5-6)

1 × 15ml spoon (1 tbs) oil
2 lge chopped onions
1 lge green pepper, chopped
350-500g (¾-1 lb) boned, raw chicken in large dice
500g (1 lb) tomatoes, chopped
350g (12 ozs) sweetcorn kernels
250 ml (8 fl.ozs) water
1 × 5ml spoon (1 tsp) salt
ground black pepper
2-3 × 5ml spoons (2-3 tsp) chili powder (to taste)

Topping:
100g (4 ozs) maize meal
4 × 15ml spoons (4 tbs or 1¼ ozs) wholewheat flour
½ × 5ml spoon (½ tsp) salt
1½ × 5ml spoons (1½ tsp) baking powder
1 × 5ml spoon (1 tsp) honey
1 egg, lightly beaten
100ml (4 fl.ozs) skimmed milk
1 × 15ml spoon (1 tbs) corn oil

Pre-heat oven to 220°C (425°F, Gas 7). Heat oil, gently sauté onion, green pepper and chicken until onion turning gold. Add all other ingredients and simmer gently for 15 mins. Pour into greased oven-proof casserole.

Topping: Combine first 4 ingredients. In separate bowl combine remaining ingredients, then pour wet into dry and stir just until you have a thick batter. Don't overmix or beat. Gently spoon and spread batter over chicken mixture in a layer without worrying if some appears to sink. Bake for 20-25 mins till golden brown and crisp on top.

This Mexican dish combines hot and sweet, juicy and crunchy, in an irresistible manner. And it has eye-appeal, too !

97
Paella
(6)

Serve this Spanish dish Spanish-style by putting the 'paella pan' right on the table and serving from it. You will need a large, deep frying pan with a lid for this (about 10 in-12 in). Use this pan for step number 3.

1 × 15ml spoon (1 tbs) oil
1 red pepper, sliced in rings
1 green pepper, sliced in rings
250g (8 ozs) any fish, cubed, sprinkled with paprika and salt

1 × 15ml spoon (1 tbs) oil
6 portions chicken, halved
1 × 5ml spoon (1 tsp) paprika
1 × 5ml spoon (1 tsp) salt
2 cloves garlic, crushed
4 tomatoes, sliced
250ml (8 fl.ozs) chicken stock
Pinch saffron (optional)

1 × 15ml spoon (1 tbs) oil
1 lge onion, chopped
350g (12 ozs) brown rice, washed and drained
800ml (28 fl.ozs) chicken stock
1 × 5ml spoon (1 tsp) salt
½ × 5ml spoon (½ tsp) turmeric

225g (8 ozs) fresh or frozen peas

1. In casserole with lid heat 1 tbs oil and sauté peppers till crisp-tender. Then sauté fish till just browned. Remove both, set aside.
2. In same casserole heat 1 tbs oil. Sprinkle chicken with paprika and salt then sauté, with garlic, till golden. Place sliced tomatoes on top, add 250ml (8 fl.ozs) stock, and saffron if using this. Cover tightly and simmer for 45 mins.
3. In large, deep frying pan ('paella pan') heat 1 tbs oil and sauté onion till silver. Stir in rice, 800ml (28 fl.ozs) stock, salt and turmeric. Cover tightly, simmer for 40 mins.
4. Cook peas in lightly salted water till crisp-tender. Drain.
5. **To Combine:** Stir cooked peas into cooked rice. Arrange peppers, chicken and fish attractively on top and pour over juice from casserole to make rice mixture very moist. Cover tightly, simmer for 10 mins to heat everything through and serve.

This is much simpler than it appears. All the sections can be cooked early in the day and combined 10 mins before dinner for the final heat-through if you wish.

98
Moroccan Chicken
(4)

4 portions chicken, skinned, halved
1½ × 5ml spoons (1½ tsp) salt
⅛ × 5ml spoon (⅛ tsp) pepper
1 med onion, chopped

1 stick cinnamon
Pinch saffron (optional)
225g (8 ozs) prunes
1 × 5ml spoon (1 tsp) ground cinnamon
4 × 15ml spoons (4 tbs) honey
1 × 15ml spoon (1 tbs) arrowroot in
2 × 15ml spoons (2 tbs) cold water
Garnish: 4 × 15ml spoons (4 tbs) roasted flaked almonds

In soup pan boil chicken with salt, pepper, onion, cinammon stick and pinch saffron (optional). Reduce heat to simmer, cover and cook for 1 hour or until chicken tender. Remove chicken to spare plate and discard cinammon stick. Put prunes into chicken liquid and simmer uncovered for 15 mins. Stir in ground cinammon and honey, then the arrowroot which you have melted in cold water. When sauce thickens slightly, return chicken to liquid and heat it through for 10 mins, stirring occasionally but without breaking the chicken or prunes. Serve at once.

This is a really magnificent dish. Spoon the bird, the fruit and the juice on to a bed of brown rice, sprinkle toasted almonds on top and eat like a Sultan.

99
Chicken Pie
(4-6)

Filling:
1 × 5ml spoon (1 tsp) oil
1 lge onion, chopped
2 carrots, coarsely chopped
1 rib celery, sliced
1 green pepper, sliced
1 clove garlic, chopped
100g (4 ozs) mushrooms, sliced
225g (8 ozs) cooked, diced chicken
1 × 5ml spoon (1 tsp) salt
$\frac{1}{8}$ × 5ml spoon ($\frac{1}{8}$ tsp) pepper
2 × 15ml spoons (2 tbs) Tamari soy sauce
2 × 15ml spoons (2 tbs) wholewheat flour
550ml (20 fl.ozs) chicken stock
100g (4 ozs) fresh peas

Crust: 175g (6 ozs) recipe No. 272

Heat oil and stir-fry onions and then all vegetables in order given, cooking each about half a minute. Add chicken, salt, pepper and soy sauce, sprinkle the flour over and stir-fry for 1 min more. Pour in stock and bring to boil, add peas, cover and simmer gently for 10-15 mins or until peas firm-tender. Spoon filling into greased, deep oven-proof dish. Make crust, roll out thinly, wet edges of dish, spread crust over and press it firmly to seal. Make three cuts in the crust to allow steam to escape, brush with skimmed milk and bake in pre-heated oven 220°C (425°F, Gas 7), for 30 minutes or until golden brown.

100
Peking Chicken
(6)

2Kg (4 lb) chicken

Pancakes:
425g (15 ozs) wholewheat flour
250ml (9 fl.ozs) boiling water

'Jam'
1 × 15ml spoon (1 tbs) arrowroot
6 × 15ml spoons (6 tbs) water
3 × 15ml spoons (3 tbs) tomato paste

4 × 15ml spoons (4 tbs) honey
1 × 15ml spoon (1 tbs) sunflower oil
6 × 15ml spoons (6 tbs) Tamari soy sauce

12 spring onions, quartered, in 3 in lengths
2 chunks unpeeled cucumber cut in 3 in matchsticks

1. Roast chicken, see No. 81
2. Make pancakes: stir boiling water into flour, combine into a firm dough and let stand for 30 mins. Then, on well-floured board, roll with hands into a sausage shape. Cut off 18 equal-sized pieces, roll each into a ball between your palms then roll flat into 5-6 in paper-thin rounds. Heat griddle or heavy frying pan without greasing it. Put one pancake into pan, cook gently for about $1\frac{1}{2}$ mins till blisters appear on surface and brown spots underneath. Remove. DO NOT COOK SECOND SIDE ! Repeat with other pancakes, separating them with foil or greaseproof paper so you can make a stack. I always make pancakes well in advance, then steam them for 10 mins immediately before serving, which makes them tender and moist as well as warm. Just put the whole stack into your steamer, (see page 21) paper dividers and all. Serve them like that, too ; guests peel them off the top.
3. 'Jam': While pancakes are heating make jam. Stir arrowroot into cold water, then combine with all other ingredients in small saucepan and stir over med heat until sauce thickens (about 5 mins). Don't leave cooking longer than 10 mins or the arrowroot will lose it's thickening power. Serve in sauce-boat.

To Eat: Carve roast chicken into small, thin slices, barely bigger than bite-sized, and put on serving plate. Round it pile the matchsticks of spring onion and cucumber. Set out 'jam' and stack of pancakes. Now each guest takes a pancake, spreads it thinly from edge to edge with 'jam' and in the centre puts a little mound of crispy onion and cucumber. A slice or two of chicken goes on top, the pancake is rolled up around the filling, like a sausage and–voila ! Peking Chicken !

Purists may say you need the crisp, fatty duck skin to make this dish a real masterpiece, but they say *that* only until they've tasted *this*.

101
Turkey or Chicken Pasties
(4)

350g (12 ozs) pastry, No. 272

1 × 5ml spoon (1 tsp) oil
1 med onion, chopped
1 clove garlic, chopped
100g (4 ozs) mushrooms, sliced

Sauce:
1 × 15ml spoon (1 tbs) polyunsaturate margarine
2 × 15ml spoons (2 tbs) wholewheat flour
450ml (16 fl.ozs) skimmed milk
250ml (8 fl.ozs) strong chicken stock
1 × 5ml spoon (1 tsp) salt
$\frac{1}{8}$ × 5ml spoon ($\frac{1}{8}$ tsp) pepper
$\frac{1}{8}$ × 5ml spoon ($\frac{1}{8}$ tsp) grated nutmeg
1 small bayleaf

225g (8 ozs) cooked, diced turkey or chicken
2 × 15ml spoons (2 tbs) chopped fresh parsley

Gently sauté onion and garlic in oil for 2 mins. Add mushrooms and sauté for 5 mins more. Remove from heat.

Sauce: Melt margarine in saucepan, stir in flour, cook for 1 minute, then gradually stir in milk and stock. Add seasonings and simmer for 10 mins, stirring occasionally. Now add the onion mixture, the turkey (or chicken) and parsley to the sauce, remove bayleaf, heat through and adjust seasoning.

Make pastry and, without 'resting' it, divide it into 4 (for 4 large pasties) or 8 (for 8 small ones). Roll each portion between your palms, then roll each ball into a flat round about $\frac{1}{8}$ in thick. Make sure there are no holes in it. Now put a quarter (or an eighth, for small ones) of the filling into the centre of each pastry round and fold it over to a half-moon shape. Swiftly press edges together to seal them and hold in the sauce. Then stand them upright, so that the edge becomes the top, and you have a pastie. Repeat with remainder.

Pre-heat oven to 220°C (425°F, Gas 7). Place pasties carefully on greased baking tray, prick once on each side so steam can escape, brush gently with skimmed milk and bake for 25 mins till golden brown and crisp.

I put clear chicken gravy No. 75 in the sauceboat and serve a salad with these pasties, followed by a fruity dessert. No one really needs more.

102
Turkey Tortellini
(4-6)

225g (8 ozs) finely chopped cooked turkey (or chicken)
2×5ml spoons (2 tsp) grated Parmesan cheese
2×15ml spoons (2 tbs) plain low-fat yogurt
4 spring onions with green, chopped
$\frac{1}{8}$×5ml spoon ($\frac{1}{8}$ tsp) grated nutmeg
$\frac{1}{4}$×5ml spoon ($\frac{1}{4}$ tsp) grated lemon peel
Salt and pepper

$\frac{1}{2}$ recipe for noodles (No. 236)[1]

Combine first 6 ingreds. and mix well. Add salt and pepper to taste, depending on how well-seasoned turkey already is. Make noodle dough to the point of rolling out first half. Now using cutter dipped in flour, cut out 20×2$\frac{1}{2}$ in rounds. Place 1×5ml spoonful (1 teaspoonful) of turkey mixture in centre of round, moisten edges with water and fold into half-moon shape, pressing edges well to seal. For authentic Italian shape, bend the long, straight edge over your finger and draw points together to form a broken ring. Repeat with all rounds. Bring large pan of salted water to boil and drop in the tortellini one at a time to keep the water bubbling. When all are in cook for 15-20 mins or till tender, stirring occasionally to keep them separated. Drain in colander. Serve with Tomato-Garlic Sauce (No. 310) or drop into boiling chicken soup, cook for 15-20 minutes and serve in the liquid for a Main Course Soup.

This is a great dish for guests. The effort you've put in really shows, while the cost is extremely low. Counteract the calories with a Watercress Soup to start (No. 4) and fresh fruit to follow.

---

[1] I make the full noodle recipe since that's no more work than half, then I make noodles with the second half and freeze them.

Vegetables and Vegetable Main Courses

Vegetables and Vegetable Main Courses

Most of us resist the idea of vegetable meals, mainly because of the 'you can't make a meal without meat' myths. But there's another reason: vegetable meals are generally described as 'Vegetarian'. The very word suggests people munching carrots while lecturing us about the perils of eating dead flesh.

However, vegetarians are not nuts, but people who learned before the rest of us that vegetables, legumes and fruits can not only make marvellous meals, but also sustain life–and healthy life at that. So why don't we close our ears to their philosophy, if we wish, but open our minds to their diet? I've tried to do just that, and the vegetable meals given here–a really valuable part of the low-fat, high-fibre diet–are as tasty, appealing, appetising, hearty, satisfying and just plain *delicious* as any meat, chicken or fish dishes.

Many of us have a poor opinion of vegetables due to school dinners that polluted the air of our childhood, or well-meaning mothers who boiled the greens a bit longer so they'd be easier to 'get down'. Greens–or yellows or reds or beiges–have a variety of flavours and textures that make them a gourmet's delight if they're cooked properly. But the difference between 'delight' and 'yuch' is just five minutes in rapidly boiling water.

Whenever I'm asked what's in a dish that everyone's enjoying, I always say 'This and that'. Well, it's disconcerting to be told you're licking your lips over, say, cabbage, when you're convinced that you hate it. Yet vegetables, transformed into stews, pies and casseroles, can easily uphold the first law of food–that it should taste good.

Butter? Cream? Rich, fatty sauces? Forget them all. Taste the sweet, natural flavour of steamed or baked sweet corn as it comes and you'll never smother it in butter again. Broccoli with hollandaise sauce? *How* many calories? *How* much cholesterol? But broccoli steamed tender-crisp with a light sprinkling of salt, or served in a rich, spicy tomato sauce? Delightful, healthy, and a gourmet way to cut calories.

I'm going on about vegetables as if they were a treat because they are–or can be (and remember I had to break down my *own* resistance when I started putting this diet together).

To help convert my family I played a little trick on them. Having cooked a vegetable entrée, I put three small bowls in front of each person and served entrée, grain and salad, all at once, in separate bowls. This Chinese style of presentation intrigued them, and I added to the sense of occasion by handing out chopsticks instead of knives and forks. Not one complaint arose, even on those early occasions when my experiments failed and the chopsticks tasted better than the meal.

As eye-appeal and novelty are so important an element in food why not put your soup, salad and dessert bowls into service all at once in the THREE-BOWL DINNER? Its other advantage is that you automatically eat more slowly, which is good for your digestion and helps control your weight. Slow chewing and swallowing make you feel 'full' on less food, so without feeling hungry you take in less.

Another trick I borrowed from the Chinese is to stir-fry vegetables. In Chinese restaurants, despite the pitfalls of mass catering, the vegetables are always perfect–full of flavour with just the right amount of bite and no sogginess–because they are not boiled and then kept warm for

Vegetables and Vegetable Main Courses

hours, but swiftly stir-fried to order. For the basic stir-fry method, see No. 110.

Stir-fried vegetables cook in their own juice. The food value stays where it belongs, in the food, and there's no vitamin-and-mineral-rich liquid to throw away.

Peeling vegetables is another way of producing nutritious, expensive garbage. Much of the 20 per cent of food wasted in this country is attached to vegetable peel, and it's not surprising as peeling is so boring and laborious. Try scrubbing instead, using a small stiff brush for carrots, turnips, celery, parsnips, etc. All you need to take off is dirt, but you'll not miss the thin outside layer that the brush brings off. It's much easier and quicker than peeling and really saves food and money.

Don't throw away limp vegetables. Their liquid content has evaporated during storage, but unless they are actually bad you don't need to waste them. Firstly, they can be used to make stock. A handful of assorted vegetables, simmered for half an hour in seasoned water, produce good, tasty stock. Secondly, limp vegetables can be added to soups and stews. They retain most of their goodness and if you combine them with fresh ones you'll deprive only your dustbin.

Leftover cooked vegetables can be just as good second-time-around. Practically any variety can be added to today's soup or stew, chopped up into rice or other grain, sprinkled with dressing and served as a salad or just dropped into a bowl of lettuce-salad for added interest.

Vegetables must become a major part of our diet if we want to be healthy and slim and live on a reasonable budget. It's no hardship, as you'll see for yourself when you try these recipes.

Vegetables and Vegetable Main Courses

Legumes

Dried peas and beans are high-protein, high-fibre and highly delicious. They combine with just about anything–chicken, fish, vegetables, salad–and bring a satisfying taste, texture and heartiness to a meal.

Preparation is much the same for all varieties, but cooking time depends on several factors like the age of the bean and where it was grown. So the cooking times given are only approximate, but they can be helpful the first time you cook legumes. After that you can adjust the cooking time according to your own experience. Don't worry too much about timing, though, because mushy beans are great in soups and stews, while hard ones can always be given more time to soften up. Don't salt any beans until they're done, or they'll take even longer to cook and may never get really tender.

As you'll see from the cooking times, pressure cooking is a big money-saver. Some people make an entire bean stew or soup in the pressure cooker, but I think the flavour is far superior if you partly cook your vegetables and other ingredients separately, then add the pressure-cooked beans for a final simmer. Also, if you do the beans on their own you can make an extra quantity for use with other dishes on other days and cut down the cost of the slow method. I keep cooked beans in the refrigerator for about a week. They may stay good even longer than that, but in my house they don't stay uneaten.

103
Dried Beans

Slow method, in saucepan with tight-fitting lid.
Pick over the beans, take out any bad or broken ones and soak overnight in cold water to cover by about 3 in. Next day, taste the soaking water to be sure it's not bitter. If it is–throw it away. If not, pour it over the beans, add fresh water to cover them by about 1 in if necessary, then bring to the boil, reduce to a gentle simmer, cover and cook until the beans are firm-tender. More boiling water can be added to keep them covered. When tender add salt to taste and simmer for 5 minutes more, uncovered. Drain (reserving the liquid for soup) and use.

Pressure Cooker:
Soaking isn't really necessary but it can't hurt. So pick over the beans, taking out bad or broken ones and soak overnight if you wish. Next day put into pressure cooker with water to just cover, bring to boil without the lid and skim off any froth. Now bring up pressure and cook according to the times below. Let pressure drop naturally (or according to the instructions with your cooker). Remove lid, add salt to taste, simmer for 5 minutes uncovered. Drain (reserving the liquid for soup) and use.

	Slow Method	*Pressure Cooker*
Haricot Beans	1 -1½ hrs	20 mins
Butter (Lima) Beans	¾ -1½ hrs	20 mins
Black Beans	1½-2 hrs	30 mins
Black-eyed peas, Kidney Beans	½ -1 hr	10 mins

Vegetables and Vegetable Main Courses

	Slow Method	Pressure Cooker
Pinto, pea, navy, rose coco	$\frac{3}{4}$ -$1\frac{1}{2}$ hrs	20 mins
Chick peas (Garbanzo beans)	$2\frac{1}{2}$-$3\frac{1}{2}$ hrs[1]	45 mins

1 cup (250ml) medium sized dried beans= 175g. 1 cup dried will yield about $2\frac{1}{2}$ cups cooked.

Lentils

Though they're legumes lentils deserve a separate heading. Each lentil dish I try, I want to call 'Lentil Surprise', because it's always a surprise that such a maligned food should be so delicious.

Like brown rice and wholewheat bread, lentils are used to ridicule 'health food nuts' and we thus turn our backs on a highly nutritious and very versatile food.

Lentils bring protein, iron and B vitamins to roasts and stews, loaves, salads, curries, fritters–an almost endless list of appetising dishes. They come in three main colours, red, greenish-brown and brown, are sometimes split and sometimes whole, but however they come–*use them.*

When asked what's in your lentil dishes, reply: 'This and that'. And don't tell the children that lentils are 'good for them'. Just put Lentilburgers before them (Nos. 163 and 164) and watch the food vanish.

[1] This extra hard bean needs special treatment if you're using the slow method. Soak overnight, bring to boil in water to just cover and let boil for five minutes. Remove from heat and let stand for one hour. Bring to boil again (adding more boiling water if needed to cover) reduce heat to simmer, put on the lid and cook for $1\frac{1}{2}$-2 hours, or until tender. Don't make them mushy–they should keep their shape and be firm.

104
To Cook Lentils

(if you're not following one of these recipes)

First pick over the lentils. They seem to attract little pebbles, which must be removed, but be sure to use dry hands or you'll be studded with limpet-like lentils. Now, wash them in cold water (soaking isn't necessary), drain, put them in a pan with water to cover, put on lid and simmer until tender. Red lentils will take 20 minutes to get tender, 30 to get mushy or dissolve. Green and brown take about 1 hour. I usually add salt towards the end of the cooking time unless the recipe says otherwise. Again, use the drained-off cooking liquid in soup or stews. It's highly nutritious.

Nuts

This delicious, high-fibre food is an important part of our diet, but we shouldn't be misled into eating nuts that aren't healthy. For example, the roasted and salted nuts you buy are much too heavily salted and almost always roasted in saturated fats.

Most supermarkets stock natural nuts ; so do grain and health food shops. I shop round for this item because prices can vary tremendously, as can the quality of the nuts. When you find good nuts at a good price buy a fairly large quantity, particularly of peanuts and hazelnuts, which are used most often, because they store well.

You'll find no coconut or cashew nuts in

this book because the oil in these nuts is saturated. Any others that you like can be eaten freely, not only in cooked foods and salads, but as between-meals snacks instead of biscuits and chocolate. A dish of nuts and raisins is not only tremendously satisfying to a sweet-tooth, it's also high-fibre and high-protein, which means you'll want less dinner after eating it.

105
To Roast Nuts
(or seeds)

Simply spread the nuts in a single layer on a baking tray and pop them under a hot grill. Or put the tray in the oven when you're cooking something else at about 190°C (375°F, Gas 5). Shake and turn the nuts once or twice. In a few minutes they'll be a lovely golden colour and they're done. Please don't add salt. The nuts don't need it and neither do you. No oil is necessary, either.

106
To Skin Nuts

Almonds: drop into boiling water for 5 minutes, drain, rinse in cold water...and the skins will slide off.
Hazelnuts and Peanuts: after roasting roll the nuts on a damp cloth and the skins will rub off. (We usually eat the skins–we like them!)

107
To Chop Nuts

One or two seconds in your grinder will give excellent coarsely chopped nuts. If you forget to switch off try Nut Pâté (No. 23).

108
To Remove Bitterness

The little packets of walnuts from the supermarket are often slightly bitter. Cover them with boiling water, soak for half an hour and drain. Cover them with cold water, soak for one hour, then drain and use.

The fibre won't be harmed by this soaking, but it doesn't help the vitamins and minerals, so I use these only in an emergency. They're more expensive, anyway, in their little brand-named packets.

Chestnuts

I always use dried chestnuts because they're ready-peeled, easy to handle and available all year round. The cheapest are found in Chinese markets, the most expensive in health food shops though the nuts are the same.

109
To Cook Chestnuts:

Slow Method: Soak chestnuts overnight in water to cover well. In fresh water bring the nuts to the boil, reduce heat to simmer,

Vegetables and Vegetable Main Courses

cover and cook until tender–about 1-1½ hours. Drain and use.

Pressure cooker: No soaking necessary. Rinse the nuts in cold water, drain, put into pressure cooker with water to just cover. Cook for 35 minutes. Bring down pressure under cold tap. Drain and use.

500g raw=750-900g (1½-2 lbs) cooked.

Simply-cooked vegetables make a perfect accompaniment to many of the recipes in this book. This is how I cook, simply, the vegetables we enjoy:

110
To Stir-Fry

Use a saucepan or frying pan with a tight-fitting lid. Put 1×5ml spoon (1 tsp) corn oil into the pan and heat over medium-to-high heat. Drop in your vegetables and stir them round the oil, keeping them moving all the time. In two minutes you'll have silvered onion and garlic, in three or four minutes golden onions and garlic, and tender sweet peppers or courgettes. For longer-cooking vegetables, like cauliflower, carrots, etc. (see individual listings below), you stir-fry for three or four minutes, then put on the tight-fitting lid, turn the heat down to the barest minimum and simmer the vegetables in their own juice until they are tender–which means just a few minutes more.

111
To Steam

(See page 21 for home-made steamer). Just make sure the water in the base (pan) is boiling steadily over medium heat before you put in the vegetable basket (or colander). Steaming time depends on the age of the vegetables, but allow 5-10 mins more than for cooking in boiling water.

112
Asparagus

Cut away some of the thick, white stem, making stalks all approx. same length. Wash green tips under cold running water and scrape stems clean with sharp knife. If you don't have a special pan (I don't), simply place asparagus stalks in your steamer, cover tightly and steam for about 15 mins.

Asparagus doesn't need butter when you serve it–just a light sprinkling of salt to bring out the natural flavour.

113
Aubergine Slices

Peel aubergine very thinly and cut into ½ in slices cross-wise. Paint a little corn oil on each slice, sprinkle with salt, pepper and some chopped herbs (if you like them), plus a sprinkling of lemon juice. Now pop under hot grill for 7 mins, turn, oil second side and grill for 5 mins more. *Or* slices can be baked in oven for 15 mins, turning once, at 200°C (400°F, Gas 6).

Vegetables and Vegetable Main Courses

114
Aubergine Fritters

Peel and slice aubergine as for Aubergine Slices, paint lightly with oil, then dip into wholewheat breadcrumbs to collect a thick coating. Heat 2-3×15ml spoons (2-3 tbs) corn oil and gently sauté until fritters are brown and crisp. Drain well and serve.

Beans

115
Broad

Bring ½ in lightly salted water to boil, drop in the podded beans and boil for about 3 mins. If the beans are young, slice up some of the pods (removing any string) and boil the pods with the beans. Economical and delicious.

116
French, Green, Runner, Snap

I treat all long, thin green beans alike: snip off tops and tails, draw out strings, if any ; leave beans whole if they're of manageable length and snap into shorter lengths if they're not. Then, 1. Stir-fry ; or 2. Pop into steamer for about 10 minutes ; or 3. Drop them into ½ in boiling, lightly salted water and cook, partly covered, for about 5 mins. Whichever method you choose make sure there's some 'bite' left in the bean.

117
Green Beans and Almonds

Cook any of the green beans by any of the above methods. When crisp-tender, drain, put into serving dish and sprinkle generously with toasted, flaked almonds. Or sprinkle with crisp wholewheat breadcrumbs for crunchy fibre, or a few spoons of fresh, chopped herbs.

118
Bean Sprouts

Rinse under cold tap and drain as well as possible. If you have a centrifugal salad drier use that. Stir-fry bean sprouts for 1 or 2 minutes and serve immediately. They should be just as crisp as when raw, since you're not really cooking but merely heating this delicious vegetable. Or, 2. put two 15ml spoons (2 tbs) Tamari soy sauce into a saucepan and heat it to boiling, drop in the washed, drained bean sprouts and stir-fry them for 1-2 mins. Or, 3. use bean sprouts raw in salads.

119
Beetroot

Even small ones can take up to 2 hours to soften, but they're worth it. Choose small ones, scrub them (but don't break skin or the colour will run), drop them into a large pan of cold, lightly salted water, bring to boil, cover and simmer until tender, adding more boiling water if necessary. Or, 2. Pressure-cook, which is much quicker, easier and cheaper. Put into pressure cooker with 250ml (8 fl.ozs) water, bring up

Vegetables and Vegetable Main Courses

pressure and cook for 15-20 mins. Cool under cold tap, remove lid, and wonderfully tender beetroots are ready to be cooled, slipped out of their skins and eaten.

120
Hot Sweet Beets
(4)

1 × 5ml spoon (1 tsp) oil
1 med onion, chopped
2 eating apples, chopped
Salt and pepper
500g (1 lb) cooked beetroot, sliced
1 × 15ml spoon (1 tbs) wine vinegar
1 × 15ml spoon (1 tbs) honey

Heat oil, stir-fry onion for 2 mins, add apple, stir-fry for 1 min, sprinkle with salt and pepper. Place sliced beetroot on top in 1 layer, sprinkle salt and pepper then trickle vinegar and honey over the slices. (If you have to make 2 layers, season and 'trickle' each). Cover with tight-fitting lid and simmer gently for 10 mins. Serve moist, sweet-and-sour beets with a crispy heap of vegetables on top.

121
Broccoli

This delicious vegetable can easily lose its lovely colour. I find the best method is to bring ½ in of lightly salted water to the boil, drop in broccoli and cook partly covered for about 10 mins, at which time the heads should be tender and the stems tender-firm. Some people recommend adding 1 × 5ml spoon (1 tsp) lemon juice to the water to help keep the colour. Don't trim off too much stalk; it tastes good and you've paid for it. Just cut away bruised outer leaves and stalk-ends, cook the rest and eat it.

122
Brussels Sprouts

These can easily be murdered. Little ones need only be washed and have a scrap trimmed off the root. Large ones need outer, damaged leaves pulled off and a gash cut into the root. Then drop sprouts into a pan of lightly salted, boiling water and simmer, uncovered, for 5-10 mins. They should be bright green and firm and have bite. No mush!

123
Brussels Sprouts and Chestnuts
(4)

Have all ingredients ready before cooking sprouts so that the second they're done, they can be combined with the other ingredients without getting cold.

150g (5 ozs) cooked chestnuts
500g (1 lb) brussels sprouts
Boiling, salted water
50ml (2 fl.ozs) chicken stock
3 × 15ml spoon (3 tbs) wholewheat breadcrumbs
1 × 15ml spoon (1 tbs) Parmesan cheese
1 × 15ml spoon (1 tbs) polyunsaturate margarine

Grease baking dish, put in the chestnuts. Drop sprouts into boiling, salted water and cook till firm-tender. Drain immediately and combine sprouts with chestnuts. Spoon stock over to moisten, sprinkle with crumbs and cheese, dot top with margarine. Bake at top of oven pre-heated to 190°C (375°F, Gas 5) for 20 mins,

124
Carrots

Scrub with stiff brush, rinse under cold tap, then 1. Stir-fry, whole if they're small and new, sliced if not. When you've had them tightly covered for about 10 mins check them. New ones should be done. If still a bit hard see if they need a spoonful of water–they should cook in their own juice but old carrots sometimes dry out. Or, 2. Drop carrots, whole or sliced, into about 250ml (8 fl.ozs) cold, salted water. Bring to boil, cover, simmer for about 15 mins. Drain (keeping liquid for stock) and serve.

125
Glazed Carrots

Best with new baby carrots, but sliced old ones taste great too. Boil carrots as 2. above. When tender drain.

Cooked, drained carrots
1 × 15ml spoon (1 tbs) polyunsaturate margarine
2 × 15ml spoons (2 tbs) honey
Salt
Paprika

In frying pan melt margarine and stir honey into it plus a sprinkling of salt and paprika. When bubbling add the carrots and turn them over and over until they are golden. This vegetable is good enough to serve as a dessert !

126
Cabbage

Heads of cabbage, green or 'white'.
1. Pressure cook. Remove damaged outer leaves and cut head into quarters (or eighths if very large). Put into rack in cooker with 250ml (8 fl.ozs) salted water and cook for 4-5 minutes, bringing down pressure under cold tap. Or, 2. Stir-fry. Shred the cabbage, stir-fry as usual for 2 mins, cover tightly and simmer for 10 mins. Or (a very poor third choice) 3. Drop into boiling salted water for the shortest possible time, just until hardness goes and tender-firmness is achieved.

127
Chinese Cabbage

Responds best to stir-fry method, exactly as cabbage 2. above. Try cutting the celery-like leaves in quarters, then stir-frying, for a more knife-and-fork vegetable. It will need to simmer, covered, for about 10 mins to become firm-tender. Also–this is marvellous–cut into little chunks or shreds and eat raw in salads.

128
Cauliflower

1. Steam for about 10-15 minutes. This produces beautifully white, tasty cauliflower with bite to it. Or 2. Drop into ½ in lightly salted, boiling water for 5-10

Vegetables and Vegetable Main Courses

minutes. Or 3. Break into small florets and stir-fry, allowing about 5 mins once you've covered the pan. This changes the flavour slightly, but it's a nice change and don't forget to leave the vegetable slightly undercooked.

129
Braised Celery

(4)

4 large or 8 short ribs celery or celery hearts
100ml (4 fl.ozs) chicken or vegetable stock
Sprinkling salt and pepper
1 × 15ml spoon (1 tbs) lemon juice
½ × 5ml spoon (½ tsp) honey
2 × 15ml spoons (2 tbs) Parmesan cheese

Scrub celery with stiff brush, trim ends, pull off any coarse strings. In shallow pan with lid combine stock, seasoning, lemon juice and honey. Put in the celery and bring to boil. Reduce heat, cover and simmer till tender–about 30 mins. Remove from liquid, arrange on heatproof plate, sprinkle with cheese and pop under hot grill until golden. (Or use wholewheat breadcrumbs for gratinée.)

130
Corn on the Cob

If you can find corn with its leaves and silk intact, you'll have a treat. 1. Gently peel down the leaves from the cob and pull away the silk. Dunk the ear in cold water, retaining as much water as possible, and press the leaves back into their original position. Now wrap the ear securely in aluminium foil. Repeat with other ears and bake in a pre-heated oven 200°C (400°F, Gas 6) for 20-25 mins. (You can cook on a barbecue in exactly this manner.) Or, 2. Drop trimmed ears into 1 in boiling water, cover and cook for 5-10 mins until firm-tender.

Don't put butter or cream sauces on corn ; it needs only a light sprinkling of salt to be a king among vegetables.

131
Courgettes
(sometimes called Zucchini)

Top and tail the little marrows, cut them into ½ in slices and 1. Stir-fry for about 3 mins, whereupon they'll be ready to eat. (No covering and simmering needed with this delicate vegetable). Or 2. Pop whole or halved courgettes into your steamer for about 10 minutes, sprinkle with salt and pepper (I use garlic salt) and serve. Or try slicing them thinly, lengthways, sprinkling with garlic salt or celery salt and pepper, chilling for an hour or so and just eating raw. Lovely !

132
Jerusalem Artichokes

Taste like delicious, savoury potatoes–but are much lower-calorie. Scrub the knobbly vegetables with your stiff brush, then 1. Steam them for about 25 mins. Or 2. Drop them into lightly salted boiling water with 1 × 5ml spoon (1 tsp) lemon juice added, and simmer covered for 15 mins–then test them. If tender drain and serve–they'll get tough again if left to cook on. Or 3. Pressure cook in 250ml (8 fl.ozs) water, for 8 mins.

Vegetables and Vegetable Main Courses

Once cooked they can be skinned very easily. The knobbles make it virtually impossible when they're raw.

133
Kale

Mature leaves should be torn in pieces, dropped into lightly salted water, part covered and cooked till tender. We like it chopped, with a little oil and garlic added. Young leaves should be cooked as fresh spinach.

134
Kohlrabi

Trim and scrub, or very thinly peel, and slice. Stir-fry for about 3 mins, then pour into the pan about 175ml (6 fl.ozs) well-seasoned chicken or veg. stock. Cover pan tightly and simmer for about 30 mins or till tender. Or cook exactly as turnips.

135
Braised Leeks
(4)

4 leeks
100ml (4 fl.ozs) chicken stock
Sprinkling salt
1 × 15ml spoon (1 tbs) lemon juice
½ × 5ml spoon (½ tsp) honey
2 × 15ml spoons (2 tbs) wholewheat breadcrumbs

Trim dark green root, cut leeks in half lengthways and wash well in cold water to remove grit from between leaves, but don't separate the leaves. In shallow pan with lid, combine stock, salt, lemon juice and honey. Put the leek halves into pan, bring to gentle boil, cover and simmer until leeks tender, 20-30 mins. Either serve now, with a spoonful of cooking liquid poured over, or carefully remove leeks from liquid, put on heatproof plate, sprinkle with breadcrumbs and pop under a hot grill until crisp and golden.

136
Mange Tout
(sometimes called snow peas)

Are eaten pods-and-all. I use them raw, chopped up in salads. Also added to stuffed aubergines or peppers to bring natural sweetness. Or eat them as a vegetable, alone or mixed with beansprouts. Simply stir-fry for 2 mins and serve at once, crisp, crunchy and sweet.

137
Mushrooms

Are used extensively in these recipes. To eat as a vegetable accompaniment, just wipe them with a damp cloth and 1. Stir-fry for 1-2 mins, cover and simmer gently for 2 mins, then serve. Or 2. Melt a spoonful of polyunsaturate margarine, drop in the mushrooms (whole if they're small, sliced if large) and gently sauté until they're golden, sprinkling with salt and pepper just before they're done.

Vegetables and Vegetable Main Courses

138
Okra

Best, I think, combined with tomatoes, stews or curries, but try it this way, too: top and tail small okra, slice larger ones into 1-2 in slices. Melt 1 × 15ml spoon (1 tbs) polyunsaturate margarine, add okra, cover and simmer for 10 mins, shaking pan frequently. Remove cover, season with salt and pepper and simmer uncovered until golden and tender.

139
Onions

Lend flavour to just about every savoury dish. On their own? Try them steamed whole. Peel 1 med size onion per person, place in steamer and cook until tender, about 30 mins. Make white sauce (No. 311) and pour over, sprinkle with Parmesan cheese and pop under the grill until golden. Or sprinkle with wholewheat crumbs for a really crisp topping.

140
Parsnips
(4)

500g (1 lb) parsnips
½ × 5ml spoon (½ tsp) salt
175ml (6 fl.ozs) chicken stock
1 × 15ml spoon (1 tbs) polyunsaturate margarine

Scrub or thinly peel parsnips and cut in half lengthways. Put into greased baking dish, sprinkle with salt, pour stock into dish. Dot margarine on top of vegetable, cover and bake in pre-heated oven 190°C (375°F, Gas 5) for 45 mins. (Cook at the same time as an entreé to save fuel costs.)

141
Pumpkin

If you have a continental market near you it'll have beautiful orange pumpkins, or huge green 'squash', which are members of the same family. These are wonderfully sweet vegetables and they're usually sold in halves or quarters, so you can buy small to give them a try. Cut the pumpkin or squash into slices about 1 in thick, scoop out and discard seeds. Place slices on greased baking tray (or aluminium foil), dot with polyunsaturate margarine, sprinkle salt and pepper and bake in pre-heated oven at 190°C (375°F, Gas 5) for about 30 mins or until very tender.

Variation: 1. If you like glazed carrots, try glazed pumpkin. Spread melted honey on top then season and bake as above.
2. For Deep South style bake with honey-glaze, then mash the flesh with 2-3 spoonfuls of orange juice and a pinch of ground ginger.

142
Spinach

Wash spinach very well in several changes of cold water, then dry thoroughly–your centrifugal salad drier will do it perfectly. Break leaves into pieces (or use young spinach) then 1. In a pan with tight-fitting lid, heat 1 × 5ml spoon (1 tsp) oil and 1 × 5ml spoon (1 tsp) polyunsaturate margarine. Add the spinach, cover at once and cook over medium-high heat until steam creeps round the lid. Immediately reduce heat to minimum and cook for about 5 mins more. Sprinkle spinach with salt and pepper and serve.

Variation: When the fats are hot, drop in 1 or 2 chopped cloves of garlic, then add spinach and proceed as above.
2. For really mature spinach, break into pieces and drop into lightly salted boiling water. Cover tightly and simmer for about 20 mins or until tender. Chop the cooked spinach and add a spoonful of oil and some garlic (if liked) or just salt and pepper.

143
Swede

Cook as Turnip, or

144
Creamed Swede
(4)

1 × 5ml spoon (1 tsp) oil
500g (1 lb) swedes, peeled, sliced
1 med onion, chopped
250ml (8 fl.ozs) water
½ × 5ml spoon (½ tsp) salt
Grating pepper
¼ × 5ml spoon (¼ tsp) grated nutmeg
2 × 15ml spoons (2 tbs) natural yogurt
3 × 15ml spoons (3 tbs) skimmed milk powder
2 × 15ml spoons (2 tbs) fresh parsley, chopped (optional)

Heat oil, stir-fry swedes and onions for 5 mins. Add water, salt and pepper, bring to boil, then cover and simmer till swede tender, about 20 mins. Put nutmeg, yogurt, milk, milk powder and half the liquid from vegetables into blender and blend well. Add vegetables and remaining liquid and blend until thick and creamy. Pour into serving bowl and sprinkle with parsley.

145
Swiss Chard Leaves

Cook exactly as Spinach

146
Turnips

Delicious raw in salads. For cooking scrub or thinly peel. 1. Slice and stir-fry for 2 mins, then cover and simmer gently for about 7 mins more until tender. 2. Drop sliced turnip into lightly salted boiling water and simmer, covered, until tender. Test after 10 minutes because it should be eaten firm-tender, not mushy.

147
Vegetable Stock

1 × 5ml spoon (1 tsp) oil
1 med onion, finely chopped
2 carrots, thinly sliced
2 ribs celery, thinly sliced
3 sprigs parsley, chopped
Pinch salt and pepper
1 litre (36 fl.ozs) water

Vegetables and Vegetable Main Courses

Heat oil, stir-fry onion till turning golden, then add other vegetables and stir-fry for 2 mins more. Add all other ingredients, bring to boil, reduce heat and simmer gently for 30-45 mins. Strain and use.

Too many vegetables can spoil a stock. This simple one has a really lovely flavour.

Rich Vegetable Stock:
As Vegetable Stock, but add some mushroom trimmings when stir-frying vegetables and a bayleaf when adding liquid. A little yeast extract is good if the stock is to be used for a stew or casserole.

148
Stuffed Aubergine

(4)

2 med aubergines, halved lengthways
1 × 5ml spoon (1 tsp) corn oil
1 med onion, chopped
1 green pepper, seeded, chopped
8 mange tout (optional)
2 ribs celery, chopped
1 clove garlic
100g (4 ozs) mushrooms, chopped
500g (1 lb) ripe tomatoes, chopped
½ × 5ml spoon (½ tsp) salt
½ × 5ml spoon (½ tsp) paprika
Wholewheat breadcrumbs
1 × 15ml spoon (1 tbs) Parmesan cheese

With grapefruit knife cut out aubergine pulp, leaving ¼ in case. Chop pulp. Heat oil, stir-fry onion for 2 mins then aubergine pulp for 1 minute. Gradually add all other vegetables, stir-frying briefly between additions. Season with salt and pepper, reduce heat, cover tightly and simmer for 15 minutes. Fill aubergine cases with the mixture. Sprinkle tops generously with breadcrumbs and lightly with cheese and pop under hot grill till golden and crisp.
Cals: 112

Variation: Replace mushrooms and mange tout with a cup of cooked brown rice or other grain, or a cup of cooked dried beans.

149
Aubergine Casserole

(main dish–3/starter–6)

1 med aubergine
3 med courgettes
2 × 5ml spoons (2 tsp) oil
1 lge onion, thinly sliced
1 lge green pepper, seeded, thinly sliced
2 cloves garlic, chopped
3 lge, ripe tomatoes, sliced
Salt and pepper
½ × 5ml spoon (½ tsp) paprika

Thinly peel aubergine, cut into slices approx 2 in × 1 in × ¼ in. Halve courgettes lengthways, then cut into 2 in slices. Heat oil in casserole (with lid). Stir-fry aubergine until golden, then remove. Stir-fry courgettes till golden, then remove. Stir-fry onion and green pepper, add garlic. When onions brown, return aubergine and courgettes to pan, add tomatoes, salt, pepper and paprika and stir well. Bring to boil, reduce heat to minimum and cook, covered, for 20 mins. This should be juicy but not swimming, so simmer uncovered for 5 mins if too liquidy.

This is good hot or cold: serve it as a starter, chilled, with home-made rye crackers (No. 209).
Cals: 3=95

Vegetables and Vegetable Main Courses

150
Aubergine and Beans
(4)

350g (12 ozs) cooked brown rice or wheat
275g (10 ozs) aubergine, peeled, thinly sliced
100g (4 ozs) mushrooms, sliced
1 med onion, thinly sliced, in rings
1-2 cloves garlic, chopped
175g (6 ozs) cooked dried beans
225g (8 ozs) tomatoes, chopped
3×15ml spoons (3 tbs) Tamari soy sauce
Salt and pepper
Bayleaf

Grease casserole (with lid). Spread rice at bottom then arrange in layers the aubergine, mushrooms, onion, garlic and beans, seasoning each layer with salt and pepper. Make aubergine the top layer. Pour over tomatoes and soy sauce. Cover and bake in oven pre-heated to 180°C (350°F, Gas 4) for 45 mins.
Cals: 184

151
Aubergine and Wheat Gratinée
(4)

1×5ml spoon (1 tsp) corn oil
1 med onion, chopped
1 med aubergine, unpeeled, diced
2 cloves garlic, chopped
1 green pepper, chopped
225g (8 ozs) tomatoes, chopped (or tin)
1×5ml spoon (1 tsp) salt
½×5ml spoon (½ tsp) dried oregano
ground black pepper
250g (9 ozs) cooked wholewheat berries
3×15ml spoons (3 tbs) wholewheat breadcrumbs
2×15ml spoons (2 tbs) grated Parmesan cheese

Heat oil, stir-fry onion till silver, add aubergine, garlic and green pepper and stir-fry until onion is golden. Add tomatoes, seasoning and herbs, stir in cooked wheat. Bring to boil, then reduce heat and simmer gently, uncovered, till vegetables are firm-tender, about 10 mins. Pour into heat-proof serving dish, sprinkle crumbs and cheese on top and pop under hot grill until brown and crisp.

Home made Noodles (No. 236) are good with this, or macaroni, and a crisp Cabbage Salad (No. 279).
Cals: 160

152
Broccoli Provençale
(4)

1×5ml spoon (1 tsp) corn oil
1 med onion, sliced
1-2 cloves garlic, chopped
225g (8 ozs) mushrooms, sliced
500g (1 lb) ripe tomatoes, chopped
½×5ml spoon (½ tsp) salt
ground black pepper
½×5ml spoon (½ tsp) dried basil
500g (1 lb) broccoli, trimmed
Salted water
2×15ml spoons (2 tbs) grated strong cheese
2×15ml spoons (2 tbs) roasted peanuts

Heat oil, stir-fry onion, then garlic, then mushrooms until all golden. Add tomatoes, seasoning and herbs, bring to boil, then reduce heat and simmer, covered, for 15

Vegetables and Vegetable Main Courses

mins. Meanwhile, bring ½ in lightly salted water to boil, drop in broccoli and cook, partly covered, until firm-tender, about 8 mins. Drain 100ml (4 fl.ozs) of water from broccoli into sauce and stir well. Put broccoli into serving dish, pour sauce over, sprinkle top with cheese and nuts, and serve.
Cals: 136

153
Red Cabbage
Main Dish–3/Vegetable–6

1 med red cabbage
2×5ml spoons (2 tsp) corn oil
2 med onions, sliced
2 med cooking apples, peeled and sliced
2 med eating apples, peeled and sliced
1×15ml spoon (1 tbs) honey
1×15ml spoon (1 tbs) wine vinegar
½×5ml spoon (½ tsp) ground cloves
1×5ml spoon (1 tsp) salt
ground black pepper

Shred cabbage, wash and drain without drying. In casserole (with lid) heat oil, stir-fry sliced onions until tender, then add the moist cabbage, apples and all other ingredients. Bring to the boil, reduce heat to minimum, cover and simmer for 1½-2 hours, until soft and mushy. Stir occasionally and add a little water if necessary.
Cals: 3=200

154
Cabbage Special
(5)

1×5ml spoon (1 tsp) corn oil
1 lge onion, thinly sliced
1 green pepper, seeded, sliced
750g (1½ lbs) lt green cabbage, shredded
350g (12 ozs) tomatoes, chopped
1½×5ml spoons (1½ tsp) salt
ground black pepper
1 bayleaf
1×5ml spoon (1 tsp) honey
1×5ml spoon (1 tsp) paprika
½-1×5ml spoon (½-1 tsp) crushed caraway seeds
150g (5 fl.ozs) natural yogurt
1×15ml spoon (1 tbs) polyunsaturate margarine
50g (2 ozs) rolled oats

Heat oil, stir-fry onion for 2 mins, add green pepper, stir-fry for 2 mins, add cabbage, stir-fry for 2 mins. Add tomatoes, salt and pepper, bayleaf, honey and paprika, cover, simmer gently for 15 mins. Stir in caraway seeds and yogurt and heat through without boiling. Remove bayleaf and pour mixture into heatproof dish. Combine margarine with oats, sprinkle oats on top of cabbage and pop under hot grill until brown and crisp but keep an eye on it to prevent burning.
Cals: 133

155
Stuffed Cabbage
(5)

1 lge-leafed cabbage, about 750g (1½ lbs)

Stuffing:
2 leeks (or 1 med onion) chopped
1 clove garlic, chopped
1×15ml spoon (1 tbs) polyunsaturate margarine

Vegetables and Vegetable Main Courses

100g (4 ozs) mushrooms, chopped
200g (7 ozs) cooked chestnuts (No. 109)
175g (6 ozs) cooked brown rice
$\frac{3}{4}$×5ml spoon ($\frac{3}{4}$ tsp) salt
$\frac{1}{4}$×5ml spoon ($\frac{1}{4}$ tsp) ground black pepper

Sauce:
350g (12 ozs) tin tomatoes
100ml (4 fl.ozs) apple cider
2×15ml spoons (2 tbs) apple vinegar
$\frac{1}{2}$×5ml spoon ($\frac{1}{2}$ tsp) honey
$\frac{1}{4}$×5ml spoon ($\frac{1}{4}$ tsp) salt
ground black pepper

Boil cabbage whole in lightly salted water, covered, for 5 mins. Drain, dunk under cold tap to freshen. Separate 10 large leaves, set aside. Chop remaining cabbage. Wash and chop leeks (or onion), chop garlic, then gently sauté both in melted marge till tender. Add chopped cabbage, mushrooms and cooked chestnuts, sauté for 5 mins more. Remove from heat, stir in rice and seasoning. Divide mixture roughly into ten, put a portion in centre of each cabbage leaf and roll up firmly. Put rolls in greased baking dish. In saucepan, combine and heat sauce ingredients, pour over rolls. Bake in oven pre-heated to 190°C (375°F, Gas 5) for 45 mins.
Cals: 2 rolls 200.

This is worth the effort, really filling and satisfying, with a delightful sweet-and-sour taste to liven up the palate.

156
Courgette Combination
(3)

1×5ml spoon (1 tsp) corn oil
1 lge onion, chopped
4 courgettes, sliced
1 green pepper, sliced
100g (4 ozs) mushrooms, sliced
4 lge ripe tomatoes, sliced
1×15ml spoon (1 tbs) Tamari soy sauce
Generous sprinkle salt, paprika and garlic powder

Heat oil, stir-fry onion until just changing colour, add courgettes and pepper, then mushrooms, and stir-fry until all golden brown. Add tomatoes and seasonings, cover and simmer gently for 5-10 mins. (Courgettes should have a little bite.)
Cals: 74

157
Courgettes Cheese
(3)

450ml (16 fl.ozs) water
500g (1 lb) courgettes in $\frac{1}{2}$ in slices
1 egg, well beaten
225g (8 ozs) low-fat cottage cheese
175g (6 ozs) cooked wholewheat berries
1 med onion, finely chopped
1×5ml spoon (1 tsp) salt
$\frac{1}{2}$×5ml spoon ($\frac{1}{2}$ tsp) paprika
Pinch nutmeg
1×15ml spoon (1 tbs) grated Parmesan cheese
1×15ml spoon (1 tbs) broken roasted peanuts

Bring water to boil, drop in sliced courgettes and cover. Blanch for 5 mins, drain, freshen under cold water. Beat egg and cottage cheese together till creamy, stir in wheat, onion and seasoning, then two-thirds of the courgettes. Spoon mixture

Vegetables and Vegetable Main Courses

into greased casserole, arrange remaining courgette slices on top, sprinkle with Parmesan and nuts. Bake in pre-heated oven at 180°C (350°F, Gas 4) for 45 minutes, top of oven.

If your nutmeg isn't freshly ground, put in two pinches; it adds a gourmet flavour to this delicate, delicious dish.
Cals: 226

158
Courgette and Mushroom Casserole
(5)

1 × 5ml spoon (1 tsp) corn oil
1 med onion, chopped
1 clove garlic, chopped
350g (12 ozs) cooked brown rice
500g (1 lb) courgettes, halved lengthways then in 2 in slices
100g (4 ozs) mushrooms, thickly sliced
1 × 5ml spoon (1 tsp) salt
$\frac{1}{8}$ × 5ml spoon ($\frac{1}{8}$ tsp) ground black pepper

Topping:
150g (5 fl.ozs) natural yogurt
$\frac{1}{4}$ × 5ml spoon ($\frac{1}{4}$ tsp) salt
ground black pepper
$\frac{1}{4}$ × 5ml spoon ($\frac{1}{4}$ tsp) dried oregano
1 × 5ml spoon (1 tsp) wholewheat flour

2 med tomatoes, sliced
4 × 15ml spoons (4 tbs) roasted peanuts

Heat oil, stir-fry onion and garlic for 5 mins. Grease casserole and put in ingredients in layers, as follows, seasoning each layer lightly with salt and pepper. 1: $\frac{1}{2}$ rice, 2: $\frac{1}{2}$ courgettes, 3: all mushrooms, 4: $\frac{1}{2}$ courgettes, 5: $\frac{1}{2}$ rice, 6: fried onion/garlic, 7: topping. Arrange tomato slices on top, sprinkle peanuts and bake in oven pre-heated to 190°C (375°F, Gas 5) for 30 minutes.
Cals: 168

159
Red Lentils and Sprouts
(4)

1 × 5ml spoon (1 tsp) corn oil
1 med onion, chopped
175g (6 ozs) red lentils, picked over, washed, drained
450ml (16 fl.ozs) boiling water
1 × 5ml spoon (1 tsp) salt
500g (1 lb) brussels sprouts

In saucepan (with lid) heat oil and stir-fry onion until just changing colour. Add lentils and boiling water, stir in salt. Reduce heat to minimum–use heat diffuser–cover and cook for 10 mins. Add sprouts, stirring them in, replace lid. Simmer for 20 mins more.

When sprouts are out of season, use frozen ones and divide cooking time in half: 15 mins before adding sprouts, 15 mins after.
Cals: 190

160
Peperonata
(4)

1 × 5ml spoon (1 tsp) corn oil
2 med onions, chopped
1-2 cloves garlic, chopped
2 sweet red peppers, seeded, sliced
2 green peppers, seeded, sliced

Vegetables and Vegetable Main Courses

2 lge tomatoes, chopped
½ × 5ml spoon (½ tsp) lemon juice
½ × 5ml spoon (½ tsp) salt

Heat oil, stir-fry onion and garlic till turning brown. Add and stir-fry peppers, for 2 mins, then stir in all other ingredients. Cover and simmer very gently for 10 mins.
Cals: 62

161
Chestnut Roast
(4)

1 × 15ml spoon (1 tbs) polyunsaturate margarine
1 med onion, finely chopped
1 rib celery, finely chopped
1 med green pepper, seeded, chopped
175g (6 ozs) cooked brown rice
4 lge ripe tomatoes, chopped
175g (6 ozs) cooked chestnuts (No. 109)
25g (1 oz) wholewheat breadcrumbs
2 × 15ml spoons (2 tbs) fresh parsley, chopped
¾ × 5ml spoon (¾ tsp) salt
½ × 5ml spoon (½ tsp) paprika
1 egg, beaten OR 50ml (2 fl.ozs) water

Melt marge and gently sauté onion, celery and green pepper until tender. Remove from heat, stir in all other ingredients thoroughly. Press into greased loaf-tin and bake in pre-heated oven 190°C (375°F, Gas 5) for 30 mins.
Cals: 180

162
Corn Fritters
(4)

225g (8 ozs) wholewheat flour
250ml (8 fl.ozs) water
1½ × 5ml spoons (1½ tsp) salt
ground black pepper
175g (6 ozs) sweetcorn kernels
1 small onion, finely chopped
1 carrot, finely chopped
½ green pepper, finely chopped

Oil to shallow-fry.

Combine flour, water, salt and pepper into a thick batter. Stir in other ingredients (except oil) and let stand for ½ hour or more. Heat oil to smoking. Drop in spoonful of well-stirred batter, press it flat. Repeat until pan full. When first side golden brown turn and brown second side. Drain well and blot dry on kitchen paper.

I make eight fritters with this mixture, frying in two halves. Keep first batch warm in a medium oven, on a wire rack, and they'll stay nice and crisp.

163
Lentilburgers
(4)

225g (8 ozs) green lentils
700ml (24 fl.ozs) water
½ bayleaf
1 × 5ml spoon (1 tsp) salt
1 × 5ml spoon (1 tsp) corn oil
1 clove garlic, chopped
1 green pepper, chopped
1 carrot, chopped
1 lge onion, chopped

Vegetables and Vegetable Main Courses

$\frac{1}{2}$ × 5ml spoon ($\frac{1}{2}$ tsp) celery seeds
1 × 5ml spoon (1 tsp) chili powder
1 × 15ml spoon (1 tbs) tomato paste
Salt (if needed)
50g (2 ozs) wholewheat breadcrumbs

Oil to shallow-fry.

Pick over lentils, wash and drain. In saucepan (with lid) bring lentils, water and bayleaf to boil. Cover tightly, reduce heat and simmer for 50 minutes. Add salt, stir, cover and cook until lentils tender, about 10 mins more. Remove bayleaf. When lentils are soft, all water should have been absorbed. If not, stir over med heat until dry. While lentils are cooking, heat oil and stir-fry chopped vegetables until crisp-tender. Remove from heat. Lightly mash cooked lentils, stir in stir-fried vegetables, add celery seeds, chili powder, tomato paste and a little more salt if needed. Let cool, form into patties (8) and dip into breadcrumbs to coat thoroughly. Heat oil to smoking and fry until burgers golden and crisp on both sides. (Or they can be grilled, but these aren't quite so good.)

Serve with grilled tomatoes and a crisp salad.

164
Red Lentilburgers
(4)

175g (6 ozs) red lentils
75g (3 ozs) whole millet
700ml (24 fl.ozs) water
1$\frac{1}{2}$ × 5ml spoons (1$\frac{1}{2}$ tsp) salt
1 med onion, chopped
1 carrot or turnip, shredded
ground black pepper
2 × 15ml spoons (2 tbs) fresh parsley, chopped
wholewheat crumbs to coat
oil to shallow-fry

Pick over lentils, wash and drain. In saucepan (with lid) toast millet by shaking it over medium heat until it begins to deepen in colour. Add lentils, water and salt, bring to boil, then reduce heat to minimum–use heat diffuser– cover and cook for 30 mins. Cool slightly, then stir in vegetables and pepper. Form into patties, dip in crumbs to coat thoroughly. Heat oil to smoking and fry patties until golden and crisp on both sides. Drain well, blot dry on kitchen paper.

Children always love burgers, but these are for the more discerning adult palate. This mid-Eastern recipe has a really delicate, savoury flavour.

165
Vegetable and Millet Mix
(4)

1 × 5ml spoon (1 tsp) corn oil
1 med onion, chopped
175g (6 ozs) whole millet
3 carrots in $\frac{1}{8}$ in slices OR 3 slices pumpkin, diced
$\frac{1}{2}$ med cabbage (about 225g, 8 ozs) shredded
3 × 15ml spoons (3 tbs) fresh parsley, chopped
350g (12 ozs) fresh green beans (whole)
1 × 5ml spoon (1 tsp) salt
$\frac{1}{2}$ × 5ml spoon ($\frac{1}{2}$ tsp) celery seeds
$\frac{1}{4}$ × 5ml spoon ($\frac{1}{4}$ tsp) dried oregano
ground black pepper
750ml (26 fl.ozs) water plus

Vegetables and Vegetable Main Courses

1 veg stock cube (or 750ml veg stock, No. 147)

In a casserole heat oil, stir-fry onion until silver. Add millet, stir-fry until deepening in colour. Add all other ingredients, bring to gentle boil, then reduce heat to minimum –use heat diffuser–and cook, covered, for 30 minutes. The vegetables should be tender and virtually all the water absorbed, so that millet is firm but moist. If it seems dry add a little boiling water and stir in before serving.

This is a very sweet dish and is excellent served with Spiked Kidney Beans (No. 176) and a crisp salad.

166
Gnocchi

(4)

1 × 15ml spoon (1 tbs) corn oil
225g (8 ozs) maize meal
625ml (22 fl.ozs) water
350ml (12 fl.ozs) skimmed milk
$1\frac{1}{4}$ × 5ml spoons ($1\frac{1}{4}$ tsp) salt
$\frac{1}{8}$ × 5ml spoon ($\frac{1}{8}$ tsp) nutmeg
$\frac{1}{8}$ × 5ml spoon ($\frac{1}{8}$ tsp) ground pepper
Grated Parmesan cheese

Heat oil in frying pan. Pour in maize meal and stir until beginning to turn golden. Remove from heat. In saucepan bring water to boil. Meanwhile, in a bowl combine milk, maize meal and salt and pour this into the boiling water, stirring continuously until it comes back to boil. Cover tightly, reduce heat to minimum–use heat diffuser–and cook for 20 mins. Remove lid, raise heat and stir mixture until it is thick enough to support a spoon. Stir in nutmeg and pepper, remove from heat. Grease baking tray approx 14 in × 10 in and spread maize mixture on to it, using back of a wet spoon (or wet fingers) to make flat, even layer. Let cool, then refrigerate for 1-2 hours. Pasta will set solid. Cut it into 1 in squares, tilting and disarranging squares as you go. Sprinkle with Parmesan cheese and pop under hot grill until gnocchi are golden.

Serve with Tomato Sauce (No. 309) spooned over, or Peperonata (No. 160).

167
Pease Pudding

(4)

1 × 5ml spoon (1 tsp) corn oil
1 lge onion, chopped
2 ribs celery, chopped
1 lge carrot, chopped
400g (14 ozs) green split peas, washed, drained
900ml (32 fl.ozs) water
1 × 5ml spoon (1 tsp) salt
$\frac{1}{8}$ × 5ml spoon ($\frac{1}{8}$ tsp) pepper
Pinch dried thyme
1 egg, beaten (optional)

Heat oil, stir-fry vegetables for 5 mins. Add peas, water and seasoning, bring to boil, then reduce heat, cover and simmer till peas tender, 30-45 mins. Drain (reserving liquid for soup) pour mixture into blender and purée. Add egg (if using) then pour mix into well-greased loaf tin, smoothing top. Bake in pre-heated oven 180°C (350°F, Gas 4) for 30 mins. Serve with Tomato Sauce (No. 309) or Creamy Onion Sauce (No. 314).

A traditional high-protein dish with a little extra fibre–and flavour–from the

Vegetables and Vegetable Main Courses

vegetables. With a sauce over and a salad accompaniment it makes a meal. Or serve it plain with grilled or steamed fish.

168
Lentil Loaf
(4)

175g (6 ozs) red lentils, picked over, washed, drained
425ml (14 fl.ozs) water
$\frac{1}{2}$ × 5ml spoon ($\frac{1}{2}$ tsp) salt
100ml (4 fl.ozs) boiling veg stock
75g (3 ozs) oatmeal
1 clove garlic, finely chopped
1 med onion, chopped
2 × 15ml spoons (2 tbs) fresh parsley
$\frac{1}{4}$ × 5ml spoon ($\frac{1}{4}$ tsp) dried rosemary, crushed
1 egg, lightly beaten

In saucepan combine first three ingredients, bring to boil, then cover and simmer over minimum heat–use heat diffuser–for 20 mins. Meanwhile pour boiling stock over oatmeal and let stand. When lentils ready combine with oats and stir in all other ingredients. Pour into well-greased and floured loaf tin. Bake in pre-heated oven 190°C (375°F, Gas 5) for 45 mins.

Nutritious and delicious, but made really marvellous by serving with Peanut Sauce (No. 312).
Cals: 240

169
Nut Bake
(4)

1 × 15ml spoon (1 tbs) corn oil
1 lge onion, chopped
1 green pepper, seeded, chopped
2 ribs celery, chopped
2 × 15ml spoons (2 tbs) fresh parsley, chopped
100g (4 ozs) mushrooms, chopped
2 carrots, finely chopped
1 clove garlic, chopped
25g (1 oz) wholewheat breadcrumbs
75g (3 ozs) walnuts, finely ground
1 egg, beaten
$\frac{3}{4}$ × 5ml spoon ($\frac{3}{4}$ tsp) salt
ground black pepper
$\frac{1}{2}$ × 5ml spoon ($\frac{1}{2}$ tsp) chili powder
175g (6 ozs) cooked brown rice
$\frac{1}{4}$ × 5ml spoon ($\frac{1}{4}$ tsp) dried rosemary, crushed

Heat oil in large frying pan, gently sauté onions till silver, add all other vegetables and cook very gently, stirring occasionally, for 15 mins. Add all other ingredients and stir well. Spoon into well-greased loaf tin and bake in pre-heated oven 180°C (350°F, Gas 4) for 30 mins.
Cals: 276

When I first tasted this I lost all my preconceived notions about nuts. I think you'll like it too.

170
Cauliflower Casserole
(4)

1 × 5ml spoon (1 tsp) corn oil
1 med onion, chopped
1 carrot, grated
1 clove garlic, chopped
1 green pepper, seeded, sliced
1 large cauliflower, in florets
500g (1 lb) ripe tomatoes, chopped (or tin)

1-1½ × 5ml spoons (1-1½ tsp) salt
ground black pepper
½ × 5ml spoon (½ tsp) dried rosemary, crushed
25-50g (1-2 ozs) grated strong cheese
50g (2 ozs) roasted peanuts

Heat oil in frying pan. Stir-fry onion till silver, then add carrot, garlic and green pepper. Stir-fry for 2 mins, then add cauliflower and stir till coated. Add tomatoes, salt, pepper and rosemary, bring to boil, then reduce heat and simmer, covered, for 15 mins. Transfer to heat-proof dish. Sprinkle cheese and nuts on top and put under hot grill until nuts toasty and cheese melted.

If you're having a baked dessert–and you can, after this low-calorie main dish–you can also bake the casserole and cut fuel costs. Pre-heat oven to 180°C (350°F, Gas 4) bake for 30 mins.
Cals: 202

171
Curried Cauli and Split Peas
(4)

225g (8 ozs) yellow split peas, picked over, washed, drained
800ml (28 fl.ozs) water
1 × 5ml spoon (1 tsp) salt

In saucepan bring peas and water to boil, cover, reduce heat to minimum–use heat diffuser–and cook till tender, about 40 mins. Add salt and stir peas well to make them into a thick sauce.
Meanwhile prepare vegetables.

1 × 15ml spoon (1 tbs) corn oil
1 med onion, chopped
1 clove garlic, chopped
1 large cauliflower, in florets
2 lge tomatoes, sliced
1 × 5ml spoon (1 tsp) salt
2-3 × 5ml spoons (2-3 tsp) curry powder
100ml (4 fl.ozs) water
2-3 × 15ml spoons (2-3 tbs) raisins

In casserole (with lid) heat oil, stir-fry onions and garlic till turning brown, then add cauliflower, stir-fry for 1 minute. Add tomatoes, salt and curry powder, stir-fry for 5 minutes over medium heat. Pour in water, stir in raisins, reduce heat, cover and simmer gently for 5-10 minutes till cauliflower crisp-tender. When vegetables and pea mixture are ready either combine them and serve, OR make a bed of the pea mixture and spoon the vegetables and liquids over. Either way this is a very satisfying meal.
Cals: 275
Serve with Minted Apple Salad (No. 295)

172
Mixed Vegetable Curry
(4-6)

Any vegetables in season can be used in a curry. I use about 6, usually, varying the quick-cooking ones like beans and corn, but sticking with onions, carrots and cauliflower as a base, since they're usually available. So:

1 × 5ml spoon (1 tsp) corn oil
1 lge onion, chopped
2 × 15ml spoons (2 tbs) curry powder
2 lge carrots, sliced
½ small cauliflower, florets

Vegetables and Vegetable Main Courses

2 lge ripe tomatoes, sliced
700ml (24 fl.ozs) water
50g (2 ozs) whole hazelnuts
50g (2 ozs) raisins

Choice of:
100g (4 ozs) sweet corn kernels
100g (4 ozs) runner beans
2 courgettes, sliced
100g (4 ozs) fresh peas
100g (4 ozs) mushrooms, sliced
100g (4 ozs) okra

Heat oil, stir-fry onions till just changing colour, add curry powder, stir-fry for 2 mins, then add carrots and cauliflower. Stir briefly and add water, bring to boil, then reduce heat, cover and simmer for 15 minutes. (If using okra put in at the same time as carrots.) Now add tomatoes, salt and any of the 'choice' vegetables, cover, simmer gently for 10 minutes more. Add nuts and raisins, cover, simmer for 5 mins more. Serve.

The purpose of adding veg in stages is to keep a little bite–and individual flavour–in each one. Serve on a bed of Brown Rice (No. 227) with Yogurt-Cucumber Salad (No. 296).
Cals: 100-200, depending on vegetables selected.

173
Okra, Country Style
(4)

350g (12 ozs) okra
1 × 5ml spoon (1 tsp) oil
1 med onion, chopped
1 clove garlic, chopped
225g (8 ozs) tomatoes (tin)
1 × 5ml spoon (1 tsp) lemon juice
1 × 5ml spoon (1 tsp) honey
100ml (4 fl.ozs) water
Salt and pepper

Cut off stems and wash okra, leaving whole if small and cutting in 2 in chunks if large (small whole ones are nicer). Heat oil, sauté onion and garlic till silver, add all ingredients *except* okra. Simmer, uncovered, for 10 mins, till fairly thick. Add okra, cover tightly, simmer very gently for 30 mins *or* heat 250ml (8 fl.ozs) Tomato Sauce (No. 309) with 250ml (8 fl.ozs) water. When bubbling add okra, reduce heat, cover and simmer for 30 mins.
Cals: 60

174
Tempura
(4)

This is a Japanese dish: bite-sized vegetables dipped in batter and deep-fried until they are crisp and golden. A choice of 4 from the following is sufficient, and you should allow about 4 pieces of each (16 'bites') per person.

Vegetables
cauliflower florets
carrot slices
celery chunks
courgette slices or strips
onion rings
green pepper rings
broccoli clusters

Wash and drain the vegetables, cut to size and refrigerate for about an hour.

Vegetables and Vegetable Main Courses

Batter
As Recipe No. 241, Eggless Crêpe or Corn Crêpe batter.

Mix batter and refrigerate for about an hour. Stir before using and add a little more water if it seems thick.

To Prepare
Put a few spoonfuls of wholewheat flour into a bag, drop in the chilled vegetables a few at a time to coat them, then shake off surplus flour and drop them into the batter. In deep-fryer or wok heat oil to smoking point, drop in the battered vegetables a few at a time and turn frequently. Fry until the batter turns golden–the vegetables inside should be firm. Drain well. Repeat with remaining vegetables, adding a little more water to the batter if it thickens. To keep the food hot and crisp until it's all done, pop it into a hot oven on a rack.

Dip
Mix together
50ml (2 fl.ozs) Tamari soy sauce
50ml (2 fl.ozs) cold water

To serve
A platter of hot, crisp Tempura and a bowl of dip are placed in the centre of the table. Bowls of steaming brown rice and a set of chopsticks are put before each person. The Tempura is picked up, dipped–and eaten with the rice.

This isn't a low-calorie meal, but it's certainly low-cost and is a treat even when the novelty of the presentation has worn off. At dinner parties a small bowl of dip between two guests is more convenient.

175
Chop Suey
(5)

500g (1 lb) beansprouts
225g (8 ozs) mushrooms
2 ribs celery
8 spring onions
1 med green pepper
2 cloves garlic, 1 crushed, 1 chopped
1 × 5ml spoon (1 tsp) oil
1 × 5ml spoon (1 tsp) grated ginger root
2 × 15ml spoons (2 tbs) Tamari soy sauce
4 × 15ml spoons (4 tbs) water

To prepare vegetables:
Bean sprouts: wash in cold water and drain well.
Mushrooms: wipe with damp cloth, slice.
Celery: scrub with stiff brush, cut into matchsticks.
Spring Onions: wash and trim, retaining green stem, cut into quarters lengthways then matchsticks.
Green pepper: wash, de-seed, cut into thin slices.
Heat oil, then stir-fry prepared vegetables (med-high heat) as follows: Onion, crushed garlic and ginger: 2 mins. Add mushrooms and 1 spoonful soy sauce, stir-fry for 2 mins. Remove to spare dish, keep warm. In same pan stir-fry celery and green pepper for 2 mins, add beansprouts, 1 spoonful soy sauce, stir-fry for 1 min. Add water. Return mushroom mixture to pan and stir-fry all together for 1 minute more. Serve at once.
Cals: 90
This has crisp and soft textures, spicy and sweet flavours–an exotic meal, completed by a bowl of Rice and Pumpkin Seeds (No. 240).

Vegetables and Vegetable Main Courses

With so few calories, you can follow Chop Suey with a good, English Prune Sponge (No. 267).

176
Spiked Kidney Beans
(4)

1 × 5ml spoon (1 tsp) oil
1 lge onion, thinly sliced
1 green pepper, seeded, chopped
1 lge clove garlic, chopped
2 ripe tomatoes, chopped
250ml (8 fl.ozs) cider
½ × 5ml spoon (½ tsp) salt
¼ × 5ml spoon (¼ tsp) ground allspice
ground black pepper
500g (1 lb) cooked red kidney beans (No. 103)

Heat oil, stir-fry onion till silver, add green pepper and garlic, stir-fry till all golden. Add all other ingredients and bring to gentle boil, reduce heat and simmer, uncovered, for 20 minutes. Liquid should be gone, but beans moist and juicy.
OR if you're baking something else, cook this in the oven at 180°C (350°F, Gas 4) for about 35 minutes.

177
Brilliant Bean Dish
(4-6)

2 × 5ml spoons (2 tsp) corn oil
1 sweet red pepper, seeded, diced
500g (1 lb) courgettes, diced
350g (12 ozs) sweetcorn kernels
275g (10 ozs) cooked red kidney beans
½ × 5ml spoon (½ tsp) salt
1 × 15ml spoon (1 tbs) Tamari soy sauce

Heat oil, stir-fry pepper and courgettes until turning golden. Reduce heat, add sweetcorn, beans and salt and simmer for 10 minutes, stirring occasionally. Add soy sauce, simmer for 5 mins more, serve.

Pile this on one side of the plate and home-made Noodles (No. 236) or macaroni elbows at the other side, and have a meal as eye-catching as it is tasty.

178
Mexican Beanfeast
(6)

150g (5 ozs) maize meal
250ml (8 fl.ozs) cold water
1 × 5ml spoon (1 tsp) oil
1 lge onion, chopped
1 clove garlic, chopped
275g (10 ozs) cooked butter beans (No. 103)
75g (3 ozs) sweetcorn kernels
1 egg, beaten
2 × 5ml spoons (2 tsp) baking powder
½ × 5ml spoon (½ tsp) salt
1-2 × 5ml spoons (1-2 tsp) chili powder
6 drops Tabasco (hot sauce)

In saucepan bring cornmeal and water to boil, stirring constantly until it becomes a thick, fairly dry paste. Set aside for 10 mins, to cool. Meanwhile heat oil, sauté onion and garlic till turning brown. Add beans and corn, remove from heat. Into cornmeal paste mix egg, baking powder, salt, chili powder and hot sauce, stir well, then combine with the bean mixture and stir again. Spoon into an oiled deep baking dish.

Vegetables and Vegetable Main Courses

Topping:
50g (2 ozs) grated strong cheese
1 green pepper in thin rings
2 tomatoes, sliced

Sprinkle cheese on to pie and arrange pepper and tomato slices attractively. Bake in pre-heated oven 180°C (350°F, Gas 4) for 25 minutes.

179
Celery Cheese
(4)

1×5ml spoon (1 tsp) oil
1 lge onion, sliced
½ green pepper, sliced
½ red pepper, sliced
500g (1 lb) celery cut in 1 in chunks (8 stalks)
1×5ml spoon (1 tsp) salt
ground black pepper
⅛×5ml spoon (⅛ tsp) ground nutmeg
225g (8 ozs) low-fat cottage cheese
1×15ml spoon (1 tbs) natural yogurt
1×5ml spoon (1 tsp) wholewheat flour
2×15ml spoons (2 tbs) chopped fresh parsley
1×15ml spoon (1 tbs) grated Parmesan cheese
25g (1 oz) roasted peanuts
25g (1 oz) wholewheat breadcrumbs

Heat oil, stir-fry onion for 1 min, then peppers and celery for about 4 mins, till onion brown. Add salt and pepper, reduce heat, cover and simmer for 10-15 mins, or till celery is tender. Meanwhile sprinkle nutmeg into cottage cheese and beat in yogurt and flour to a creamy consistency. When celery done, stir in cheese mix, add parsley, heat through without boiling, then transfer to heat-proof serving dish. Sprinkle cheese, peanuts and crumbs on top and pop under hot grill until golden.
Cals: 170

180
Jerusalem Artichokes in Pink Sauce
(4)

500g (1 lb) Jerusalem artichokes
225g (8 ozs) whole baby onions (or 2 med cut into eighths)
350ml (12 fl.ozs) vegetable stock
1 bayleaf

Sauce:
1×15ml spoon (1 tbs) polyunsaturate margarine
2×15ml spoons (2 tbs) wholewheat flour
250ml (8 fl.ozs) skimmed milk
250ml (8 fl.ozs) water from artichokes
1×15ml spoon (1 tbs) tomato paste
Salt and pepper
2×15ml spoons (2 tbs) fresh chopped parsely to garnish

Scrub artichokes, cut into chunks, peel onions, put both into saucepan with stock and bayleaf. Bring to boil, cover tightly, reduce heat and simmer till tender. Drain, reserving water for sauce. Artichokes may now be peeled if you wish. In separate saucepan, melt margarine, stir in flour and cook for 1 minute, then gradually add milk and 250ml water from artichokes. When sauce thickens stir in tomato paste. Add artichokes and onions to sauce, adjust seasoning, simmer gently for 5 mins. Garnish with parsley and serve.

Vegetables and Vegetable Main Courses

This is good with crisp-steamed broccoli (No. 121) and Bulgur Salad (No. 303).

181
Baked Leeks
(3)

500g (1 lb) leeks
1 × 5ml spoon (1 tsp) oil
1 clove garlic, chopped
1 green pepper, seeded, chopped
350g (12 ozs) tomatoes, chopped
½ × 5ml spoon (½ tsp) salt
ground black pepper
1 × 5ml spoon (1 tsp) dried dill weed
½ × 5ml spoon (½ tsp) dried basil
50ml (2 fl.ozs) cold water
3 slices wholewheat bread, toasted
2 × 15ml spoons (2 tbs) grated Parmesan cheese

Trim only the coarse dark green stems off leeks, halve lengthways and wash well in cold water to remove grit from between leaves. Cut into ¼ in slices. In frying pan, heat oil, stir-fry leeks, garlic and green pepper till turning golden. Add tomatoes, salt, pepper and herbs, stir, cover, simmer for 10 mins. Remove, stir in the cold water. Grease baking dish, line bottom with toast and pour leek mixture over. Sprinkle cheese on top. Bake in pre-heated oven 180°C (350°F, Gas 4) for 20 minutes.

182
Spinach and Cheese Tart
(4)

Pastry case: 100g (4 oz) recipe No. 272, fully baked blind.

Filling:
1 × 5ml spoon (1 tsp) oil
½ med onion, chopped
225g (8 ozs) fresh spinach, washed, drained, chopped
½ × 5ml spoon (½ tsp) garlic salt
225g (8 ozs) low-fat cottage cheese
Few spoons skimmed milk
¼ × 5ml spoon (¼ tsp) salt
¼ × 5ml spoon (¼ tsp) paprika

2 tomatoes
Sprinkling roasted peanuts

Heat oil, stir-fry onion for 2 mins, stir in spinach, cover and reduce heat at once, simmer for 7 minutes. Stir in garlic salt, remove from heat and set aside. Beat cottage cheese and milk to thick sauce, beating in salt and paprika. Stir cheese mixture into *cool* spinach mixture and spread into *cool* pastry case. Decorate top with tomato slices, sprinkle with nuts. Bake in pre-heated oven 180°C (350°F, Gas 4) for 30 mins.

This is great for a party. All ingredients can be prepared early in the day and popped into pastry case for baking 30 minutes before serving time. It looks lovely, too.

183
Vegetable Pie
(4-6)

1 lge onion
2 ribs celery
¼ white cabbage
2 lge carrots
1 courgette
½ green pepper

Vegetables and Vegetable Main Courses

½ small cauliflower
½ × 5ml spoon (½ tsp) salt
¼ × 5ml spoon (¼ tsp) ground black pepper
1 × 5ml spoon (1 tsp) garlic powder
1 × 5ml spoon (1 tsp) paprika
2 × 15ml spoons (2 tbs) Tamari soy sauce
1 × 15ml spoon (1 tbs) yeast extract (optional)
2 × 5ml spoons (2 tsp) corn oil
175g (6 ozs) cooked chickpeas (No. 103)
2 tomatoes, chopped
100ml (4 fl.ozs) cold water

Dice all vegetables separately, floret cauliflower. Heat oil, lightly brown onions, add other vegetables, lightly cooking each before adding the next. When all are in reduce heat, cover and simmer for 10 mins, then add tomatoes, chickpeas and all seasonings. Simmer uncovered for 5 mins, stir in water, then pour into greased casserole and set aside.

Crust:
100g (4 ozs) wholewheat flour
25g (1 oz) barley flour
25g (1 oz) maize meal
good pinch salt
75g (3 ozs) polyunsaturate margarine
5 × 15ml spoons (5 tbs) cold water

(or use all wholewheat flour, 175g, recipe No. 272.)

Combine flours and salt, rub in margarine until texture of breadcrumbs, stir in water, using cool fingers or a fork. Combine pastry into a ball, roll out on board lightly floured with maize meal. Spread pastry over casserole, pressing well on to greased rim. Make three gashes in crust, or puncture in several places, to let steam escape, then brush lightly with skimmed milk. Bake in pre-heated oven 200°C (400°F, Gas 6) for 30-40 mins, till crust golden.

All you'll need is a Spinach Salad (No. 278) and a Fruit Whip (No. 250) for a very satisfying meal.

184
Stuffed Tomatoes
(3-6)

6 ripe tomatoes, 3-4 in across
75g (3 ozs) wholewheat breadcrumbs
1 × 15ml spoon (1 tbs) fresh parsley, chopped
1 × 5ml spoon (1 tsp) dried basil
1 lge clove garlic, chopped
1 × 5ml spoon (1 tsp) salt
ground black pepper
1 × 5ml spoon (1 tsp) corn oil

Cut 'lid' off each tomato, remove seeds and reserve. Sprinkle salt into shell and turn upside down to drain for ½ hour. Combine other ingreds., add seeds and pack into tomato shells. Replace 'lids', sprinkle drops of oil on tops, place in greased baking dish. Bake in pre-heated oven 180°C (350°F, Gas 4) for 20-30 minutes till just tender. Serve 1 per person as starter, 2 each as main dish. *Cals:* 3 servings=94 each.

Variation: Stir 1 × 5ml spoon (1 tsp) wholewheat flour into 150g (5 fl.ozs) natural yogurt and pour into dish round tomatoes, sprinkling with fresh, chopped chives.

Vegetables and Vegetable Main Courses

185
Stuffed Cucumbers
(4)

4 × 4 in lengths cucumber, un-peeled
1 med onion, chopped
1 lge clove garlic, chopped
½ sweet red pepper, chopped
1 × 5ml spoon (1 tsp) salt
100g (4 ozs) ground almonds
4 ripe tomatoes
½ × 5ml spoon (½ tsp) honey
1 × 5ml spoon (1 tsp) hot water
½ × 5ml spoon (½ tsp) lemon juice
100ml (4 fl.ozs) buttermilk
1 × 5ml spoon (1 tsp) wholewheat flour

Halve cucumbers lengthways and scoop seeds and pulps from middle, leaving ¼ in shell. Combine the chopped vegetables with salt, add almonds and pound into a thick paste. Fill cucumber shells with mixture and arrange in greased baking dish in one layer. Melt honey in hot water, add lemon juice, buttermilk and flour and stir well, then pour over cucumbers. Cover with lid. Bake in pre-heated oven 180°C (350°F, Gas 4) about 45 minutes.
Cals: 215

186
Stuffed Green Peppers
(4)

2 large or 4 small green peppers
1 × 5ml spoon (1 tsp) corn oil
1 med onion, chopped
1 sweet red pepper, chopped
250g (9 ozs) sweetcorn kernels
175g (6 ozs) cooked butter beans (No. 103)
1 lge ripe tomato, chopped
½ × 5ml spoon (½ tsp) salt
generous ground black pepper
100ml (4 fl.ozs) skimmed milk
1 egg, lightly beaten

Cut the green peppers in half, cutting through stems too. Without cracking shell de-seed and rinse under cold tap. Bring a pan of water to the boil and drop in peppers. Cover pan tightly, reduce heat to medium and cook (blanch) for 5 mins. Immediately plunge peppers into cold water to prevent further cooking. They should now be tender enough to eat but firm enough to stuff.

Stuffing:
Heat oil, stir-fry onion until changing colour, then add red pepper and stir-fry for 1 min more. Add all ingredients except beaten egg, stir until beans get a bit mushy, then add the egg and cook until the mixture thickens slightly. Stuff into pepper shells, pop under grill to heat the shells through and serve.

There are lots of stuffings in this book which would be lovely in pepper shells prepared as above. Try: Chicken Pie Filling, No. 99. Millet with Nuts and Raisins, No. 237. Mixtures for making Lentilburgers Nos. 163 or 164 stuffed into peppers instead of coating and frying.

187
Stuffed Onions
(4)

4 med whole onions
Salted, boiling water
225g (8 ozs) cooked brown rice
1 tomato, chopped

½ green pepper, chopped
50g (2 ozs) roasted, chopped nuts or seeds
2 × 15ml spoons (2 tbs) raisins (optional)
Salt and pepper
50ml (2 fl.ozs) chicken stock

Peel onions, drop into boiling water, cover and cook for 10 mins. Drain and plunge into cold water to freshen. Cut a slice from top of each onion and scoop out centres. Combine remaining ingredients and stuff into centres. Place onions on greased baking dish, pouring chicken stock over to keep them moist. Bake in pre-heated oven, 190°C (375°F, Gas 5) for 30 mins, basting occasionally.

188
Barley Stew and Biscuits
(4-6)

1 × 5ml spoon (1 tsp) oil
1 med onion, chopped
1-2 cloves garlic, chopped
3 ribs celery, sliced
3 carrots, sliced
500g (1 lb) tomatoes (or tin)
350-450ml (12-16 fl.ozs) water
½ × 5ml spoon (½ tsp) dried basil
1½ × 5ml spoons (1½ tsp) salt
¼ × 5ml spoon (¼ tsp) ground black pepper
75g (3 ozs) raw barley

In ovenproof casserole heat oil, sauté onion, garlic, celery and carrots gently for about 10 mins. Add tomatoes, 350ml (12 fl.ozs) water, seasoning and barley. Stir, cover, simmer for about 1 hour, till everything tender. Add remaining water if there isn't generous quantity of liquid.

Biscuits:
225g (8 ozs) wholewheat flour
50g (2 ozs) maize meal
2½ × 5ml spoons (2½ tsp) baking powder
1 × 5ml spoon (1 tsp) salt
50g (2 ozs) polyunsaturate margarine
175ml (6 fl.ozs) skimmed milk
Pinch grated nutmeg

Combine first 4 ingredients. Rub or cut in marge. Add milk all at once and combine. Knead dough literally ½ minute, then pat or roll on floured board to ½ in thickness. With floured pastry cutter cut out 2½ in rounds and place them gently on top of stew, touching each other (there will be some gaps). Brush tops with skimmed milk, put casserole at top of oven pre-heated to 230°C (450°F, Gas 8) and bake for 15 minutes till golden and crisp on top.

These are American style 'biscuits', delicious savoury scones to add texture and fibre to a good stew.

189
Ravioli
(20 lge 'envelopes')
(4)

Casing: Make up half recipe Noodles (No. 236) up to and including making soft ball of the dough. Now divide dough in two and roll first half on floured board to about 12 in square, *without leaving holes*.

Filling:
1 × 5ml spoon (1 tsp) oil
½ med onion, chopped
1 clove garlic, chopped
1 × 15ml spoon (1 tbs) flour
½ × 5ml spoon (½ tsp) salt

ground black pepper
$\frac{1}{4}$×5ml spoon ($\frac{1}{4}$ tsp) dried oregano
100ml (4 fl.ozs) vegetable stock
500g (1 lb) frozen chopped spinach, cooked and drained

3×250ml cups (3 cups) Tomato-Garlic Sauce (No. 310) Parmesan cheese to sprinkle on top

Heat oil, sauté onion and garlic till just changing colour. Stir in flour, cook gently for 2 mins. Add salt, pepper and oregano, then gradually stir in stock until sauce thickens. Fold in spinach, adjust seasoning, and leave to cool. When cool, put spoonfuls of filling 2 in apart on rolled-out dough (I use 5ml spoons). Roll second half of dough, place it on top and press firmly between the bumps of filling. Now cut along these indentations, making squares, and trim dough fairly close to filling. Re-roll and re-use any dough you trim off. Now press edges of envelopes together with fork tines for a tight, attractive seal, and let ravioli rest, to dry out, for 1-2 hours.
To cook: Bring a large saucepan of salted water to boil, drop in ravioli and boil for 15-20 minutes. Remove to plates with slotted spoon, pour over a generous quantity of Tomato-Garlic Sauce, sprinkle with Parmesan Cheese.

I only have time to make these occasionally, but they're always high on our list of 'special requests'.

190
Italian Beans
(pasta e fagioli)
(4-6)

2×5ml spoons (2 tsp) corn oil
1 med onion, chopped
1 rib celery, chopped
2 small carrots, matchsticks
2 cloves garlic, chopped
3 lge ripe tomatoes, chopped
$\frac{1}{2}$×5ml spoon ($\frac{1}{2}$ tsp) dried basil
$\frac{1}{8}$×5ml spoon ($\frac{1}{8}$ tsp) grated nutmeg
$\frac{1}{2}$×5ml spoon ($\frac{1}{2}$ tsp) paprika
Salt and pepper
600g (1$\frac{1}{4}$ lbs) cooked haricot beans
100ml (4 fl.ozs) tomato juice
250ml (8 fl.ozs) water
100g (4 ozs) wholewheat macaroni
Salted water to cover
2×15ml spoons (2 tbs) grated Parmesan cheese

In large pan, heat oil and stir-fry onion, celery, carrots and garlic, in that order, for about 1 min each. Add tomatoes and seasoning, then cooked beans and liquids. Simmer, uncovered, for 10 mins. Meanwhile drop macaroni into lightly salted boiling water to cover and cook till tender, about 7 mins. Drain, add to bean mixture and adjust seasoning. Transfer to serving dish, sprinkle with Parmesan.

Stick to the Italian practice–just serve a large leafy salad with the *pasta e fagioli*, and fresh fruit to follow.

Vegetables and Vegetable Main Courses

191-2
Pizza
2 × 10 in pizzas

Dough:
225g (8 ozs) wholewheat flour
½ × 5ml spoon (½ tsp) salt
200ml (6-7 fl.ozs) warm water (46°C)
½ × 5ml spoon (½ tsp) honey
1 × 5ml spoon (1 tsp) dried yeast
½ × 5ml spoon (½ tsp) corn oil

Sift flour and salt into mixing bowl, then throw into bowl the grains left behind in sieve. In half warm water stir honey and sprinkle yeast. Let stand for 12 minutes, stir. Make well in flour, pour in yeast mixture, oil and most of remaining warm water, reserving a little to see if you need it to make a soft (not sticky) dough. Make into 2 balls between palms. On floured board roll out each ball into 10 in round, place on greased trays, cover with a cloth and stand in a warm place for 30 mins. When risen press flat again and build up a little ridge around edge to contain filling.

Fillings:
(each makes 1 pizza)

1: Cheese Pizza
225g (8 ozs) low-fat cottage cheese
2 × 15ml spoons (2 tbs) natural yogurt
1 × 15ml spoon (1 tbs) grated Parmesan cheese
¼ × 5ml spoon (¼ tsp) garlic salt
175ml (6 fl.ozs) Tomato Sauce (No. 309)
1 med onion, in rings, browned in corn oil
A few halved olives
1-2 × 15ml spoons (1-2 tbs) sunflower seeds

Beat together first 4 ingredients to make thick sauce, adding a few spoons skimmed milk if necessary. On to prepared, risen dough, spread tomato sauce, then cheese mixture. Arrange onion rings on top, decorate with olives, sprinkle seeds. Bake in pre-heated oven 230°C (450°F, Gas 8) for 20 minutes.

2: Anchovy Pizza
1 × 15ml spoon (1 tbs) grated Parmesan cheese
1 × 250ml cup (1 cup) Tomato Sauce (No. 309)
25g (1 oz) anchovy fillets, rinsed well and drained
8 black olives, halved
50g (2 ozs) sliced mushrooms
OR 1 med green pepper in rings, sauteed in oil for 5 mins
1-2 × 15ml spoons (1-2 tbs) broken roasted peanuts.

Stir cheese into Tomato Sauce, spread on to prepared, risen dough. Place other ingredients on top, attractively. Bake as Cheese Pizza.

Bread and Breakfast

Bread and Breakfast

Bread

Few of us can spend the time on cooking or baking that our mothers and grandmothers did, and few of us want to. At the end of a hard day it's infuriating to pick up a recipe suggesting another two hours of labour so that we can enjoy 'the glorious aroma of baking bread'. I used to enjoy the glorious aroma of burning recipe instead until I began experimenting with bread recipes and found that with minimal effort I could turn out perfect loaves, well-risen, nutty and rich in flavour and wonderfully chewy in texture. Light as air? Blow it away? Not likely ! This bread is *food !*

The work involved in Basic Bread (No. 193), Bran-Wheat Bread (No. 194) and Wheat Germ Bread (No. 195) is finished exactly 15 minutes after assembly of the ingredients. After that the yeast and oven take over and the resulting bread is a rich reward for so little labour. I've never had a failure, even in the early days, when I wasn't sure what quantities to put in or quite what to do with them when they *were* in. Since then I've learned a few basic rules, and here they are.

Yeast. I always use dried yeast. It's available in most supermarkets, keeps for months in an airtight container and gives good results. And there's nothing tricky in handling it. Simply measure out the warm water called for in the recipe, sprinkle the correct amount of yeast on top and go away for 10-15 minutes (I usually leave it for 12), then stir the foamy mixture and pour it into the flour.

The water temperature is important, for yeast is a living thing. Cold water won't wake it up and hot water kills it. You need water at about blood heat, or 43°C (110°F). Generally speaking, if the water feels gentle and comfortable when you stir it with your finger it's right. I was very unsure at first, so I dipped a thermometer in the water (ignoring ribald comments from the front stalls), adding hot or cold water until I got a reading of 43°C (110°F)–and then I stirred with my finger to find out exactly how it should feel. I didn't need to use the thermometer after that, but if you want to it only adds 60 seconds to preparation time.

Flour always means whole grain flour (or meal, which is coarsely ground flour). It means whole wheat, whole barley, whole rye, whole maize (corn) and so on, whole flours that contain all the goodness of the grain, with nothing removed.

Flour is best when it's fresh, so don't buy more than you need for the week's baking and try to buy where there's a fairly fast turnover, not a slowly ageing stock. Usually the lowest-price flour sells fastest, so you kill two birds with one stone. I find grain shops cheaper than supermarkets, but they haven't opened in many areas yet.

The flour for your day-to-day needs should be kept in a totally airtight container.

Bran and Wheat Germ are also better fresh, so buy in small quantities and store, like flour, in airtight containers. Both should stay in pretty good condition for 2-3 months, while treated wheat germ (from the chemist) stays good for about 6 months.

Warmth is a very important ingredient in bread-making. First, as already mentioned, for the yeast-water, and secondly for the flour, bran, wheat-germ or whatever dry ingredients you're using. I combine these with salt in the mixing bowl, according to the recipe, then pop the bowl under the grill for the 12 minutes or so the yeast takes to dissolve, stirring frequently to warm it

Bread and Breakfast

through. Being absent-minded, I sometimes forget to stir and the top gets toasty, but I just stir in the toasty bits and proceed. Leaving the bowl (covered) in a warm airing cupboard for a few hours, or even overnight, will work, too.

Warming is particularly important in cold or wet weather, and it definitely improves the bread.

Warmth is also needed later, when you want the dough to rise, but we'll discuss that when we get there.

Measurements should be accurate when you're making bread. A scale, a measuring cup and a set of measuring spoons are vital. (See Kitchen Equipment section for the best way to use these aids. Page 20.)

It may happen, once in a while, that though you have used the amount of water specified in the recipe the dough is dry and rather hard instead of soft and spongy. This is no fault of yours. Flours vary from time to time, depending on the grain. Just measure another 25-50ml water (1-2 fl.ozs) and gradually work as much as you need into the dough to achieve a soft sponge. Dough rather sticky? That's all right too. Sprinkle a little extra flour on the dough as you mix it, and on the board when you shape the loaves to go into the tins. Again, a very small amount–25-50g (1-2 ozs) will make all the difference.

The Mixing Bowl should be bigger than you think you need. When I began I put half a kilo of flour into a bowl and found I couldn't get my hands in at the same time. It's so much easier to combine flour, yeast and liquid if you're not ankle-deep in spillage !

So...to bake bread you simply melt yeast in warm water, add it to flour with salt and a little oil, let the resultant dough rise and bake it.

Above I've suggested methods of getting together the ingredients you need. Below–how to combine them.

To mix: Your flour and other dry ingredients are warmed in your large bowl, the yeast is foamy, the additional water and the oil are already–so make a well in the dry ingredients, pour in the wet ones and combine them. I generally start with a large spoon, stirring flour from the sides of the bowl towards the centre until the liquid is partly absorbed. Then it's in with the hands, stirring and pressing with a kneading motion until all traces of dry flour have gone and a uniformly soft and spongy dough is achieved. This takes about 3-5 minutes. Now grease your tins with corn oil and warm them.

With traditional recipes this is where the kneading starts. With Basic Bread (and its two variations) you skip kneading altogether and go to the final stage.

To shape: Divide the dough into the number of loaves you're making. Press and fold each piece into an oblong, then flatten it, roll it up like a Swiss Roll and flatten it into an oblong again, slightly larger than the tin. Place it in the tin–it should fill every corner–and gently press the dough round all the edges so that the centre becomes slightly concave. Stand the tins in a warm place, covered with a cloth, and the dough will rise. The height it reaches is the height your baked loaf will be, about double the original bulk. If your warm place isn't warm enough it won't rise as much as it could. As a rule of thumb the centre mound should peek over the top of the tin. If it doesn't, return the tins to the warm place for another 10 minutes or so.

I use the warming cupboard of my stove for the rising (or 'proving', as it's called), but a cosy draught-free corner of a warm kitchen or linen cupboard will do. And when the dough has risen the loaves are ready to go into the pre-heated oven for 40 minutes.

To test if done: take loaf out of the oven and tip it out of the tin, then rap the bottom of the loaf with your knuckles. If you get a hollow sound the loaf is baked. If you don't–put it back in the tin and the oven for five minutes more.

To cool: Remove from tins immediately and stand on wire rack.

Even your washing-up is minimal–a bowl, a cup, a few spoons–and the famous aroma of baking bread surrounds you as you do it.

Everything sounds difficult until you try it yourself, but Basic Bread is fiasco-proof. Stick with it until you're confident enough to bake it in your lunch break or on the day guests are coming. Try using honey this week, molasses next, and eat a completely different-tasting bread. Try the two variations on no-knead Basic Bread: Bran-Wheat and Wheat Germ. Then, when you're really experienced and can sense the need for a drop more water or a bit more rising time–and when you think a little kneading won't ruin your day–try the other yeast breads given here. You'll find it difficult to choose a favourite.

To store: The bread I'll use during the next few days goes into a polythene bag in the bread box. The remainder I freeze (slicing one loaf so that in an emergency–like unexpected starvation, or forgetting to take out a loaf in time for lunch–I can pop frozen slices into the toaster and have instant toast).

When bread has been frozen it dries out quickly, so take out only what you'll need right away. Remember, a whole loaf will thaw out in 1-2 hours at room temperature (leave it in the polythene, to keep it moist), so it isn't necessary to take out too much at one time. To freshen bread that's been hanging around for a while wrap it in foil, leaving one end open for steam to escape, put the package in a pre-heated oven at 200°C (400°F, Gas 6) and bake for 20 minutes for a lovely crisp crust and moist middle.

Talking of moistness brings me to the final bonus brought by all the breads in this book. They are so full of flavour, so chewy and moist, that they don't need butter or margarine at all. Be like the French and serve your bread just the way it comes. You'll love it !

... And Breakfast

Since we learned that sugar-and-crackle type breakfast cereals were deficient in vitamins, vast numbers of us have switched to 'health food' cereals like muesli. Though the commercial brands can be very high in sugar, muesli certainly provides a high-fibre breakfast and, eaten with skimmed milk, it's also a low-fat one. But if you check the list of ingredients in some cereals marked 'healthy' or 'natural' you'll see they are made with coconut oil or palm oil, which means saturated fat. In this situation skimmed milk won't help, but switching to home-made Bran Crunch (No. 216) will. This is a toasted, honey-sweet, satisfying cereal that contains no sugar, chemicals or unhealthy fats and has the added bonus of hearty heapings of bran. It's quick and easy to make and it keeps well in airtight jars.

Bread and Breakfast

I love hot, cooked breakfast cereals, even in the summer, and I think it's a shame that we've virtually forgotten about them– except for soggy oatmeal smothered in sugar, whole milk and butter. Oats have a wonderful flavour, as do cracked wheat, rice cream and cornmeal. All they need is gentle cooking in water with a little salt and they become all *we* need for a really natural, healthy, low-fat, high-fibre start to the day. Compared with the sugar-filled cereals they're low-calorie, too.

Try the recipes given here. Try varying the 'plain' cereals (which are far from plain, really) by adding chopped fresh fruit, nuts and raisins or dried fruits that have been soaked overnight. You'll be adding extra fibre as well as sweet, fruity flavours to your breakfast.

If you like to start the day with a knife and fork you'll love whole grain Pancakes (Nos. 221 and 222). Or why not try smoked fish now and then? But do serve home-made high-fibre bread or toast with it. Don't let a breakfast go by without eating *some* fibre. It's what gets the system going.

Bread and Breakfast

For perfect results, please read page 110, 111, 112 before you start

193
Basic Bread
3 × 1Kg loaves

1.5Kg (3 lbs 3 ozs) wholewheat flour
5 × 5ml spoons (5 level tsp) salt
1025ml (36 fl.ozs) warm water (46°C)
2½ × 5ml spoons (2½ tsp) honey
25g (1 oz) dried yeast
2 × 15ml spoons (2 tbs) corn oil

In a large mixing bowl combine flour and salt, warm thoroughly. Pour about 1 cup of the measured warm water into a basin, stir in the honey. Sprinkle yeast on top and let stand for 10-15 minutes till yeast is foaming. Stir the mixture, add oil, stir again. *Make a well in flour, pour in yeast mixture and remaining warm water and combine into a soft, spongy dough. Separate dough into three (using a little flour on board and hands if necessary). Grease and warm tins. Shape the dough and press into tins, then cover with a cloth and stand them in a warm place for 30 mins. Pre-heat oven to 190°C (375°F, Gas 5). Bake for 35-40 mins, test if done and cool on a wire rack.

To mix, To shape, To test if done — see pages, 111, 112
To glaze — see page 121

194
Bran-Wheat Bread
3 × 1Kg loaves

1.5Kg (3 lbs 3 ozs) wholewheat flour
75g (3 ozs) wheat bran
5 × 5ml spoons (5 level tsp) salt
1025ml (36 fl.ozs) warm water (46°C)
2½ × 5ml spoons (2½ tsp) molasses
25g (1 oz) dried yeast
2 × 15ml spoons (2 tbs) corn oil

In a large mixing bowl combine flour, bran and salt, warm thoroughly. Pour about 1 cup of the measured warm water into a basin, stir in the molasses. Sprinkle yeast on top and let stand for 10-15 mins till yeast is foaming. Stir mixture, add oil, stir again. Now proceed exactly as **Basic Bread** from *

195
Wheat Germ Bread
3 × 1Kg loaves

1.5Kg (3 lbs 3 ozs) wholewheat flour
75g (3 ozs) wheat bran
100g (4 ozs) wheat germ
5 × 5ml spoons (5 level tsp) salt
1075ml (38 fl.ozs) warm water (46°C)
2 × 5ml spoons (2 tsp) honey
25g (1 oz) dried yeast
2 × 15ml spoons (2 tbs) corn oil

In a large mixing bowl combine flour, bran, wheat germ and salt, and warm thoroughly. Pour about 1 cup of the measured warm water into a basin, stir in the honey. Sprinkle yeast on top and let stand for 10-15 mins till yeast is foaming. Stir the mixture, add oil, stir again.
Now proceed exactly as **Basic Bread** from *

Bread and Breakfast

196
Oat Bread

1 × 1Kg loaf

100g (4 ozs) rolled oats
250ml (8 fl.ozs) boiling water
1 × 15ml spoon (1 tbs) corn oil
1 × 15ml spoon (1 tbs) honey

1 × 15ml spoon (1 tbs) dried yeast
100ml (4 fl.ozs) warm water (46°C)

2 × 5ml spoons (2 tsp) salt
3 × 15ml spoons (3 tbs) wheat germ
375g (13 ozs) wholewheat flour

Place oats in mixing bowl, pour boiling water over, stir in oil and honey. Let cool to hand-heat.
Sprinkle yeast into the warm water, let stand for 10-15 mins until foamy, then stir into the oats mixture. Add salt and wheatgerm and stir well. Gradually add warmed wholewheat flour, reserving about 4 × 15ml spoons (4 tbs) for kneading. Mix with hands until the dough holds together, then transfer it to a floured board and knead for about 10 mins.

Lightly oil the mixing bowl, place the dough in it and turn the dough over so that all surfaces are lightly oiled. Cover bowl with a cloth and stand it in a warm place for 1 hour. Grease and warm large tin, shape the dough and put it into tin, then cover with cloth and let stand in a warm place for 45 mins. The dough should now have roughly doubled in bulk and be nicely rounded on top. Bake in pre-heated oven 190°C (375°F, Gas 5) top of the oven, for 40 mins. Test if done and cool on a wire rack.

To mix
To shape
To test if done } see pages 111, 112
To glaze see page 121

This is a chewy, moist bread that's good straight out of the oven or several days later.

197
Rye Bread

3 × 1Kg loaves

1Kg (2 lbs) wholewheat flour
500g (1 lb) rye flour
4 × 5ml spoons (4 tsp) salt
3 × 15ml spoons (3 tbs) caraway seeds
850-900ml (30-32 fl.ozs) warm water (46°C)
1 × 15ml spoon (1 tbs) honey
25g (1 oz) dried yeast
25g (1 oz) polyunsaturate margarine

Combine the flours, salt and caraway seeds in mixing bowl and warm thoroughly. Pour about 1 cup of the measured warm water into a basin and stir in the honey. Sprinkle yeast on top and let stand for 10-15 mins till yeast is foaming. Rub the margarine into the flours, then make a well in centre and pour in yeast mixture and *most* of the remaining warm water, retaining about 50ml (2 fl.ozs). Combine into a spongy dough. If the dough seems a little hard or dry, add the last of the water and work it in. Transfer dough to a board and knead for about 5 minutes. Lightly oil the mixing bowl, place dough in it and turn the dough over so that all surfaces are lightly oiled. Cover bowl with a cloth and stand it in a warm place for 1 hour. Grease and warm tins, shape the dough and put it into tins, cover with a cloth and let stand in a warm place for 30 mins. The dough should have roughly doubled in bulk and be nicely rounded on top. Bake in pre-heated oven, top of the oven, for 40 minutes at 190°C (375°F, Gas 5).

For a nice hard crust put a flat pan containing about a cup (250ml) of boiling water at the bottom of the oven when you put bread in. Ten minutes before bread is baked, remove the water and brush the crusts with hot salt water: 1×5ml spoon (1 tsp) salt to 100ml (4 fl.ozs) water. Test if done and cool on a wire rack.

To mix
To shape
To test if done } see pages 111, 112

This is a lovely, tasty light rye–but don't let your supplier sell you rye *meal* instead of rye flour or you may have a darker, richer flavour than you bargained for. For a darker, richer flavour...use rye meal !

198
Corn and Wheat Bread

1 large loaf

150g (5 ozs) yellow maize meal
250ml (8 fl.ozs) boiling water
2×5ml spoons (2 tsp) salt
2×15ml spoons (2 tbs) corn oil
1×15ml spoon (1 tbs) honey
1×15ml spoon (1 tbs) dried yeast
100ml (4 fl.ozs) warm water (46°C)
425g (15 ozs) wholewheat flour, warmed

Put maize meal into mixing bowl and pour boiling water over. Stir in salt, oil and honey. Let cool while preparing yeast. Sprinkle yeast on to 100ml warm water and let stand for 10-15 mins till yeast is foaming. Stir, then add to the cornmeal mixture and stir well. Gradually add wholewheat flour to make a soft, spongy, but not sticky, dough. Reserve about 4 spoons of flour for kneading. Knead on floured board for about 10 minutes. Lightly oil the mixing bowl, place dough in it and turn dough over so that all surfaces are lightly oiled. Cover bowl with a cloth and stand it in a warm place for 1 hour or until doubled in bulk. Punch down, shape into a loaf and put into greased, warmed tin. Cover with a cloth and let stand in a warm place until doubled in bulk–about 30-45 minutes–when loaf should have a nicely rounded top. Bake in pre-heated oven 190°C (375°F, Gas 5), top of the oven, for 35-40 minutes. Test if done and cool on a wire rack.

To mix
To shape
To test if done } see pages 111, 112
To glaze see page 121

This is a wonderfully delicate, cake-like bread that's irresistible. Just double all the ingredients for two large loaves.

199
Barley Bread

2×1Kg loaves

500g (1 lb) barley flour
500g (1 lb) wholewheat flour
3×5ml spoons (3 level tsp) salt
650ml (23 fl.ozs) warm water (46°C)
2×5ml spoons (2 tsp) honey
4×5ml spoons (4 tsp) dried yeast
1×15ml spoon (1 tbs) corn oil

In mixing bowl combine flours and salt and warm thoroughly. Pour about 1 cup of the measured warm water into a basin, stir in the honey. Sprinkle yeast on top and let stand for 10-15 mins till yeast is foaming. Stir the mixture, add oil, stir again. Make a well in flour, pour in yeast mixture and remaining warm water and combine to a soft, spongy dough. Turn out on to a well-floured board and knead for 5 minutes, sprinkling extra flour if needed. Lightly oil mixing bowl, place the dough in it and turn the dough over so that all surfaces are lightly oiled. Cover bowl with a cloth and stand it in a warm place for about 45 minutes. Grease and warm two tins. Punch down the dough, divide, shape into loaves and put into tins, then cover with a cloth and stand in a warm place for 35 minutes or until nicely rounded on top. Bake in pre-heated oven 190°C (375°F, Gas 5), for 40 minutes. Test if done and cool on a wire rack.

To mix
To shape
To test if done } see pages 111, 112
To glaze see page 121

This bread has a very unusual, delicate flavour, and it makes the best toast I ever tasted.

200 Rolls

about 22.

725g (1½ lbs) wholewheat flour
50g (2 ozs) wheat bran
50g (2 ozs) wheat germ
2½ × 5ml spoons (2½ level tsp) salt
550ml (19 fl.ozs) warm water (46°C)
1 × 5ml spoon (1 tsp) honey or molasses
1 × 15ml spoon (1 tbs) dried yeast
1 × 15ml spoon (1 tbs) corn oil

In mixing bowl combine flour, bran, wheat germ and salt and warm thoroughly. Stir honey or molasses into the warm water, sprinkle yeast on top and let stand for 10-15 mins till yeast is foaming. Stir the mixture, add oil, stir again. Make a well in the flour, pour in yeast mixture and combine to a spongy dough.

If you wish to make Raisin Bread (No. 265) now is the time to set aside 500g (1 lb) of this dough.

To shape rolls: Cut dough into equal 50g (2 ozs) pieces. To avoid weighing each one, try taking a big piece of dough and weighing it, then work out how many 50g (or 2 ozs) pieces it should make. Cut the dough in halves, quarters, and so on, until you have the right number. They'll be equal enough for your needs, and this saves time.

Snails: Roll 50g (2 ozs) dough into a rope about ½ in thick and 8-10 in long. Hold one end down and coil the other end around it. Tuck end under and press firmly.

Cottage Loaf: Break 50g (2 ozs) dough into one-third and two-third pieces. Make both into balls between your palms and press the smaller one firmly into the centre of the larger.

Crescents: Take 225g (8 ozs) dough and roll it into a circle about ¼ in thick. Cut circle into quarters. Each 'slice' should be rolled up from wide end to pointed end, then points pulled round to form a crescent.

Wheat tops: Form 50g (2 ozs) dough into a small, thick circle. Scatter cracked wheat on the board, place the circles on the wheat and press firmly, so that you have a somewhat flatter circle with wheat embedded in its surface. If the wheat is too crunchy for you try soaking it in hot water for 1 hour, then toasting in a pan till it's dry before using on the rolls.

Clover Leaf: Take 50g (2 ozs) dough and roll into a ball between your palms. Put on board and with back of knife blade make a cross, cutting about ¼ in into surface.

Put rolls on to greased baking trays, leaving space for them to approx. double in size. Cover with cloths and stand in a warm place for 30 minutes.

Glaze: Using soft pastry brush, paint tops with skimmed milk. Bake for 15 minutes in pre-heated oven, 220°C (425°F, Gas 7). (Top shelf will be crustier, so switch trays round for last 5 minutes.)

201
Pocket Bread

When making Wheat Germ Bread or Wheat-Bran Bread separate ½-1Kg (1-2 lbs) of dough before setting it to rise in tins. Divide this dough into 50g (2 ozs) pieces and roll into balls between the palms. Then roll on floured board to ovals about ¼ in thick. With soft pastry brush paint corn oil lightly all over one oval, leaving ½ in dry all round edge. Take second oval and place on top of first, pressing edges firmly to seal. Repeat until all ovals are used up. Place on greased baking trays, cover with cloths and put in warm place for 30 mins, then brush with skimmed milk to glaze and bake for 15 minutes in pre-heated oven, 220°C (425°F, Gas 7). Take out and immediately transfer to wire rack to cool.

To serve: Cut each 'loaf' in half crossways. Gently insert thumb and wiggle to hollow out the centre. Fill these pockets with chopped lettuce and tomato, sardines and onion–anything you would enjoy in a thick, juicy sandwich-with-a-difference.

Dessert: Fill the pockets with chopped fruit, nuts and raisins, dribble honey over the top and pop under the grill for 5 minutes to make glazing sizzle.

202
Soda Bread

275g (10 ozs) wholewheat flour
¾ × 5ml spoon (¾ level tsp) bicarb. of soda
¾ × 5ml spoon (¾ level tsp) salt
25g (1 oz) polyunsaturate margarine
1 × 15ml spoon (1 tbs) honey, melted
150-175ml (5-6 fl.ozs) buttermilk

Combine first three ingredients. Rub in margarine, making breadcrumb texture, then stir in honey and mix well. Gradually add buttermilk until you achieve a very soft, but not sticky, dough, holding back 1 or 2 spoons if necessary. Press and knead the dough briefly until you can form a nicely-shaped round. Grease a baking tray, put the round on it and cut a cross along the top and down the sides. Brush lightly with skimmed milk to glaze and bake in pre-heated oven 190°C (375°F, Gas 5), top of oven, for 45 minutes.

It takes literally 5 minutes to prepare this bread for the oven–almost an 'instant' high-fibre loaf. It's fantastic eaten hot, quite good next day, and worth any effort necessary to find buttermilk, which makes all the difference.

Bread and Breakfast

203
Mexican Corn Bread

200g (7 ozs) yellow maize meal
75g (3 ozs) wholewheat flour
1 × 15ml spoon (1 tbs) baking powder
1 × 5ml spoon (1 tsp) salt
1 egg, lightly beaten
1 × 15ml spoon (1 tbs) honey
2 × 15ml spoons (2 tbs) corn oil
300ml (10 fl.ozs) skimmed milk

1 slice of onion, finely chopped
½ sweet red pepper, finely chopped
1 × 15ml spoon (1 tbs) fresh green chili-pepper, chopped

In mixing bowl combine dry ingredients. In separate bowl combine liquids and stir in honey. Pour liquids into dry ingredients and combine swiftly, stirring just enough to wet the flour. Don't beat or worry about lumps. Now fold in vegetables and pour batter into greased 8 in × 8 in tin. Bake in pre-heated oven for 20-30 minutes 220°C (425°F, Gas 7), until golden on top and crisp at the edges. Serve right out of the oven.

This moist, tender delicacy with a spicy bite to it is perfect with soup or a salad for a high-fibre, nutritious lunch or supper.

Alternative: Leave out the vegetables and serve slices of delicious corn bread Deep South style.

204
Corn Tortillas

An almost-instant bread from Mexico–and you can slap the tortillas between your palms instead of rolling them, if you've seen enough Westerns.

150g (5 ozs) yellow maize meal
250ml (8 fl.ozs) boiling water
¾ × 5ml spoon (¾ tsp) salt
150g (5 ozs) wholewheat flour

Put maize meal in mixing bowl, pour boiling water over and let stand for 10 minutes. Stir in salt, then gradually add wholewheat flour until you have a heavy dough. Let it rest for 10 minutes or longer, then roll a little piece into a ball between your palms. Sprinkle maize meal on your board and roll the ball into a flat, thin round. Heat a griddle or lightly grease a heavy frying pan and heat to medium-high, then cook tortillas for 2 minutes on each side.

205
Indian Bread

8 × 6 in rounds

275g (10 ozs) wholewheat flour
¾ × 5ml spoon (¾ tsp) salt
2 × 15ml spoons (2 tbs) corn oil
Pinch ground cumin (optional)
175ml (6 fl.ozs) cold water

Combine flour, salt and cumin (if using), rub oil through flour then gradually add water. Knead for a few minutes until the dough feels elastic, then rest it for half an hour. Heat griddle, or dry, heavy-based frying pan, to medium-high. On lightly floured board roll dough into thin rounds, then place in hot pan and cook until blisters appear on top and brown spots underneath. Turn and cook second side. Serve hot.

Variations: When rolling, sprinkle dried,

ground garlic on to bread, or chopped fresh garlic; or sprinkle generously with toasted sesame seeds. Roll in the garlic or seeds until embedded, then cook as above.

206
Breadcrumbs

Use up any stale, dry bread this way. Thinly slice a wholewheat loaf and place the slices on a baking tray. When you're cooking something in the oven pop the tray in at the same time and allow the bread to become dry and crisp but not brittle and burnt. At 180°C (350°F, Gas 4), this will take about 15 minutes. Break the slices into your grinder, reduce to fine crumbs and store in airtight jars.

Soft Breadcrumbs

Day-old bread is best, but simply slice as much as you need off a wholewheat loaf and reduce to little lumps, either by chopping, pulling to bits with a fork, or popping into the grinder for literally seconds–you don't want fine crumbs this time. If you use a grinder be sure its dry or you'll wind up with paste. Don't store soft crumbs in jars, but you can freeze them if you wish.

Any of the yeast breads in this book will give you excellent, tasty breadcrumbs or soft breadcrumbs.

207
Sesame Crackers
(about 36)

225g (8 ozs) wholewheat flour
50g (2 ozs) maize meal
$\frac{1}{2}$ × 5ml spoon ($\frac{1}{2}$ tsp) salt
75ml (3 fl.ozs) corn oil
75ml (3 fl.ozs) water
Toasted sesame seeds

Combine flours and salt, stir in oil, then gradually add water until dough holds together in a ball. Sprinkle maize meal on board and roll dough to about $\frac{1}{4}$ in thick. Sprinkle generously with toasted sesame seeds, then roll to $\frac{1}{8}$ in thick, so seeds are embedded. Cut into 2 in squares or rounds, bake on greased trays, top of the oven pre-heated to 190°C (375°F, Gas 5), for 20-30 mins or until lightly browned. Cool on a wire rack, store in airtight container.

These toasty-tasting crackers are high-fibre and high-protein too.

208
Oatcakes
(about 26)

200g (7 ozs) med rolled oats
100g (4 ozs) wholewheat flour
$1\frac{1}{4}$ × 5ml spoons ($1\frac{1}{4}$ tsp) salt
$\frac{1}{4}$ × 5ml spoon ($\frac{1}{4}$ tsp) bicarb. of soda
$\frac{1}{2}$ × 5ml spoon ($\frac{1}{2}$ tsp) honey
50ml (2 fl.ozs) corn oil
175ml (6 fl.ozs) boiling water

In bowl combine oats, flour, salt and bicarb. Stir honey and oil into boiling water, then pour this liquid into oats to form a soft, not sticky, dough. On floured board (use a little extra flour if dough slightly sticky) roll out to $\frac{1}{4}$ in thick, then cut into 2 or $2\frac{1}{2}$ in rounds. Bake on ungreased trays, top of the oven pre-heated to 220°C 425°F, Gas 7) for 15 minutes. Cool on a wire rack, store in airtight containers.

209
Rye Crackers
(about 24)

150g (5 ozs) wholewheat flour
150g (5 ozs) rye flour
1 × 5ml spoon (1 tsp) baking powder
1 × 5ml spoon (1 tsp) salt
1 × 15ml spoon (1 tbs) caraway seeds
100ml (4 fl.ozs) skimmed milk
4 × 15ml spoons (4 tbs) corn oil
1 × 5ml spoon (1 tsp) honey
1 × 5ml spoon (1 tsp) grated orange peel

Combine dry ingredients. In separate bowl combine milk, oil, honey and peel. Stir liquids into flours to make a fairly dry, firm dough. Let rest for 15 mins, then on floured board roll out to ⅛ in thick and cut into 2 in squares or rounds. Put on greased trays, brush with skimmed milk and bake at top of oven pre-heated to 220°C (425°F, Gas 7) for 15 mins. Cool on wire rack, store in airtight containers.

These are so filled with flavour, we eat them by themselves instead of sweet biscuits.

210
Corn Crispies
(about 45)

150g (5 ozs) maize meal
75g (3 ozs) wholewheat flour
¾ × 5ml spoon (¾ tsp) salt
⅛ × 5ml spoon (⅛ tsp) chili powder
¼ × 5ml spoon (¼ tsp) bicarb. of soda
75ml (3 fl.ozs) milk
2 × 15ml spoons (2 tbs) corn oil
1 × 5ml spoon (1 tsp) honey

Combine first five ingredients. In separate bowl combine milk, oil and honey. Pour liquids into flours, stir and knead briefly until you have a pliable dough. Let rest for 15 minutes, then sprinkle board with maize meal and roll out dough, parchment thin. Cut into 2 in rounds and bake on ungreased trays, top of oven pre-heated to 180°C (350°F, Gas 4), for 10-12 minutes until pale golden brown. Cool on a wire rack, store in airtight containers.

These are as crisp and munchy as potato crisps, but with no unhealthy grease.

To Glaze Bread

Most bread looks better with a nice, golden crust. If you have a really delicate hand and a soft pastry brush you can glaze the risen loaves before you put them into the oven to bake. However, if you press on the loaf at this stage it will flatten and lose some of its rise, so until you're really experienced it might be best to glaze the safer way, 10-15 minutes before the bread is baked. So, have ready.
1. a lightly beaten egg white
or
2. a bowl of skimmed milk.
Dip your pastry brush into egg white *or* milk, swiftly paint a coating on the hot bread and immediately pop it back into the oven to complete its baking time. Another glaze is 1 × 5ml spoon (1 tsp) salt stirred into 100ml (4 fl.ozs) hot water. This is painted on 10 minutes before baking time is complete, and *again* immediately the baked bread is removed from oven. It will

glaze, and also harden the crust, so I use it only for rye bread. For a really crusty crust (again, I use this for rye bread) put a pie tin containing about ½ in boiling water at the bottom of the oven when you put your bread in to bake. For the prettiest bread of all use cracked wheat. Either buy cracked wheat cereal–not flakes, but actual whole wheat that's been cracked–or crack your own whole wheat in your grinder, giving it about 7 seconds, then pouring it into a sieve and shaking away loose flour. Scatter a layer of this wheat on your board when you have almost finished shaping the bread. When you are at the last stage press the loaf firmly into the scattered cracked wheat, which will become embedded in the dough. Put bread in tin wheat-side up and bake as usual. Result: a beautiful-looking loaf with a delightfully crunchy toasted topping. But the crunch may be a little too much for you, so take care. Some people soften the wheat before use. Pour boiling water over the cracked wheat and let it stand, cooling, for half an hour. Then drain, put into a dry frying pan and toast over medium heat until the grain is dry and beginning to change colour. Now scatter it on to board and proceed as above. For decoration with a difference: scatter sesame seeds or sunflower seeds on to your board and press the shaped loaf into the seeds. You'll be adding protein as well as flavour and appearance to your bread. I emphasise 'pressing firmly' and 'embedding' because if the wheat or the seeds are just sitting on top of the loaf, they'll brush off after it's baked.

211
Croutons

Cut any of your whole-grain loaves into slices, then cut the slices into cubes about ½ in square. Spread in single layer on baking tray, sprinkle generously with corn oil and bake at 180°C (350°F, Gas 4) until they are very crisp–about 20 mins.

I keep these in an airtight jar for about a week and sprinkle them on to every thin, clear or light soup. They add a wonderful crunchy texture, plus fibre and protein. If you're a garlic-lover try sprinkling with garlic powder as well as oil before baking.

212
Oatmeal

(3)

1×250ml cup (1 cup) rolled oats or oatmeal
3×250ml cups (3 cups) water
¼-½×5ml spoon (¼-½ tsp) salt

Bring salted water to boil, pour in oats. Reduce heat to minimum (use heat diffuser), cover and simmer from 4 to 30 minutes, depending on size and coarseness of oatmeal. (See packet, or ask your supplier for actual cooking time. Rough guide–pinhead oats: 4 minutes, coarse oats: 10 minutes, large rolled oats: 30 minutes.)
Cals: 113

213
Cornmeal Mush

(4)

1×5ml spoon (1 tsp) corn oil
1×250ml cup (1 cup) maize meal

3×250ml cups (3 cups) water
$\frac{1}{2}$×5ml spoon ($\frac{1}{2}$ tsp) salt

Heat oil in frying pan. Pour in maize meal and toast over med heat, stirring until it begins to deepen in colour and smell nutty. Transfer meal to saucepan, let cool slightly, then pour in water, stir in salt and bring to gentle boil. Immediately reduce heat to minimum (use heat diffuser), cover and simmer for 30 mins. Stir and serve.

Alternative: make as above the night before, spread into a flat dish to cool and refrigerate overnight. Next morning cut into slices and fry lightly in a spoonful of corn oil until golden and crispy on the outside.

Either way this is a traditional American Deep South breakfast, with the lovely gritty bite of cornmeal and a flavour that needs no fruit or nuts to improve it.
Cals: 118

214
Rice Cream Breakfast
(4)

175g (6 ozs) rice cream (No. 234)
800ml (28 fl.ozs) water
$\frac{1}{2}$-$\frac{3}{4}$×5ml spoon ($\frac{1}{2}$-$\frac{3}{4}$ tsp) salt

In saucepan combine ingredients, bring to gentle boil, cover tightly and reduce heat to minimum, using heat diffuser. Simmer for 20 mins then remove from heat and let stand, still covered, for 5 mins more. Stir and serve.

If you like Scottish-style oatmeal you'll find this perfect as it is. However, you may add chopped, dried or fresh fruit, raisins or dates, or a little skimmed milk. Try it all ways and ring the changes.

215
Muesli

225g (8 ozs) whole oat flakes
225g (8 ozs) whole wheat flakes
225g (8 ozs) whole barley flakes
100g (4 ozs) millet flakes
100g (4 ozs) wheat germ
225g (8 ozs) mixed nuts (hazelnuts, peanuts, walnuts, sunflower seeds), chopped
100g (4 ozs) chopped dried fruits
100-225g (4-8 ozs) raisins

Combine and store in airtight jars, or buy the muesli grains already mixed, from supermarkets and health stores, and add your own fruit, nuts and raisins. Don't forget to use skimmed milk !

216
Bran Crunch

75ml (3 fl.ozs) corn oil
100ml (4 fl.ozs) honey
1×15ml spoon (1 tbs) vanilla essence
$\frac{1}{2}$×5ml spoon ($\frac{1}{2}$ tsp) salt
3×15ml spoons (3 tbs) sesame seeds
3×15ml spoons (3 tbs) wheat germ
75g (3 ozs) sunflower seeds
50g (2 ozs) hazelnuts, chopped
100g (4 ozs) wheat bran
700g (1$\frac{1}{2}$ lbs) rolled oats
150g (5 ozs) raisins
75g (3 ozs) chopped dates or dried fruit

Pre-heat oven to 180°C (350°F, Gas 4).
In large saucepan combine and heat oil,

honey and vanilla. Remove from heat and gradually stir in other ingredients in order given. *Do not include* raisins and dates.[1] When all other ingreds. are thoroughly mixed and moistened spread into shallow roasting tin and bake for 25 minutes, stirring and turning the mixture over every 10 minutes. Cool, stir in raisins and dates and store in airtight jars.
Cals: 1oz=110

217
Cracked Wheat
(4)

1×250ml cup (1 cup) cracked wheat (No. 229)
4×250ml cups (4 cups) water
1×5ml spoon (1 tsp) salt

In saucepan with tight-fitting lid combine ingredients, bring to boil, then reduce to minimum heat, using heat diffuser. Cover and simmer for 40 mins., stir and serve.

Like oats, this cereal is so tasty naturally that it needs no fruit or milk to improve it.

218
Sweet Rice
(4)

400g (14 ozs) cooked brown rice
300ml (10 fl.ozs) skimmed milk
1-2×15ml spoons (1-2 tbs) honey
1 lge eating apple, coarsely chopped
1×5ml spoon (1 tsp) lemon juice
$\frac{3}{4}$×5ml spoon ($\frac{3}{4}$ tsp) cinnamon
Pinch salt

Combine all ingredients in saucepan and simmer gently for 5-10 mins. Apple should still have a little bite to it.

This cereal is also delicious cold: cook at night, refrigerate and have a lovely 'instant' breakfast on a warm morning.

219
Prunes and Grains
(4)

12 prunes soaked in 450ml (16 fl.ozs) water, overnight
150g (5 ozs) bulgur wheat, washed and drained
500ml (18 fl.ozs) water (from prunes)
$\frac{1}{2}$×5ml spoon ($\frac{1}{2}$ tsp) salt
1×5ml spoon (1 tsp) grated orange peel
1×15ml spoon (1 tbs) honey

Measure water from soaked prunes and make up to 500ml (18 fl.ozs). Pour into saucepan with tight-fitting lid, stir in all other ingreds. and bring to boil. Reduce heat immediately to minimum, using heat diffuser, and cover. Cook for 15 mins, stir and serve.
Cals: 185

220
Sweet Millet
(4)

350g (12 ozs) cooked millet (No. 233)[1]
300ml (10 fl.ozs) skimmed milk

---

[1] Raisins will become rocky and dates dry out if baked with cereal.

[1] This is 100g (4 ozs) raw.

Bread and Breakfast

1 × 15ml spoon (1 tbs) honey
50g (2 ozs) raisins
50g (2 ozs) chopped nuts
Pinch salt
A few drops almond essence (optional)

Combine all ingredients in saucepan and gently heat through for 5-10 mins, stirring frequently.

Any cooked grains you have in the refrigerator can be turned into a breakfast cereal in exactly this way. Try adding chopped dried apples and apricots, or dates and sunflower seeds–or fresh fruits, of course.

221
Wholewheat Pancakes
(serve 4)

150g (5 ozs) wholewheat flour
$\frac{1}{2}$ × 5ml spoon ($\frac{1}{2}$ tsp) salt
$\frac{1}{2}$ × 5ml spoon ($\frac{1}{2}$ tsp) baking powder
$\frac{1}{2}$ × 5ml spoon ($\frac{1}{2}$ tsp) bicarb. of soda
250ml (8 fl.ozs) buttermilk[1]
1 egg, lightly beaten
1 × 15ml spoon (1 tbs) honey
1 × 15ml spoon (1 tbs) sunflower oil

Combine first four ingreds. in mixing bowl. In separate bowl combine last four. Stir wet into dry swiftly and briefly, not worrying about lumps.
To cook: Heat lightly oiled griddle or heavy frying pan. It's hot enough when a drop of water leaps across it, hissing. Now drop a generous spoonful of batter and wait till bubbles appear on top. Turn and lightly brown second side. Repeat with all batter.

Serve cakes warm with melted honey or Apricot Preserve (No. 276), Pancake Topping (No. 223) or any warm fruit purée.

[1] Almost as good with skimmed milk, but omit the bicarb. of soda and increase the baking powder to 1 × 5ml spoon (1 tsp).

222
Buckwheat Pancakes
(serve 4)

100g (4 ozs) buckwheat flour
4 × 15ml spoons (4 tbs-about $1\frac{1}{4}$ ozs) wholewheat flour
$1\frac{1}{2}$ × 5ml spoons ($1\frac{1}{2}$ tsp) baking powder
$\frac{1}{4}$ × 5ml spoon ($\frac{1}{4}$ tsp) salt
250ml (8 fl.ozs) skimmed milk
1 egg, lightly beaten
2 × 15ml spoons (2 tbs) honey
1 × 15ml spoon (1 tbs) sunflower oil

To combine ingredients, to cook and to serve, see Wholewheat Pancakes (No. 221).

Any pancake expert will tell you the sharp, distinctive flavour of buckwheat cakes can't be beaten.

223
Pancake Topping, Pear
(4)

3 ripe pears, peeled, chopped
2 × 15ml spoons (2 tbs) honey
1 × 5ml spoon (1 tsp) polyunsaturate margarine
$\frac{1}{4}$ × 5ml spoon ($\frac{1}{4}$ tsp) cinnamon
50ml (2 fl.ozs) water

Combine all ingredients in saucepan and

simmer gently till very tender. Stir to a sauce texture and spoon over pancakes while still warm.

Treat any fruit this way (peaches or raspberries are really luscious), adjusting honey/cinnamon to taste.

224
Wheat Berries and Bananas
(4-6)

350g (12 ozs) cooked whole wheat (No. 228)
50g (2 ozs) coarsely chopped roasted peanuts
50g (2 ozs) raisins (or more)
2 bananas, thinly sliced
(or seedless grapes)

Topping:
150g (5 ozs) natural yogurt
1 × 15ml spoon (1 tbs) honey

Combine the cereal ingredients and spoon into serving bowls. Stir honey into yogurt and put a dollop on each portion.

This is our favourite cold cereal, wonderfully chewy, with surprise textures in it (the nuts and raisins), and very sweet and satisfying. We use the topping only occasionally–it's so good without.
Cals: 6=192

Muffins

...are a great favourite with Americans and they make a sweet and nourishing high-fibre breakfast. Of course they're good at tea time, too, and as a dessert.

225
Apple and Fruit Muffins
(about 20)

225g (8 ozs) wholewheat flour
$2\frac{1}{2}$ × 5ml spoons ($2\frac{1}{2}$ tsp) baking powder
$\frac{3}{4}$ × 5ml spoon ($\frac{3}{4}$ tsp) salt
50g (2 ozs) raisins or currants
1 lge eating apple, chopped
2 × 15ml spoons (2 tbs) wheat germ
1 egg, lightly beaten
350ml (12 fl.ozs) skimmed milk
3 × 15ml spoons (3 tbs) honey
1 × 15ml spoon (1 tbs) corn oil

In mixing bowl combine first six ingredients. In separate bowl combine remaining four. Then pour wet into dry and combine in a few strokes. Too much stirring spoils the tender crumb, so don't worry about a few lumps. Spoon into well-greased $2\frac{1}{2}$ in tins, filling each only about two-thirds full of batter.
Bake: oven pre-heated to 220°C (425°F, Gas 7) for 20 minutes.

226
Bran Muffins

175g (6 ozs) wholewheat flour
50g (2 ozs) wheat bran
1 × 5ml spoon (1 tsp) salt
1 × 15ml spoon (1 tbs) baking powder
75g (3 ozs) chopped dates
3 × 15ml spoons (3 tbs) chopped hazelnuts
1 egg, lightly beaten
350ml (12 fl.ozs) skimmed milk
1 × 15ml spoon (1 tbs) corn oil

Bread and Breakfast

1 × 15ml spoon (1 tbs) molasses } melted in 2 × 15ml spoons (2 tbs) boiling water
1 × 15ml spoon (1 tbs) honey }

Mix and spoon into well-greased tins exactly as Apple and Fruit Muffins (No. 225). Bake in pre-heated oven 200°C (400°F, Gas 6) for 20-25 mins till golden.

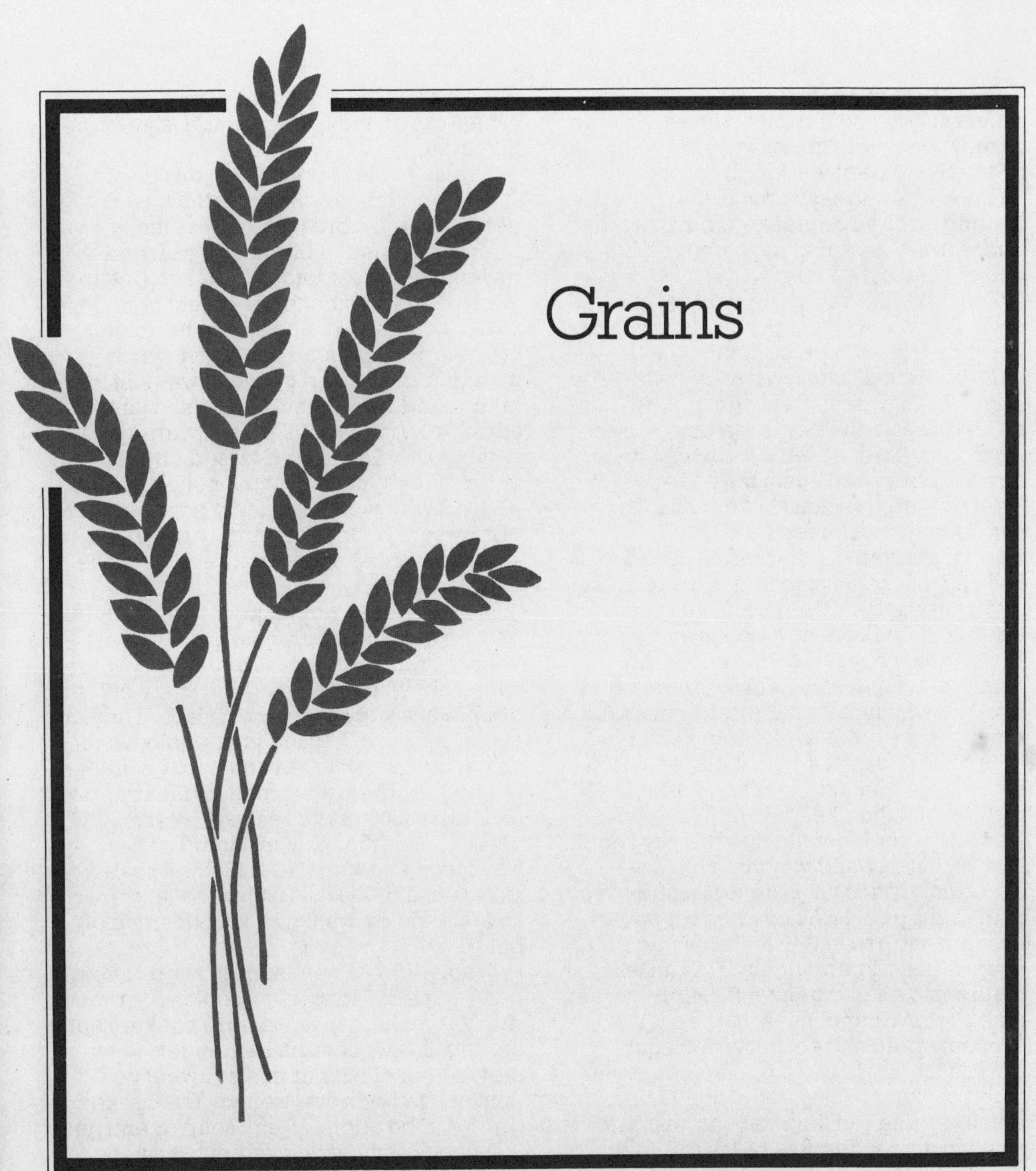

Grains

Grains

There are many different kinds of grain, different tastes, different textures. As long as they are *whole* grains they are all an invaluable part of your high-fibre diet. 'Whole' grains doesn't mean they can't be ground, broken or cracked, but that the *entire* grain, with nothing removed, is cooked and eaten.

Polished rice and barley, degerminated corn and wheat, refined grains of all kinds, leave their goodness behind in the mill–whereupon it's sold separately in the form of rice bran, wheat bran, wheat germ and so on. We actually pay three times for the same bag of wheat: once for white flour, again for bran and again for wheat germ !

Grains are delicious hot or cold. They can be boiled or pressure cooked, casseroled with vegetables or baked with fish and chicken, eaten in dozens of different ways–but they must be eaten. They contain protein, vitamins and *fibre*.

Generally speaking, one cup of raw whole grain gives you about three cups cooked, which makes all grains, even the apparently expensive Couscous, very economical to use. You can buy grains in fairly large quantities, cutting cost even further, and they keep well.

I always cook double the quantity I think I'll use that day and wind up with a selection of cooked grains, in airtight plastic boxes, in the refrigerator. They keep for a week or more and are handy to throw into a thin soup, a stuffed pepper, a chestnut roast ; or to turn into a salad or heat through (perhaps with a sprinkling of pumpkin seeds) to accompany an entrée. Because of this double life, try to use the minimum of salt when cooking grains. They don't need much to bring out their flavour, and salt's really not good for you, so try to avoid over-salting (as you avoid over-sweetening) and let the natural taste come through.

Grains replace potatoes in this diet. There's nothing wrong with the basic potato, a high-fibre food, unless there's been some kind of blight or it's turned green. But we seldom eat a naked potato. We dress it with butter or cream or cheese, adding oodles of calories and harmful saturated fats. I found that a diet which included grains and potatoes was just too heavy, and since grains bring so many additional bonuses (like great variety without needing to be dressed up at all) I cut out the potatoes without noticing they'd gone. If you want to eat them now and then, of course you may–but simply scrub the skin, boil or bake the potato and eat it the way it comes.

Bulgur Wheat, sometimes called Bulghur or Burghul, and Couscous, a pretty, pale-yellow grain, are very popular in the East where they're eaten hot, with spicy entrées, or cold in a wide variety of salads. They are rather more processed than whole wheat, since they are cracked and partly softened, but nevertheless they contain dietary fibre and are a tasty as well as healthy and versatile addition to your diet. Try Couscous Pudding (No. 263) for a real surprise–a dessert as fruity and tender as any sponge pudding but with no trace of butter, sugar or eggs.

Whole Wheat, sometimes called Wheat Berries, needs long, slow cooking (or much shorter cooking in a pressure cooker) but the result is well worth it–a tender, juicy 'berry', full of flavour and so sweet you'd think it had been sweetened. The cooked grain can be added to any soup or entrée that needs a chewy ingredient, it can be

Grains

stirred with soy sauce or yeast extract for a savoury cold salad, mixed with fruit and honey for a filling, chewy breakfast–even added to Basic Bread (replacing an equal volume of flour) for a heavy, unusual bread that's great with a soup or salad meal.

We've already talked about Brown Rice, (see p. 3 and p. 14), arguably the most versatile grain of all, but do try the others.

Maize Meal, or Corn Meal (not to be confused with corn flour or corn starch, the thickening agents) is very popular in America and is the basis of many traditional Southern and Mexican dishes and breads. I use it a lot, as Cornmeal Mush for breakfast, as a 'biscuit' topping for stews, as flour in pancakes and melt-in-your-mouth baking powder breads. It has a pleasantly gritty bite and a flavour that's irresistible once you've tried it. Don't forget, though–whole grain, not degerminated.

Barley, in its whole form, (not pearled or polished), makes wonderful stuffings, soups and even breakfasts, because it's so easy to digest. It takes the flavour of the other ingredients so that you can make it sweet or savoury according to your needs–but it's always tender, chewy and satisfying.

Rolled oats, flaked barley, millet, wheat and rye are all high-protein, high-fibre grains which combine, uncooked, to form muesli.

Buckwheat (Kasha) is a dark, richly flavoured grain, much favoured in Eastern Europe. It is improved and sweetened by roasting before you boil it. Simply pour your measured quantity into a heavy, dry frying pan and stir and shake the pan over medium heat until the grain smells nutty and turns a rich, dark colour, then transfer to your saucepan and cook, (No. 230) .Or you can actually roast in the saucepan, if it has a thick, heavy bottom.

Most grains benefit from light roasting, especially if they've been stored for a while but I always roast Millet, even when it's fresh, because stirring over heat until the grain smells nutty and deepens in colour improves the flavour of this, one of the highest-protein, lowest-calorie, lightest and most appetising of grains. You'll find Whole Millet in health food shops.

Some people are quick to point out that you'll also find millet in pet shops, as I was informed by my sister, who insisted it was bird seed and treated us to budgie impressions at the slightest provocation. One evening I innocently served Millet with Nuts and Raisins (No. 237) at dinner. (Sister: 'What's in it?' Me: 'This and that.') She insisted on having the recipe, so I typed on it 'He who tweets last, tweets longest'. It didn't make too much sense but I got satisfaction out of it.

Grains

227
Brown Rice

1×250ml cup (1 cup) brown rice
2×250ml cups (2 cups) water
$\frac{1}{2}$×5ml spoon ($\frac{1}{2}$ tsp) salt

Wash rice under cold water and drain. In saucepan with tight-fitting lid combine rice, water and salt, bring to the boil, reduce heat to minimum–use heat diffuser–and cook for 35-45 mins. Water should be completely absorbed and rice firm-tender.
Pressure cooking: Combine ingredients as above and pressure cook for 25 minutes. Bring pressure down under cold tap, or grain will overcook and turn yellow at the bottom.
To double this quantity:
2×250ml cups (2 cups) brown rice
3$\frac{1}{2}$×250ml cups (3$\frac{1}{2}$ cups) water
1×5ml spoon (1 tsp) salt
Cooking methods and times remain the same.

228
Whole Wheat
(Wheat Berries)

1×250ml cup (1 cup) whole wheat
3×250ml cups (3 cups) water
1×5ml spoon (1 tsp) salt

Wash wheat under cold water and drain. In saucepan with tight-fitting lid combine wheat, water and salt, bring to the boil, reduce heat to minimum–use heat diffuser–and cook for 1$\frac{1}{2}$-2 hours, until wheat is firm-tender.
Pressure cooking:
Combine ingredients as above and pressure cook for 1 hour. Allow heat to fall gradually.
If you have time you'll improve the flavour of whole wheat by putting it into a dry frying pan and stirring over medium heat until the grain turns golden and smells nutty. Then boil or pressure-cook as above.

229
Cracked Wheat

This is whole wheat berries which have been cracked. If you can't find it in the shops put whole wheat into your grinder and crack it yourself in a few seconds. Put the cracked cereal into a sieve, shake away loose flour, then cook as No. 217.

230
Buckwheat
(Kasha)

1×250ml cup (1 cup) buckwheat groats
2×250ml cups (2 cups) boiling water
$\frac{1}{2}$×5ml spoon ($\frac{1}{2}$ tsp) salt

In dry pan toast the buckwheat over medium heat until it turns a deep colour and smells nutty. Pour boiling water over, add salt, cover tightly, reduce heat to minimum–use heat diffuser–and cook for 15 mins.

231
Bulgur Wheat

1×250ml cup (1 cup) bulgur wheat
2×250ml cups (2 cups) cold water
$\frac{3}{4}$×5ml spoon ($\frac{3}{4}$ tsp) salt

Grains

Combine ingredients in saucepan with tight-fitting lid. Bring to boil, cover, reduce heat to minimum–use heat diffuser–and cook for 15 mins.

232
Couscous

$1\frac{1}{2}$ × 250ml cups ($1\frac{1}{2}$ cups) water
1 × 250ml cup (1 cup) couscous
$\frac{1}{2}$ × 5ml spoon ($\frac{1}{2}$ tsp) salt

Bring water to boil, add salt and couscous, return to boil, cover tightly. Reduce heat, simmer for 2 mins. Remove from heat, let stand for 10 minutes. Serve.

233
Millet

1 × 250ml cup (1 cup) whole yellow millet
3 × 250ml cups (3 cups) water
1 × 5ml spoon (1 tsp) salt

In dry pan toast the millet until it begins to deepen in colour and smell nutty. Pour in water, add salt and bring to gentle boil. Cover tightly, reduce heat to minimum–use heat diffuser–and cook for 20 mins.

234
Rice Cream

350g (12 ozs) brown rice

Wash rice in cold water and drain well. Pour into a heavy, dry frying pan and toast over medium heat, stirring and shaking the pan until the rice first dries, then turns brown and pops enthusiastically. Remove pan from heat, let rice cool slightly, then put it into your grinder, a little at a time, and grind to a coarse meal rather like crushed biscuit crumbs. Store rice cream in air-tight jar and use according to recipe.

Don't make too much at once. Fresh roasting and grinding improve the flavour.

235
Popcorn

Popping corn
Corn oil
Salt

In large saucepan with tight-fitting lid heat enough oil to cover bottom of pan with a thin coating. When oil is smoking pour in enough corn just to cover the bottom of the pan in one layer. Put on the lid and at the first 'pop' begin to shake the pan over the heat. The popping gets fast and furious (don't, whatever happens, lift the lid at this stage, or you'll have a kitchen full of popcorn !) When the popping *stops* your corn is ready. Pour the fluffy white buds into a large bowl, sprinkle lightly with salt and eat American-style popcorn which, incidentally, is a healthy, high-fibre treat containing only about 25 calories per whole cup-full. Buy your corn from a health food shop because it *is* a health food. A tub of corn containing a big lump of lard (or something !) is *not* a health food–and anyway, it costs more.
Cals: 25 per cup-full

236
Noodles

575g (1¼ lbs) wholewheat flour
1 × 5ml spoon (1 tsp) salt
1 × 15ml spoon (1 tbs) corn oil
350ml (12 fl.ozs) cold water

Pile the flour on pastry board and with fingers stir in the salt. Make a well in the middle, pour in oil and rub into flour. When absorbed, make a well again and pour in a little water. Combine with flour, then repeat until all water is used up and dough is a soft but not sticky ball. (This can be done in a suitable mixer.) Now using plenty of wholewheat flour on the board and on top of your dough, roll half the dough into a rectangle as thin as paper, set aside. Roll second half, set aside. Let dry for 30 minutes, roll up the dough like a Swiss Roll, starting from narrower edge, then cut the roll into ¼ in strips with a sharp knife repeatedly dipped in flour. Unroll strips and lay on a baking tray. With knife cut strips about 2 in long. Put trays of noodles into oven heated to 100°C (200°F, Gas ¼) and bake for about 30 minutes. Use within a day or two or store in polythene bags in the freezer. They come out as fresh and delicious as the day you made them.

To Cook: Bring a good quantity of lightly salted water to boil, drop in noodles and boil for 5-6 minutes, or until *'al dente'*– which means they have a bit of bite to them.

I wouldn't make noodles every day but one baking gives me enough for several noodle dishes including my favourite, Pasta Pudding (No. 271).

237
Millet with Nuts and Raisins
(4)

175g (6 ozs) whole millet
550ml (20 fl.ozs) water
1½ × 15ml spoons (1½ tbs) Tamari soy sauce
½ × 5ml spoon (½ tsp) salt
1 clove garlic, chopped finely
1 × 5ml spoon (1 tsp) oil
½ med onion in thin rings
2 × 15ml spoons (2 tbs) raisins, halved
1 × 15ml spoon (1 tbs) flaked, toasted almonds
1 × 15ml spoon (1 tbs) toasted sunflower seeds

Roast millet in saucepan over med heat until turning golden. Pour in water, soy sauce, salt and garlic. Cover tightly, reduce heat to minimum–use heat diffuser–and cook for 15 mins. Meanwhile heat oil in frying pan and stir-fry thinly sliced onion rings until golden. When millet is cooked, stir into it the onions, raisins, nuts and seeds. Warm through and serve.

This is great with Vegetable Curry (No. 172) and Yogurt-Cucumber Salad (No. 296) as a Three-Bowl Dinner.

238
Millet and Chickpeas
(4-6)

1 × 5ml spoon (1 tsp) oil
1 med onion, chopped
175g (6 ozs) whole millet
700ml (24 fl.ozs) water
175g (6 ozs) cooked chickpeas (No. 103)
1½ × 5ml spoons (1½ tsp) salt

Heat oil in frying pan, and stir-fry onion until golden. Meanwhile, in saucepan, toast millet until it deepens in colour and smells nutty. Pour in water, add chickpeas and salt and the cooked onions. Return to boil, cover tightly, reduce heat to minimum–use heat diffuser–and cook for 20 mins. Stir and serve.

239
Fried Rice
(3-4)

Keep cooked rice in the refrigerator and use it as a 'convenience food'.

1×5ml spoon (1 tsp) corn oil
500g (1 lb) cooked brown rice

Heat oil in frying pan, add rice and stir until heated through. We like crusty bits in it, so I stir over med-to-high heat.

Variations: Lightly stir-fry onion, then add rice, or heat a cup or two of cooked dried beans with the rice, or stir in 225g (8 ozs) cooked fresh green peas, or add cooked, leftover vegetables of any kind and a sprinkling of toasted peanuts.

240
Rice and Pumpkin Seeds
(3-4)

A delicious way of adding flavour and protein to fried rice.

1×5ml spoon (1 tsp) corn oil
2×15ml spoons (2 tbs) pumpkin seeds
500g (1 lb) cooked brown rice

Heat oil in frying pan, and toast pumpkin seeds until they pop, add the cooked rice and stir until heated through, then serve.

241
Stuffed Crêpes

These crêpes are very thin, tasty 'envelopes' made with little or no egg, filled with a chicken, turkey or vegetable stuffing, or even a sweet one if you wish. French Crêpes stuffed with Warm Fruit (No. 261), topped with melted honey, make a glorious dessert. And all these crêpes are high-fibre.

French Crêpe

150g (5 ozs) wholewheat flour
½×5ml spoon (½ tsp) salt
1 egg, lightly beaten
300ml (10 fl.ozs) skimmed milk
1×15ml spoon (1 tbs) melted polyunsaturate margarine

Combine flour and salt. Stir egg into milk, add melted marge, then pour wet ingredients into dry and combine swiftly in a few strokes. Don't worry about lumps–over-mixing makes heavy cakes.

Corn Crêpe

150g (5 ozs) maize meal
¾×5ml spoon (¾ tsp) salt
250ml (8 fl.ozs) boiling water
1 egg, lightly beaten
100ml (4 fl.ozs) skimmed milk
1×15ml spoon (1 tbs) corn oil

50g (2 ozs) wholewheat flour

Mix maize meal and salt in a bowl. Pour boiling water over, stir, cover and let stand for 10 mins. Combine egg, milk and oil, pour into cooled maize meal, stir briefly, add wholewheat flour, stir briefly again.

Eggless Crêpe

150g (5 ozs) wholewheat flour
$\frac{1}{2}$ × 5ml spoon ($\frac{1}{2}$ tsp) salt
300ml (10 fl.ozs) skimmed milk
1 × 15ml spoon (1 tbs) melted polyunsaturate margarine

Combine flour and salt, add milk and marge, mix together briefly. Let batter rest an hour or more, if possible.

To Cook: Lightly oil a heavy frying pan and heat until a drop of water leaps across it, hissing. Drop a spoonful of batter into pan and swirl it so that batter spreads. Cook until golden on first side, turn and cook second side. Repeat until all batter used up– but *don't* stack the pancakes or they'll stick to each other.

To Stuff: Prepare Chicken Pie Filling, (No. 99), Unbaked Tuna Bake (No. 52), Vegetable Pie Filling (No. 183).
...or any moist, tasty fish, fowl or vegetable combination or moist, tasty fruit combination. Lay the pancake flat, place a generous spoonful of your chosen filling just below centre, roll up pancake like a sausage.

To Re-Heat: Put the filled pancakes into greased baking dish. Savoury pancakes can be sprinkled with a little Parmesan cheese or toasted sesame seeds ; sweet ones can have honey trickled over. Pop under hot grill until heated through or bake in a pre-heated oven 180°C (350°F, Gas 4) for about 15 minutes.

Desserts

Desserts

It's hard to do without desserts and we soon give up diets that ask us to, which means most diets. But as we now know, white flour and sugar, the basis of most puddings and cakes, are nothing but fat-makers, containing lots of calories but no food value, while butter, eggs, milk and cream, the other ingredients of many desserts, shoot our cholesterol intake to the sky.

The French, famous for butter and cream in their cooking, have the right idea when it comes to dessert. They eat fruit, usually simple fresh fruit and occasionally fresh fruit baked into a tart. But seldom do the extra-rich desserts which appear in French cook-books actually appear on French tables.

The fact is that the tastes and textures of fresh fruits quickly satisfy our desire for sweet things once we get used to the *idea* of cutting out sugary, creamy stodge.

I felt that by making desserts sweet and mouth-watering, but still as nutritious, low-fat and high-fibre as the rest of the meal, they could become an important element in our diet instead of just empty calories. I've used fruit a lot, to take advantage of its natural sweetness–plus some pretty unexpected ingredients–to produce desserts which are tasty, tempting and good for us.

If you plan to serve a really solid dessert, like Applesauce Cake (No. 266) or Almond Rice Cream Pudding (No. 269), adjust the rest of the meal accordingly. You'll be getting nutrition from the dessert, remember, so you can cut out the entrée altogether. Serve soup and bread, salad, then dessert, and you'll be eating a completely satisfying, nutritionally sound meal. Or have soup for lunch and at dinnertime a light vegetable entrée followed by a hearty pudding. After soup *and* an entrée try Fruit Whip (No. 250) or Honey and Lemon Water Ice (No. 255) for a perfect finale.

You'll be astonished at how few calories these fruity desserts contain compared with the sugar, cream and chocolate things we're used to.

We eat vast amounts of bread in our house so I usually serve cake-type desserts only twice a week and fruit desserts the rest of the time. At least twice a week a highly polished apple or pear and an orange, a peach, a plum or a banana–whatever is in season–appear on each plate or in a pretty bowl in the middle of the table. When I have guests I give them fruit knives and fingerbowls to play with and the simple fruit becomes an important dessert.

I keep Ginger Cake (No. 264), Banana Cake (No. 270) or a Raisin Bread (No. 265) ready-sliced in the freezer. When the craving strikes we take out a slice each, let them thaw (about an hour at room temperature) and enjoy a treat with our tea or coffee without creating the temptation to 'finish off what's left'. Sometimes, of course, a few extra slices stick to my fingers but I don't worry too much because they're 10 per cent fibre, about 25 per cent fruit and 100 per cent nutritious, with fewer calories and better food-value than might be suspected from their scrumptious taste. In spite of this gluttony my weight remains comfortingly constant.

Desserts

242
Apple Fritters
(4)

150g (5 ozs) wholewheat flour
$\frac{1}{4}$ × 5ml spoon ($\frac{1}{4}$ tsp) salt
300ml (10 fl.ozs) water
1 × 15ml spoon (1 tbs) honey
1 × 5ml spoon (1 tsp) corn oil
4 × 15ml spoons (4 tbs) wholewheat flour for coating
3 sweet eating apples
Corn oil to deep fry
Cinnamon

Combine wholewheat flour and salt, add water to make fairly thick batter, stir in honey and 1 × 5ml spoon oil. Refrigerate or stand in cool place half an hour or more. Then put 4 spoons flour in a large, strong bag. Core and peel apples, cut into $\frac{1}{4}$ in slices, then drop slices into bag a few at a time and shake to coat them with flour. Heat oil in deep fryer or wok. When a spot of batter rises instantly to surface oil is ready. Now shake surplus flour off apple slices, dip into well-stirred batter, then drop into oil a few at a time and fry until golden. Remove and drain well. Sprinkle with cinnamon and serve piping hot.

243
Applesauce, Basic

2Kg (4 lbs) mixed eating apples
500g (1 lb) tart cooking apples
100ml (4 fl.ozs) cold water
Honey
Lemon juice

Thinly peel and slice apples. Put into a large pan with water, bring to gentle boil, then cover and simmer on minimum heat–use heat diffuser–until apples have more or less dissolved. Stir well to make a thick sauce and taste. Add honey, lemon juice or both to taste–but this is a basic sauce and should not be too sharp or sweet or it will conflict when used later. I use it in Applesauce Cake (No. 266), Warm Fruit (No. 261), Applesauce Sorbet (No. 244).

I freeze applesauce in 1-cup portions (measured to 250ml line in measuring cup) and it's always available for 'instant' desserts.

244
Applesauce Sorbet
(3-4)

Take two portions (2 cups) of applesauce out of freezer and put into refrigerator for half an hour before wanted. Just before serving trickle a spoonful or two of honey over and give the mixture a swift stir to break up the ice crystals. You'll have delicious pure apple ice (sorbet) for dessert.
Cals: approx. 100

245
Baked Apples
(4)

4 eating apples
50g (2 ozs) raisins
3 × 15ml (3 tbs) chopped hazelnuts
3 × 5ml spoons (3 tsp) cinnamon
1 × 5ml spoon (1 tsp) honey
100ml (4 fl.ozs) hot water

Core apples, fill hollows with raisins, nuts and cinnamon. Stir honey into hot water. Place apples in baking dish, pour liquid over and round and bake for about 20 minutes 180°C (350°F, Gas 4) or until apples tender. Serve with juice poured over, hot or cold.
Cals: 147

246
Apple Crisp
(6)

8 eating apples, peeled and sliced
100ml (4 fl.ozs) apple juice
1-2×5ml spoons (1-2 tsp) cinnamon

Topping:
225g (8 ozs) wholewheat flour
½×5ml spoon (½ tsp) salt
4×15ml spoons (4 tbs) corn oil
75ml (3 fl.ozs) apple juice
1×15ml spoon (1 tbs) honey
3×15ml spoons (3 tbs) chopped walnuts

Place apples in greased baking dish, pour apple juice over, sprinkle with cinnamon. **Topping:** Combine flour and salt. With fingers rub in oil, then apple juice and honey, to get crumb-like texture. Add nuts, then sprinkle topping over apples and let rest for half an hour. Pre-heat oven to 200°C (400°F, Gas 6), bake for about 40 mins till apples tender and topping crisp.

247
Broiled Bananas
(4)

2×5ml spoons (2 tsp) honey
1×15ml spoon (1 tbs) polyunsaturate margarine
4 ripe bananas, peeled
3×15ml spoons (3 tbs) lemon juice
½×5ml spoon (½ tsp) ground allspice
4×5ml spoons (4 tsp) chopped nuts

Melt honey and margarine together, halve bananas lengthways, put into greased baking dish and brush lightly with some of the lemon juice. Dribble honey mixture over them, letting some run into dish, and pour in remaining lemon juice. Sprinkle with allspice and pop under hot grill for 5 mins. Sprinkle nuts over and pop under grill for another 5 mins, or until nuts turn golden.
Cals: 134

248
Frozen Banana

Simply peel a banana and put it into the freezer as it is. Remove it, frozen solid, put it into the refrigerator for half an hour–and it tastes like exotic banana ice-cream. A sprinkling of nuts (if served in a dish), or a few spoons of Bran Crunch (No. 216) adds tasty fibre topping.
Cals: 80-100

249
Stuffed Prunes

4-6 prunes per person
Blanched almonds–about the same
3×15ml spoons (3 tbs) honey

Soak prunes overnight, drain. Slit each prune, remove the stone and insert a blanched almond in its place. Just before serving, heat a bowl of honey. Spear each stuffed prune on a cocktail stick, rest it in the honey. Let guests help themselves from the bowl.

250
Fruit Whip
(4)

12 cooked prunes[1]
3 ripe bananas
3×15ml spoons (3 tbs) water from prunes
½ eating apple
½×5ml spoon (½ tsp) almond essence

Combine all ingredients in blender, whip till smooth, spoon into individual serving bowls and chill.
Cals: 115

251
Stuffed Oranges
(4)

2 lge oranges
1 apple
2×15ml spoons (2 tbs) chopped walnuts
1×15ml spoon (1 tbs) raisins

Halve oranges and carefully remove flesh with a grapefruit knife without damaging skin. Chop orange flesh and apple, add nuts and raisins and pile all back into the orange halves. Chill and serve.
Cals: 88

[1]Either soak overnight and use uncooked, or simmer for 15 mins with a slice of lemon in 100ml (4 fl.ozs) water.

252
Baked Pears
(4)

4 ripe pears
2×5ml spoons (2 tsp) honey
2×5ml spoons (2 tsp) hot water
2×5ml spoons (2 tsp) cinnamon
2×15ml spoons (2 tbs) chopped, roasted nuts
2×15ml spoons (2 tbs) fruit juice or water

Halve pears, remove cores and seeds, place in greased baking dish. Stir honey into hot water, dribble over pears. Sprinkle with cinnamon and nuts. Put two spoons juice or water into dish. Bake in pre-heated oven 180°C (350°F, Gas 4) for about 20 minutes or until pears very soft.
Cals: 135

253
Pear Tart

Pastry: 225g (8 ozs) recipe No. 272

Roll out and line 9 in tin. Bake blind until completely baked, about 20 minutes in oven pre-heated to 220°C (425°F, Gas 7).

Filling:
1×15ml spoon (1 tbs) honey
250ml (8 fl.ozs) water
2 sticks cinnamon
6 whole cloves
6 whole allspice
4 large very ripe pears

2×5ml spoons (2 tsp) plain gelatine
175g (6 ozs) Apricot Preserve (No. 276)

In poacher or large, shallow pan with a lid combine first 5 ingredients. Place pears in liquid in 1 layer, bring to gentle boil, cover and simmer until tender, about 15 mins. Remove pears without breaking and strain liquid into measuring cup. Make it up to 250ml (8 fl.ozs) with water, pour into saucepan and stir in gelatine. Warm gently until dissolved–do not allow to boil or taste will spoil–then stir in apricot preserve until mixture creamy. Remove and cool. When cool spread two-thirds mixture into baked case, arrange pears on top, spoon remaining mixture over to glaze. Chill.

I put a bowl of uncooked Meringue Topping on the table for guests to help themselves (No. 275).

254
Rhubarb Sweet-Crunch
(4-5)

500g (1 lb) rhubarb
75g (3 ozs) chopped dates
50g (2 ozs) raisins
½×5ml spoon (½ tsp) ground ginger
2×15ml spoons (2 tbs) honey
50ml (2 fl.ozs) boiling water

Cut rhubarb into 1 in chunks and put in baking dish. Sprinkle dates, raisins and ginger over and toss rhubarb to coat. Stir honey into water and pour over fruit.

Topping:
75g (3 ozs) wholewheat flour
50g (2 ozs) rolled oats
¼×5ml spoon (¼ tsp) salt
1×15ml spoon (1 tbs) honey
2×15ml spoons (2 tbs) boiling water
4×15ml spoons (4 tbs) corn oil

Combine flour, oats and salt. Combine honey and water, stir in oil, then mix liquids into flour and rub through until wet and crumbly. Sprinkle evenly over the fruit. Bake in pre-heated oven 200°C (400°F, Gas 6) for 30 minutes.

This is delightfully sweet, despite the small amount of honey, because of the dates and raisins.

255
Honey and Lemon Water Ice
(4)

100ml (4 fl.ozs) honey
1×5ml spoon (1 tsp) grated lemon peel
450ml (16 fl.ozs) water
100ml (4 fl.ozs) lemon juice

In saucepan combine honey, lemon peel and water. Bring to boil and let bubble for 5 mins. Cool and chill, then stir in lemon juice and pour into a freezer-container. Freeze until just beginning to set, then stir mixture from front to back of container, stirring in ice crystals that have formed. Return container to freezer. Repeat this freezing-and-stirring every half hour until you've stirred three times. You should now have a tender, mushy ice which is ready to serve. If you leave it in freezer for any period (hours, weeks or months) transfer the container to refrigerator and let stand for 20 mins or so, then stir ice well before serving.

Variation: Increase flavour and add fibre by sprinkling nuts and raisins on to each portion. For parties halve lemons lengthways, squeeze out juice to use elsewhere, scoop out and discard pulp,

then fill shells with the made ice and freeze. Again let stand for about 20 mins in the refrigerator before serving.
Cals: 90

256
Rhubarb Honey
(4)

500g (1 lb) rhubarb
3 × 15ml spoons (3 tbs) water
2-4 × 15ml spoons (2-4 tbs) honey

Wash rhubarb and cut into 1 in chunks. Put in pan with water and honey, bring to gentle boil, cover and simmer at minimum heat –use heat diffuser– for 10 mins. Cool, chill.
To serve: sprinkle generously with Bran Crunch (No. 216) for a delicious, high-fibre topping.
Cals: (fruit dish) 53

257
Fruit Jelly
(5)

1 × 15ml spoon (1 tbs) plain gelatin
50ml (2 fl.ozs) orange juice
2-3 × 15ml spoons (2-3 tbs) honey
400ml (14 fl.ozs) orange juice[1]
1 apple, peeled, sliced
1 pear, peeled, sliced
50g (2 ozs) raisins
2 × 15ml spoons (2 tbs) hazelnuts

In pudding basin, sprinkle the spoonful of gelatin on to the small quantity of orange juice and let stand undisturbed for 5 mins. Then sit basin in a pan containing 2 in boiling water and put on med heat until gelatin dissolved, stirring occasionally. (Or use double boiler, gelatin and juice in top, boiling water in base.) When gelatin mixture is clear and shiny remove from pan and stir in honey and remaining orange juice. Transfer to bigger bowl, if necessary, or to mould if desired. Now add fruits and nuts and let mixture cool. Refrigerate for 2-4 hours until completely set.
To un-mould: run knife around edge of the set jelly, turn over on to a damp plate (which lets you slide jelly round to centre it) and put warm, damp cloth on top of mould. Jelly should slide neatly on to plate.

Variation: change the fruit according to season–strawberries and peaches are wonderful; always use raisins or dates for sweetness–and you might reduce the amount of honey next time!
To decorate: See Lemon Jelly, No. 258.
Cals: 139

258
Lemon Jelly
(5)

1 × 15ml spoon (1 tbs) plain gelatin
3 × 15ml spoons (3 tbs) cold water
350ml (12 fl.oz) cold water
4 × 15ml spoons (4 tbs) honey
½ × 5ml spoon (½ tsp) grated lemon peel
3 × 15ml spoons (3 tbs) lemon juice
Fresh fruit

Make as *Fruit Jelly* (No. 257), soaking gelatin in the smaller amount of water and stirring

[1] (if using frozen, thaw to room temperature)

in the larger amount plus honey, lemon peel and juice when the gelatin has dissolved and is clear and shiny. Now add fresh fruit to your taste.

To decorate: For special occasions make leaves out of apple peel and use a few bright red cherries for the peaks of your mould; or try paper-thin slices of cucumber or a sprig or two of fresh mint. When jelly is mixed and ready to set put a few spoonfuls into your mould and arrange your apple-leaves, cherries and other decorations in this jelly. Refrigerate until set firmly, about half an hour. Put another 2-3 spoonfuls of jelly into mould, let that set for half an hour. Now spoon in remaining jelly, plus fruit.

If you have the patience you can arrange your fruit in layers using this method. Just don't add too much liquid jelly over the set jelly at one time or you'll melt it.

Cals: 139

259
Chestnut Pie

(6-8)

50g (2 ozs) oatmeal
75g (3 ozs) chopped dates
2×15ml spoons (2 tbs) sunflower oil

In grinder grind oats and dates together until fine. (If you've no grinder, chop dates small and use fine oatmeal.) Now rub oil through until well mixed and pack the mixture into 7-8 in greased flan tin, pressing as firmly as possible so that you make a solid, even crust. (Best way is to press a second, same sized, tin on to mixture in the first.) Bake crust in pre-heated oven 220°C (425°F, Gas 7) for 8 minutes. Cool.

Filling:
½ packet plain gelatin (to gel 300ml [10 fl.ozs])
250ml (8 fl.ozs) water
1×5ml spoon (1 tsp) vanilla essence
2×15ml spoons (2 tbs) honey
225g (8 ozs) cooked chestnuts, puréed or riced (No. 109)
½×5ml spoon (½ tsp) cinnamon
1 stiffly beaten egg white

In pudding basin sprinkle gelatin on to water and let stand undisturbed for 5 mins. Then put basin into pan containing a little boiling water and stir over med heat until gelatin dissolved–about 5 mins. When liquid clear and shiny stir in vanilla and honey, then combine with chestnuts. Add the cinnamon, then stir in 1 spoonful of beaten egg white and mix well. Gently fold in remaining egg white and pour filling into the cool crust.

Topping: (optional)
150g (5 ozs) natural yogurt
2×15ml spoons (2 tbs) honey
Pinch salt
½×5ml spoon (½ tsp) vanilla

Combine, spread over pie, chill for 1 hour.

Cals: ⅛th=170

Comparison: 1 slice apple pie without topping=216 calories

260
Apricot-Chestnut Whip

(4)

225g (8 ozs) dried apricots
250ml (8 fl.ozs) water
¼×5ml spoon (¼ tsp) ground cloves
½×5ml spoon (½ tsp) cinnamon

$\frac{1}{2}$ × 5ml spoon ($\frac{1}{2}$ tsp) vanilla
250ml (8 fl.ozs) orange juice
75g (3 ozs) cooked chestnuts plus 4 whole ones to garnish (No. 109)
1 × 15ml spoon (1 tbs) honey

Simmer apricots in water until very tender, about 40 mins. Stir in cloves, cinnamon and vanilla, simmer for 2 mins more. In blender combine orange juice, chestnuts and apricots. Blend till creamy and spoon into individual serving dishes. Dip whole chestnuts into honey and put one in centre of each dish. Chill.
Cals: 187

261
Warm Fruit Dessert
(4)

2 × 250ml cups (2 cups) Applesauce (No. 243)
1 orange, cut into small chunks
2 × 15ml spoons (2 tbs) raisins
2 × 15ml spoons (2 tbs) chopped toasted nuts
A few fresh berries (optional)

Combine in a saucepan and warm through very gently. Put into individual serving dishes and sprinkle generously with Bran Crunch (No. 216)
Cals: 130

262
Fruited Carrot Surprise
(6)

350g (12 ozs) shredded carrots
50g (2 ozs) coarsely ground mixed nuts (hazel, roasted peanuts)
25g (1 oz) soft wholewheat crumbs
100g (4 ozs) chopped dates
100g (4 ozs) chopped raisins
75-100ml (3-4 fl.ozs) honey
1 × 15ml spoon (1 tbs) lemon juice

Combine all ingredients and pile loosely into greased casserole. Bake in pre-heated oven, 190°C (375°F, Gas 5), for 40 minutes. First 30 minutes keep covered, final 10 minutes uncovered.
Cals: 230
This is wonderful with Lemon Sauce, (No. 273)

263
Couscous Pudding
(5-6)

1 cooking apple, sliced
1 eating apple, sliced
1 × 5ml spoon (1 tsp) cinnamon
2 × 15ml spoons (2 tbs) honey
$\frac{1}{2}$ × 5ml spoon ($\frac{1}{2}$ tsp) grated lemon rind
25-50g (1-2 ozs) toasted seeds or broken walnuts
50g (2 ozs) raisins
175g (6 ozs) couscous
$\frac{1}{8}$ × 5ml spoon ($\frac{1}{8}$ tsp) salt
350ml (12 fl.ozs) water or apple juice
100ml (4 fl.ozs) apple juice for topping

Peel, core and slice apples, mix into them cinammon, honey, lemon peel, nuts (or seeds) and raisins. In casserole, or pudding basin with lid, put couscous, salt and 350ml (12 fl.ozs) apple juice. Put coated apple slices on top. Cover with lid. Bake 180°C (350°F, Gas 4) for 45 mins. Before serving pour remaining 100ml (4 fl.ozs) apple juice over.

Cals: 201
Comparison: 1 portion syrup sponge pudding=416 cals.

264
Gingercake Delight

50g (2 oz) oatmeal
2×15ml spoons (2 tbs) molasses
100ml (4 fl.ozs) boiling water
100ml (4 fl.ozs) honey
4×15ml spoons (4 tbs) corn oil
225g (8 ozs) wholewheat flour
1½×5ml spoons (1½ tsp) baking powder
½×5ml spoon (½ tsp) bicarb. of soda
½×5ml spoon (½ tsp) salt
½×5ml spoon (½ tsp) ground allspice
¼×5ml spoon (¼ tsp) ground cloves
2×5ml spoons (2 tsp) ground ginger
2×5ml spoons (2 tsp) ground cinnamon
1 egg, beaten
1 eating apple, grated
2 lge carrots, grated

Put oatmeal in spare bowl. Stir molasses into boiling water, pour over oats, stir in honey and oil and let cool. In mixing bowl combine next 8 ingredients. Stir egg into cooled oats mixture, then pour this mixture into flour and stir to make a lumpy batter. Fold in apple and carrot and stir lightly. Grease and flour large loaf tin, pour in batter. Pre-heat oven to 200°C (400°F, Gas 6) put tin in centre. Immediately reduce heat to 180°C (350°F, Gas 4) and bake for 50 minutes.

This moist and mouth-watering ginger cake invariably invokes the comment 'This is much too good to be healthy !' It's healthy *and* it's good.

265
Raisin Bread

500g (1 lb) 'rolls' dough or any yeast bread dough given in this book, other than rye. When you have made rolls or bread dough separate 500g (1 lb) *before putting dough into tins to rise* and proceed as follows:

2×15ml spoons (2 tbs) honey
4×15ml spoons (4 tbs) raisins
3×15ml spoons (3 tbs) broken nuts
1×15ml spoon (1 tbs) cinammon
2×5ml spoons (2 tsp) grated lemon peel
8 chopped dates

On lightly floured board roll the dough to an oblong about ¼ in thick. Spread it with honey, then scatter remaining ingredients evenly over it. Now roll up like a Swiss Roll, starting at short edge. Press ends together firmly and gently mould loaf into shape suitable for your tin. Warm and grease tin, put loaf in, cover with cloth and stand in a warm place for 30 minutes. Bake at 200°C (400°F, Gas 6) for 30 minutes. **To glaze:** Immediately it comes out of oven remove from tin, stand on a wire rack and brush the top with honey.

266
Applesauce Cake

225g (8 ozs) wholewheat flour
½×5ml spoon (½ tsp) baking powder
½×5ml spoon (½ tsp) bicarb. of soda
½×5ml spoon (½ tsp) salt
1×5ml spoon (1 tsp) ground cinammon
½×5ml spoon (½ tsp) ground cloves
1 egg, lightly beaten
100ml (4 fl.ozs) skimmed milk

4×15ml spoons (4 tbs) corn oil
4×15ml spoons (4 tbs) honey
1×250ml cup (1 cup) Applesauce (No. 243)
2 med cooking apples, peeled, sliced
1×15ml spoon (1 tbs) honey to glaze

Combine first 6 ingredients in mixing bowl. In separate bowl combine next 4 ingredients. Briefly stir wet into dry without beating–just until flour moistens. Now fold in applesauce. Pour batter into greased 9 in flan tin and gently arrange apple slices on top (don't submerge them), then dribble the spoonful of honey over. Bake in pre-heated oven 190°C (375°F, Gas 5) for 50 minutes.

Variation: replace applesauce with 2 cups lightly cooked berries, draining off juice so that batter isn't made too soft. Pour into tin as above, omit apple slices and bake. When done paint honey on to hot crust, then sprinkle a few extra berries to decorate.

267
Prune Sponge

225g (8 ozs) wholewheat flour
½×5ml spoon (½ tsp) salt
½×5ml spoon (½ tsp) bicarb. of soda
1×5ml spoon (1 tsp) baking powder
175ml (6 fl.ozs) skimmed milk
1 egg, lightly beaten
1×15ml spoon (1 tbs) grated orange peel
4×15ml spoons (4 tbs) honey
4×15ml spoons (4 tbs) melted polyunsaturate margarine
3×15ml spoons (3 tbs) raisins or currants
225g (8 ozs) prunes, soaked overnight, stoned, roughly chopped

Combine first 4 ingredients. In separate bowl combine next 5 ingredients. Now stir wet into dry, just mixing briefly without beating. Stir in raisins (or currants) and chopped prunes until distributed evenly. Pour batter into greased 8 in or 9 in shallow cake tin. Bake in pre-heated oven 180°C (350°F, Gas 4) for 50-60 minutes.

Glaze: 1 tbs honey painted on hot crust immediately cake removed from the oven.

To serve as a dessert: put a bowl of Orange Sauce (No. 274) on table for guests to help themselves.

268
Bread Pudding
(6)

450ml (16 fl.ozs) skimmed milk
3×15ml spoons (3 tbs) honey
4 thick slices wholewheat bread (225g, 8 ozs)
50g (2 ozs) raisins
3×15ml spoons (3 tbs) broken nuts
1×5ml spoon (1 tsp) vanilla
¼×5ml spoon (¼ tsp) grated nutmeg
1×5ml spoon (1 tsp) lemon peel, grated
3×15ml spoons (3 tbs) lemon juice

In saucepan warm milk and stir in honey. Dice bread, put into mixing bowl, pour milk over. Let stand for 10 minutes, then stir in all other ingredients. Spoon into greased baking dish and stand dish in shallow pan of hot water in the oven. Bake in pre-heated oven 180°C (350°F, Gas 4) for ¾-1 hour, until firm and set. This uses up stale bread beautifully, but I use whatever bread I have made that week, excepting rye.

A moist and mouth-watering dessert, filling and high-fibre–ideal after a salad meal.
Cals: 200

269
Almond Rice Cream Pudding
(4)

75g (3 ozs) rice cream (No. 234)
450ml (16 fl.ozs) water
$\frac{1}{4}$×5ml spoon ($\frac{1}{4}$ tsp) salt
$\frac{1}{2}$×5ml spoon ($\frac{1}{2}$ tsp) grated lemon peel
$\frac{1}{2}$×5ml spoon ($\frac{1}{2}$ tsp) almond essence
1×5ml spoon (1 tsp) lemon juice
1×5ml spoon (1 tsp) vanilla
100ml (4 fl.ozs) skimmed milk
50g (2 ozs) ground almonds[1]
4×15ml spoons (4 tbs) honey

In saucepan combine first 7 ingredients and bring to gentle boil. Cover, reduce heat to minimum–use heat diffuser–and cook for 20 mins. Remove from heat but leave covered, let stand for 5 mins, then stir in milk, almonds and honey until a smooth cream. Divide into individual dishes and chill.
Cals: 230
Comparison: 1 portion suet pudding=420 cals.

If you like a topping on your desserts, this pudding is lovely with crisped Meringue Topping (No. 275).

[1] A light toasting before freshly grinding improves flavour

270
Banana Cake

225g (8 ozs) wholewheat flour
$1\frac{1}{2}$×5ml spoons ($1\frac{1}{2}$ tsp) baking powder
$\frac{1}{2}$×5ml spoon ($\frac{1}{2}$ tsp) bicarb. of soda
$\frac{1}{2}$×5ml spoon ($\frac{1}{2}$ tsp) salt
1×5ml spoon (1 tsp) grated lemon peel
75ml (3 fl.ozs) corn oil
1 egg, beaten
2 lge bananas, pulped
100ml (4 fl.ozs) honey
100g (4 ozs) chopped dates
75g (3 ozs) coarsely chopped walnuts

Combine first 4 ingredients. Beat together the next 5 ingredients. Stir liquids into flours with just a few strokes, to make a lumpy batter. Fold in dates and nuts. Grease a large loaf tin. Pour in batter. Bake in pre-heated oven 160°C (325°F, Gas 3) for 1 hour, centre of oven.

271
Pasta Pudding
(4-5)

100g (4 ozs) noodles (No. 236) or macaroni 'elbows'
$\frac{1}{4}$×5ml spoon ($\frac{1}{4}$ tsp) salt
Water to well cover

1 cooking apple
1 eating apple
1×5ml spoon (1 tsp) cinnamon
50g (2 ozs) raisins
50g (2 ozs) broken walnuts
1×15ml spoon (1 tbs) honey
100ml (4 fl.ozs) apple juice

Cook noodles or macaroni in boiling, salted

water until *'al dente'*, drain, rinse under cold water. Peel and slice apples in bowl. Sprinkle with cinammon, raisins and nuts. Dribble honey over, add apple juice and mix very well. Gently fold in cooked pasta. Grease casserole (with lid) and spoon pudding into it. Bake, covered, in oven pre-heated to 180°C (350°F, Gas 4) for 30 mins.

272
Wholewheat Pastry

225g (8 ozs) wholewheat flour
Pinch salt
100g (4 ozs) polyunsaturate margarine
50ml (2 fl.ozs) cold water (or skimmed milk)

Combine flour and salt, rub in margarine till texture is like breadcrumbs, then add liquid all at once and stir till pastry forms a rough ball. Roll out according to recipe. This pastry is most malleable when first made, so I roll it at once, line the pie tin, then pop it into refrigerator to rest for half an hour before baking. For pasties, etc. I don't rest it at all, just fill the pastry shapes and bake as recipe. *Remember to cool pastry on a rack to keep it crisp.*

For 2×8 or 9 in crusts:
350g (12 ozs) wholewheat flour
Pinch salt
175g (6 ozs) polyunsaturate margarine
75ml (3 fl.ozs) cold water

For 1×9 in crust:
175g (6 ozs) wholewheat flour
Pinch salt
75g (3 ozs) polyunsaturate margarine
2×15ml spoons (2 tbs) cold water

Sweet Pastry:
Measure water (or skimmed milk) as above, then *replace* one or two spoons of liquid with equal quantity of honey. (Honey acts as liquid when added to the flour.)

Quick Pastry:
225g (8 ozs) wholewheat flour
$\frac{1}{4}$×5ml spoon ($\frac{1}{4}$ tsp) salt
100ml (4 fl.ozs) corn or sunflower oil
50ml (2 fl.ozs) water or skimmed milk

Combine flour and salt in bowl. Mix oil and water together, pour all at once into flour and stir with fork until pastry forms a ball. Use as above.

To Bake Blind:
Line tin, prick pastry all over with fork, bake in pre-heated oven 220°C (425°F, Gas 7) for 12-15 minutes.

273
Lemon Sauce
(6-8)

1×15ml spoon (1 tbs) arrowroot
350ml (12fl.ozs) skimmed milk
1 stick cinnamon
1×5ml spoon (1 tsp) grated lemon peel
3×15ml spoons (3 tbs) lemon juice
3×15ml spoons (3 tbs) honey

In saucepan stir arrowroot into a little of the cold milk, then add remaining milk and cinnamon stick and stir over gentle heat until sauce thickens. Remove, stir in lemon juice, peel and honey. Cool, chill. Remove cinnamon stick before serving.
Cals: (8)=45

274
Orange Sauce
(6)

1 × 15ml spoon (1 tbs) arrowroot
350ml (12 fl.ozs) orange juice
½ × 5ml spoon (½ tsp) grated lemon peel
1 stick cinnamon
3 whole cloves
3 whole allspice
1 × 15ml spoon (1 tbs) honey

In saucepan stir arrowroot into a little of the juice, then add remaining juice and all other ingredients. Stir over gentle heat until sauce thickens. Remove, cool, chill. Before serving take out cinnamon, cloves and allspice.

275
Meringue Topping

1 egg white
Pinch salt
Small pinch cream of tartar
1 × 15ml spoon (1 tbs) honey
3 drops vanilla

Your bowl should be clean and dry, egg at room temperature. A balloon whisk gives greatest volume. Beat egg white to gentle peaks, add other ingredients and beat again until peaks are stiff. Use topping as it is for a soft, whipped-cream effect.

Variation: Put a dollop of topping on to dessert or spread it over tart and put under hot grill for 1-2 minutes to get golden and crisp–but watch it closely !

If dessert shouldn't be warmed–or your dishes might crack under the grill–then put dollops of topping on to aluminium foil, put the foil under the grill until topping is crisp, then slide the meringue on top of the dessert. (This is easier than it sounds.)

I make this meringue no more than 1 hour before serving, as honey eventually trickles out. This is all right except that meringue loses sweetness while the dessert it's sitting on gains it !
Cals : total 71

276
Apricot Preserve
(500g, 1 lb 2 ozs)

225g (8 ozs) dried apricots
50ml (2 fl.ozs) soaking water from apricots
75-100ml (3-4 fl.ozs) honey
1 × 5ml spoon (1 tsp) grated lemon peel

Soak apricots overnight in 250-300ml (8-10 fl.ozs) cold water. Use large-based container so they can be placed in single layer and need less water to cover them. Next day put 50ml (2 fl.ozs) of this water into blender, drain apricots and put them and all other ingredients into blender. Whip until smooth. Spoon the preserve into clean, airtight jars. *It is essential that this preserve be kept in the refrigerator.* It will remain good for weeks–if it lasts that long.

I use the smaller amount of honey. Since the peel gets a little sharper as the preserve stands, try the larger amount first time and see if you can manage with less next time.
Cals : comparison:
Commercial Apricot Jam = 1332
This Apricot Preserve = 744

Salads, Dressings and Sauces

Salads, Dressings and Sauces

Some people maintain that the finest salad is a chilled crispy lettuce lightly sprinkled with vinaigrette dressing, and it's hard to argue with that. But since we need lots more vegetables if we're to benefit from their fibre, a good way to get them is in salad.

My family eat it every single day and sometimes twice a day in the summer. Salad is frequently our lunch, it regularly fills one bowl in our three-bowl dinner ; it's served before the main course in a traditional dinner and after the main course if we don't have a dessert. It's often simple lettuce leaves, but by varying the dressing we have a very different-tasting salad each time.

Virtually any tender-crisp vegetable is delicious raw: carrot, turnip, jerusalem artichoke, beetroot, cabbage, and so on. Combine some of these with fruits–chopped apple and pear, sliced orange and grapefruit, grapes and raisins–add a sprinkling of sunflower seeds or roasted nuts–and you have a feast.

A salad can be sweet or savoury, mild or sharp, a single vegetable, shredded, or a variety of them, chopped. Vary your salads and eat them often. Raw vegetables contain their full quota of vitamins and minerals (unlike cooked ones, which lose quite a lot while cooking), they're good for the teeth, delightfully low-calorie–and best of all, they're absolutely delicious.

Try to get the salad habit now. It's never out of season.

Salads, Dressings and Sauces

277
Traditional Salad

A bowl of crisp green lettuce leaves, lightly sprinkled with dressing, tossed carefully to coat the leaves without bruising them and served before, with or after main course. Even purists won't mind if you add a few thin slices of cucumber, but that's all !

278
Spinach Salad
(4)

225g (8 ozs) young spinach
2 med leaves Chinese cabbage
50g (2 ozs) mushrooms
2 firm tomatoes
3 × 15ml spoons (3 tbs) sunflower seeds
Italian dressing

Carefully wash spinach, trim off any coarse stems, wash Chinese cabbage and tomatoes, wipe mushrooms with damp cloth. Now finely chop the vegetables, put them into salad bowl and sprinkle with seeds. Just before serving, trickle over dressing (quantity to your taste) and toss lightly.

If you can't find Chinese cabbage use a handful of bean sprouts, cauliflower florets, or mange tout. Anything crisp and delicate can go into this salad and taste great.

279
Cabbage Salad
(4)

500g (1 lb) white cabbage, shredded
1 sweet red pepper, seeded, shredded
4 spring onions, with green, finely sliced
2 × 15ml spoons (2 tbs) raisins
2 × 15ml spoons (2 tbs) freshly chopped mint

Dressing:
275g (10 ozs) natural yogurt
1 × 5ml spoon (1 tsp) French mustard
1 × 5ml spoon (1 tsp) garlic salt
generous ground black pepper

Combine vegetables in salad bowl, combine dressing ingredients, pour over and mix well. Chill before serving.

Instead of raisins and mint try: 1 sprig fresh dill weed, 1 × 5ml spoon (1 tsp) caraway seeds

280
Red Cabbage Salad
(4-6)

500g (1 lb) red cabbage, finely chopped
2 eating apples, chopped
1-2 ribs celery, thinly sliced
1 × 5ml spoon (1 tsp) caraway seeds OR
¾ × 5ml spoon (¾ tsp) fennel seeds

Dressing:
4 × 15ml spoons (4 tbs) cider vinegar
2 × 15ml spoons (2 tbs) honey, melted in
4 × 15ml spoons (4 tbs) boiling water
¼ × 5ml spoon (¼ tsp) salt

Combine dressing ingredients, pour over salad, chill before serving.

Salads, Dressings and Sauces

281
Red Cabbage-Yogurt Salad
(4-6)

500g (1 lb) red cabbage, finely shredded
2 eating apples, chopped
1-2 ribs celery, sliced
2×15ml spoons (2 tbs) raisins
2×15ml spoons (2 tbs) broken walnuts

Dressing:
$1\frac{1}{2}$×5ml spoons ($1\frac{1}{2}$ tsp) honey, melted in
2×15ml spoons (2 tbs) boiling water
2×15ml spoons (2 tbs) cider or wine vinegar
$\frac{1}{4}$×5ml spoon ($\frac{1}{4}$ tsp) ground coriander
Pinch ground cloves
$\frac{1}{4}$×5ml spoon ($\frac{1}{4}$ tsp) salt
150g (5 ozs) natural yogurt

Combine dressing ingredients, pour over salad, chill before serving.

This is a perfect winter salad, going well with most cooked dishes but very appetising served as part of a three-bowl dinner with grilled fish and a bowl of brown rice.

282
Carrot Salad
(4)

500g (1 lb) carrots, scrubbed, grated
100ml (4 fl.ozs) fresh orange juice
1×5ml spoon (1 tsp) grated orange peel
$\frac{1}{4}$×5ml spoon ($\frac{1}{4}$ tsp) salt
2×5ml spoons (2 tsp) lemon juice
2×15ml spoons (2 tbs) raisins

Mix all together, chill.

283
Green Salad
(4)

$\frac{1}{2}$ crisp lettuce
8 leaves young spinach
$\frac{1}{2}$ bunch watercress
2 in chunk cucumber
6 spring onions
2 sprigs parsley
dressing of your choice
sprinkling toasted sunflower seeds

Wash and dry all ingredients. Break lettuce, spinach and watercress into small pieces, thinly slice cucumber and onions, chop parsley. Combine in bowl, refrigerate. Immediately before serving add dressing, toss lightly and sprinkle seeds.

284
Chopped Salad
(4)

12 leaves cos lettuce
4 ripe tomatoes
4 lge radishes
4 ribs celery
4 spring onions
3 in chunk cucumber
4 ozs whole fresh peas or cooked dried beans
dressing of your choice

Wash and dry all vegetables. Set aside 4 lettuce leaves and peas or beans. Finely chop other ingredients, combine in bowl, add peas or beans and refrigerate. Before serving toss lightly with dressing, scoop into reserved lettuce leaves.

Salads, Dressings and Sauces

285
Shredded Salad
(4)

2 lge carrots
1 raw beetroot
1 Jerusalem artichoke
$\frac{1}{8}$ small red cabbage
2 ribs celery
3 ripe tomatoes
dressing of your choice
2 × 15ml spoons (2 tbs) toasted pumpkin seeds

Scrub first three ingredients, wash and dry next three. Finely shred carrots, beetroot and cabbage ; cut artichoke into matchsticks, dice celery and tomatoes. Dress, toss, chill. Before serving sprinkle in seeds and toss again.

286
Combination Salad
(6)

1 lge (2 small) lettuce
$\frac{1}{2}$ bunch curly endive
2 carrots, cut in matchsticks
4 in chunk cucumber, sliced
6 radishes, sliced
2 eating apples, chopped
1 grapefruit, in sections
Vinaigrette dressing (No. 304)

Combine vegetables and fruit, refrigerate. Before serving toss lightly with dressing.

287
Bean Salad
(4-6)

350g (12 ozs) runner, or any green beans
100ml (4 fl.ozs) Italian dressing (No. 306)
175g (6 ozs) cooked chickpeas
100g (4 ozs) cooked butter beans
$\frac{1}{2}$ small onion, diced
$\frac{1}{2}$ sweet red pepper, diced

Cut green beans into 2 in lengths and cook in lightly salted, boiling water until crisp-tender. Drain, pour dressing over, cool, then add all other ingredients. Refrigerate for at least 1 hour, stirring occasionally. This is just as good next day.

288
Jamaican Salad
(4)

1 lge lettuce (Webb's is best)
2 lge ripe bananas
4 ribs celery
1 green pepper, seeded
$\frac{1}{2}$ × 5ml spoon ($\frac{1}{2}$ tsp) honey
150g (5 ozs) natural yogurt
2 × 15ml spoons (2 tbs) toasted, flaked almonds

Reserve 4 lge lettuce leaves, shred remainder. Thinly slice bananas, celery and green pepper rings, divide into 4. On each reserved lettuce leaf pile a layer of shredded lettuce, banana, celery and green peppers. Combine yogurt and honey, put a dollop on each salad and sprinkle nuts over.

289
Beansprout Salad
(4-6)

350g (12 ozs) raw beansprouts
8 spring onions
100g (4 ozs) mange tout (snow peas)
12 olives, halved
100ml (4 fl.ozs) Vinaigrette (No. 304)

Wash beansprouts in cold water and dry thoroughly. Clean and slice onions. Remove tails and strings from peas and cut into $\frac{1}{4}$ in slices. Combine all with olives and chill. Before serving toss lightly with dressing.

290
Lentil Salad
(4)

175g (6 ozs) green lentils, washed, picked over
water to well cover
$\frac{1}{2}$ med onion, chopped
1 clove garlic, chopped
$\frac{1}{4}$ × 5ml spoon ($\frac{1}{4}$ tsp) ground mace
$\frac{1}{2}$ × 5ml spoon ($\frac{1}{2}$ tsp) salt
1 bayleaf
1 small green pepper, seeded, chopped
4 spring onions, finely sliced
3 × 15ml spoons (3 tbs) parsley, chopped
3 fresh mint leaves, chopped (optional)
3 × 15ml spoons (3 tbs) Vinaigrette (No. 304)
1 × 15ml spoon (1 tbs) lemon juice
pepper to taste

Bring lentils to boil in water, boil 2 mins, then cover, remove from heat and let stand 1 hour. Replenish water, add onion, garlic, mace, salt and bayleaf, bring to boil, cover and simmer until lentils tender, about 30 mins. Drain, cool, stir in all other ingredients and chill.

291
Smoked Pepper Salad
(4)

2 sweet red peppers
2 green peppers
12 olives, green or black, halved
4 tomatoes, cut in matchsticks
$\frac{1}{2}$ lge onion, thinly sliced in rings
3 × 15ml spoons (3 tbs) Italian Dressing (No. 306)

Quarter peppers, wash and seed them, then pop under hot grill until the skins turn black. Cool, then peel off the skins and cut flesh into chunks. Combine with other ingredients and chill for at least 1 hour before serving. (This is just as good next day, too.)

292
Sweet and Crisp Salad
(4)

50g (2 oz) walnuts, coarsely chopped
8 dates, finely sliced
2 eating apples, coarsely chopped
4 ribs celery, thinly sliced
2 in cucumber, diced

Dressing:
150g (5 ozs) natural yogurt
2 × 5ml spoons (2 tsp) lime juice (or lemon)
$1\frac{1}{2}$ × 5ml spoons ($1\frac{1}{2}$ tsp) honey
$\frac{1}{2}$ × 5ml spoon ($\frac{1}{2}$ tsp) ground coriander

Salads, Dressings and Sauces

Combine salad ingredients in bowl, stir dressing ingredients together, pour over salad, mix well and chill before serving.

This mixture of sweet and sharp, crisp and tender, is really delightful with any plain, simple entrée... or try it with a bowl of chewy whole wheat berries, for a sustaining lunch.

293
Pickled Beetroot

500g (1 lb) boiled beetroots, skinned, sliced

Pickling ingreds:
100ml (4 fl.ozs) wine vinegar
100ml (4 fl.ozs) water from beets, or plain water
2×15ml spoons (2 tbs) honey
3 whole cloves
2 whole allspice
4 whole black peppercorns
½ bayleaf
1 in stick cinnamon
½×5ml spoon (½ tsp) salt

Combine pickling ingreds. in saucepan, bring to boil, then pour liquid and spices over sliced beets in clean, airtight jars. Cool, chill.

294
Russian Beetroot Salad
(4)

½×5ml spoon (½ tsp) honey
450g (3×5 ozs cartons) natural yogurt
225g (8 ozs) pickled beetroot, diced (No. 293).
2 lge ribs celery, diced
salt and pepper
½-1×5ml spoon (½-1 tsp) caraway seeds
a few raisins (optional)

Stir honey into yogurt. Combine beets and celery. Pour yogurt over vegetables, add salt and pepper to taste. Stir in seeds and raisins, chill.

295
Minted Apple Salad
(4)

600g (4×5 oz cartons) natural yogurt
2×5ml spoons (2 tsp) honey
2 med. eating apples, diced
3×15ml spoons (3 tbs) chopped fresh mint

Stir honey into yogurt, pour over apples, stir in mint, chill and serve.

Cool and lovely with any curry or spicy dish.

296
Yogurt-Cucumber Salad
(2)

4 in chunk cucumber
275g (2×5 oz cartons) natural yogurt
½×5ml spoon (½ tsp) honey
¼×5ml spoon (¼ tsp) salt
generous grating pepper
pinch garlic powder (optional)

Thinly slice unpeeled cucumber. Combine remaining ingredients and stir well, then pour over cucumber slices and chill.

Salads, Dressings and Sauces

The following are substantial salads, suitable for lunches, light dinners and, in small portions, starters.

297
Oriental Chicken Salad
(4-6)

3 × 15ml spoons (3 tbs) sunflower oil
1 × 15ml spoon (1 tbs) wine vinegar
1 × 15ml spoon (1 tbs) Tamari soy sauce
½ × 5 ml spoon (½ tsp) grated ginger root
2 portions chicken, cooked, boned, shredded
4-6 leaves Chinese cabbage, shredded
1 white radish, thin slices
100g (4 ozs) beansprouts
25g (1 oz) chopped roasted peanuts

Combine first four ingredients, pour over chicken and marinate approx. 1 hour in refrigerator. Keep prepared vegetables cold, too, and just before serving mix them into the chicken, to distribute dressing, and sprinkle with nuts.

298
Chicken and Rice Salad
(4)

1 × 5ml spoon (1 tsp) corn oil
½ med onion, chopped
175g (6 ozs) cooked brown rice
175g (6 ozs) cooked chicken, diced
1 green pepper, seeded, chopped
50g (2 ozs) roasted hazelnuts, chopped
2 × 15ml spoons (2 tbs) raisins
1 × 5ml spoon (1 tsp) curry powder
100ml (4 fl.ozs) Vinaigrette (No. 304)
salt and pepper
lettuce leaves

Heat oil, stir-fry onions till golden, set aside to cool, then combine with next 5 ingredients. Stir curry powder into dressing and pour over. Adjust seasoning and chill. Serve on bed of crisp lettuce leaves.

299
Avocado Salad
(4)

1 lettuce, divided into leaves (Webb's is best)
500g (1 lb) low fat cottage cheese
2 ripe avocado pears, peeled, sliced
4 slices pineapple, in chunks
toasted nuts or seeds to garnish

On each plate make a bed of lettuce leaves. In centre put a scoop of cottage cheese, to the left slices of avocado (sprinkled with lemon juice), to the right chunks of pineapple. Garnish and serve very cold.

300
Macaroni Cheese Salad
(4)

100g (4 ozs) macaroni (1 in pieces)
boiling, salted water to cover
500g (1 lb) low fat cottage cheese
2 × 15ml spoons (2 tbs) Parmesan cheese
½ red pepper, chopped
½ green pepper, chopped
2 ribs celery, thinly sliced
½ small onion, chopped
2 ripe tomatoes, chopped
salt and pepper

Salads, Dressings and Sauces

lettuce leaves

Cook macaroni in water until tender, drain, cool. Thoroughly mix cottage and Parmesan cheese, then stir in cool pasta and vegetables. Adjust seasoning, chill and serve on lettuce leaves.

301
Salad Niçoise
(4-6)

1 lge lettuce, shredded
½ bunch watercress, small sprigs
4 ripe tomatoes, quartered
4 fillets anchovy, soaked, drained, chopped
200g (7 ozs) tin tuna fish, well drained, flaked
2 × 15ml spoons (2 tbs) Parmesan cheese
10 olives, sliced
2 in chunk cucumber, diced
100ml (4 fl.ozs) Italian dressing (No. 306)

Lightly mix all ingredients to distribute dressing, but don't make into a 'mush'. Serve in individual bowls, very cold.

302
Rice Salad
(4)

500g (1 lb) cooked brown rice
1 rib celery, finely sliced
1 small beetroot, peeled, finely diced
3 tomatoes, chopped
½ med. onion, finely chopped
2 × 15ml spoons (2 tbs) roasted nuts or seeds
3 × 15ml spoons (3 tbs) Italian Dressing (No. 306) *or* Vinaigrette (No. 304)

Combine all ingredients, toss well and chill before serving. This salad needs only a soup before and a dessert after to make a satisfying, nutritious meal.

303
Bulgur Salad
(4)

150g (5 ozs) bulgur wheat (raw)
Boiling water to cover
1 × 5ml spoon (1 tsp) salt
3 in cucumber, diced
½ green pepper, diced
3 tomatoes, chopped
4 spring onions, incl green, sliced
2 × 15ml spoons (2 tbs) fresh parsley or mint, chopped
Or 1½ × 15ml spoons (1½ tbs) fresh tarragon, chopped
3 × 15ml spoons (3 tbs) Vinaigrette (No. 304)
Or Italian Dressing (No. 306)

Put wheat into basin, pour boiling water over to cover by about 3 in. Stir in salt, let stand 1 hour, then drain well in sieve. Combine all other ingredients with wheat, toss well, chill and serve.

This is traditional Eastern style, but you can add virtually any crisp vegetables or even fruit, while the herbs can be varied according to season. Or try this delicious salad with a dollop of yogurt on top for added protein.

Salads, Dressings and Sauces

Salad Dressings

304
Vinaigrette

6 × 15ml spoons (6 tbs) sunflower oil
½ × 5ml spoon (½ tsp) dry mustard
½ × 5ml spoon (½ tsp) honey
¼ × 5ml spoon (¼ tsp) salt
generous grating pepper
4 × 15ml spoons (4 tbs) wine vinegar

Mix together in a screw-top jar, shake well before use. Keep in refrigerator, but let it reach room temperature before sprinkling on salad.

Garlic Vinaigrette

Make exactly as above, but add 1 or 2 cloves of lightly crushed garlic to the jar. If you keep the dressing longer than 24 hours remove the garlic. It doesn't taste good after that.

305
Herb Dressing

½ × 5ml spoon (½ tsp) dried basil
½ × 5ml spoon (½ tsp) dried dill weed
⅛ × 5ml spoon (⅛ tsp) salt
½ clove garlic
¼ × 5ml spoon (¼ tsp) honey
2 × 15ml spoons (2 tbs) sunflower oil
2 × 5ml spoons (2 tsp) wine winegar

In mortar crush basil, dill weed and salt to a fine powder. Add garlic and crush to paste, then blend in honey, vinegar and oil, until thoroughly combined. Chill before using.

This is just enough for one salad. It's a little too pungent to keep but delicious to eat ! A plain lettuce salad is transformed by this dressing.

306
Italian Dressing

175ml (6 fl.ozs) sunflower oil
50ml (2 fl.ozs)wine vinegar
1 × 5ml spoon (1 tsp) dry mustard
¾ × 5ml spoon (¾ tsp) salt
generous ground black pepper
1 × 5ml spoon (1 tsp) honey
2 × 5ml spoons (2 tsp) finely chopped onion
2 × 5ml spoons (2 tsp) finely chopped sweet red pepper
1-2 cloves garlic, lightly crushed.

Mix all together in a screw-top jar, shake for 30 seconds before use. Keep in refrigerator and remove garlic after 24 hours.

This is a good all-purpose dressing with lots of flavour to it.

Low Calorie Dressings

307
Yogurt Dressing
(about 150ml: 5 fl.ozs)

150g (5 ozs) natural yogurt
1 × 15ml spoon (1 tbs) chopped celery
1 × 15ml spoon (1 tbs) chopped parsley
1 × 5ml spoon (1 tsp) chopped onion
½ clove garlic
¼ × 5ml spoon (¼ tsp) salt
ground pepper
½ × 5ml spoon (½ tsp) honey

Combine all ingredients in blender and blend until smooth. Refrigerate at least half an hour, then just before serving pour over salad and toss lightly.

308
Tomato Dressing
(about 250ml: 8 fl.ozs)

3 × 15ml spoons (3 tbs) tarragon vinegar
175ml (6 fl.ozs) tomato juice
½ × 5ml spoon (½ tsp) dry mustard
½ × 5ml spoon (½ tsp) salt
1 clove garlic, lightly crushed

Combine all ingredients in salad shaker and shake well. Refrigerate as long as possible to develop flavour. Just before serving pour desired quantity over salad and toss lightly. Remainder keeps well, but remove garlic after 24 hours.

Sauces

309
Tomato Sauce
(about 4½ × 250ml cups)

1 × 15ml spoon (1 tbs) oil
1 lge onion, chopped
1-2 cloves garlic, chopped
1 lge carrot, chopped
1 Kg (2 lbs) tomatoes (or tins)
¾ × 5ml spoon (¾ tsp) salt
¼ × 5ml spoon (¼ tsp) ground black pepper
1 × 15ml spoon (1 tbs) tomato paste
1 × 5ml spoon (1 tsp) dried basil

Heat oil and brown onion, garlic and carrot. Add all other ingredients, bring to boil, then reduce heat and simmer gently, uncovered, for 30 mins. If you like it smooth, put through blender.
Optional: a little red wine or a dash of chili powder.

I make this in large quantities and freeze it in 250ml cup (1 cup) portions. This gives 'instant' tomato sauce and Tomato Soup (No. 9). For freezing, the smaller amount of garlic works best.
Cals: 9 portions, each 41 cals.

310
Tomato-Garlic Sauce
(about 2½ × 250ml cups)

1 × 5ml spoon (1 tsp) corn oil
1 med onion, chopped
2-3 cloves garlic, chopped
600g (1¼ lbs) tomatoes, chopped (or tin)
1 × 15ml spoon (1 tbs) tomato paste
1 bayleaf
¼ × 5ml spoon (¼ tsp) dried oregano
pinch fennel seeds, crushed
ground black pepper
1 × 5ml spoon (1 tsp) salt

Heat oil, sauté onion till silver, add garlic and sauté for 2 mins more. Add all other ingredients, bring to boil, then reduce heat and simmer very gently, uncovered, till thick–about ½ hour.

This has a really Mediterranean flavour, not over-garlicky but very full-bodied, perfect for the fairly strong taste of wholewheat pasta.

311
White Sauce
(1 × 250ml cup)

1 × 15ml spoon (1 tbs) polyunsaturate margarine
2 × 15ml spoons (2 tbs) wholewheat flour
300ml (10 fl.ozs) skimmed milk
½ × 5ml spoon (½ tsp) salt
ground pepper
¼ × 5ml spoon (¼ tsp) ground nutmeg

Melt margarine, stir in flour and cook gently, without browning, for a minute or two. Gradually add milk, stirring constantly, until sauce thickens. Add salt, pepper and nutmeg, reduce heat to minimum–use heat diffuser–and cook, stirring occasionally, for 15 mins.

312
Peanut Sauce
(2 × 250ml cups)

1 × 5ml spoon (1 tsp) corn oil
½ small onion, finely chopped
1 clove garlic, finely chopped
1 green chili pepper, seeded, finely chopped
75g (3 ozs) roasted peanuts, finely ground
1 × 15ml spoon (1 tbs) wholewheat flour
2 × 5ml spoons (2 tsp) honey
2 × 15ml spoons (2 tbs) lemon juice
pinch ground nutmeg
½ × 5ml spoon (½ tsp) salt
250ml (8 fl.ozs) skimmed milk
100ml (4 fl.ozs) water

Heat oil, stir-fry onion, garlic and chili pepper till mixture turns golden. Add ground peanuts, flour, honey and lemon juice and cook gently, stirring, for 1 minute. Add nutmeg and salt, then gradually stir in milk and water until sauce boils. Reduce heat at once, simmer gently, stirring occasionally, for 10 mins.

This piquant sauce adds flavour and texture, as well as protein and fibre, to any vegetable dish.

313
Nut-Tomato Sauce
(about 2½ × 250ml cups)

1 × 5ml spoon (1 tsp) corn oil
½ med onion, finely chopped
1 clove garlic, finely chopped
50g (2 ozs) ground hazelnuts
225g (8 ozs) tomatoes, skinned, chopped
250ml (8 fl.ozs) water
¾ × 5ml spoon (¾ tsp) salt
1 × 5ml spoon (1 tsp) paprika

Heat oil, stir-fry onion and garlic until golden. Stir in nuts, then all other ingredients and bring to boil. Reduce heat and simmer very gently for 10 mins, stirring occasionally.

I grate the hazelnuts coarsely, so the sauce has an interesting, bumpy texture. This is good on grains as well as vegetables.
Cals: ½ cup=64

314
Creamy Onion Sauce
(about 1½ × 250ml cups)

1 × 15ml spoon (1 tbs) polyunsaturate margarine
2 med onions, chopped
2 × 15ml spoons (2 tbs) fresh parsley,

chopped
300ml (10 fl.ozs) chicken stock
pinch ground nutmeg
1 × 15ml spoon (1 tbs) low fat cottage cheese
generous ground black pepper
$\frac{1}{4}$-$\frac{1}{2}$ × 5ml spoon ($\frac{1}{4}$-$\frac{1}{2}$ tsp) salt

Melt margarine and gently brown onions. Stir in parsley and stock, add nutmeg, reduce heat to minimum, simmer 20 mins. Cool slightly then pour into blender with cottage cheese. Blend till creamy. Return to pan, add salt and pepper to taste and gently warm through.
Do not boil.

315
Watercress Sauce
(about 1$\frac{1}{2}$ × 250ml cups)

Make 1$\frac{1}{2}$ cups Creamy Onion Sauce to the point of pouring sauce into blender. Put into blender with it:
50g (2 ozs) watercress, washed and well dried ($\frac{1}{2}$ bunch).
Blend until creamy. Return to pan, add salt and pepper to taste and gently warm through. *Do not boil.*

This sauce is wonderful on a whole steamed cauliflower or poured over a lentil loaf, giving eye appeal as well as flavour.

Index

Index

Index

Index

Index

Index

Index

Index

Index

Index

Index